TOTALLY TUBULAR '80s TOYS

MARK BELLOMO

Published by

Krause Publications, a division of F+W Media, Inc.
700 East State Street • Iola, WI 54990-0001
715-445-2214 • 888-457-2873
www.krausebooks.com

To order books or other products call toll-free 1-800-258-0929
or visit us online at www.krausebooks.com or www.Shop.Collect.com

Cover and inside photography by Kris Kandler

Library of Congress Control Number: 2010925139

ISBN-13: 978-1-4402-1282-6
ISBN-10: 1-4402-1282-1

Cover Design by Heidi Bittner-Zastrow
Designed by Heidi Bittner-Zastrow
Edited by Kristine Manty

Printed in China

3 1571 00285 6105

Acknowledgments

I'd like to thank Mr. Paul Kennedy for all that he's done for me personally and professionally throughout my tenure at Krause Publications. Without his guidance, encouragement, and patience… well… you—quite simply—wouldn't have this book in your hand. He is a saint, and I'll approach the Church to figure out how that gets done. While we're at it, maybe I'll obtain sainthood for Kris Kandler (the book's photographer) and Kris Manty (the book's editor) as well. Ms. Kandler's patience during our three-day-long photo shoot immediately after my car accident should count for something. And Ms. Manty's easygoing acceptance of my many suggestions and edits is truly awe-inspiring.

Big thanks to the ever-accessible Dragon's Den for selling me all of the video games included in this book at the eleventh hour. Without them, not sure our console video game section(s) would be HALF as effective as they look in print. If anyone is looking to purchase vintage video games, give Dave a call at (845) 471-1401 or visit www.dragonsdengames.com.

Chad Hucal, thank you for filming my collections for your Collectable Spectacle, now posted on Chad's Flophouse Films channel on youtube.com. Check it out if you get a chance; it's… enlightening. Soon, I'll have my own Web site, www.markbellomo.com, up and running with a link to The Collectable Spectacle, Krause Publication's Web site (shop.collect.com), and various other supporters.

When giving props, I'd be remiss without mentioning Lynn and Dick Husted at www.toystable.com. Toy Stable has awesome stuff for sale at reasonable prices, as always. And to all of the various repeat sellers on eBay I've bought from for this book over the past three years: know that my purchases have not been in vain… there was always a finish line in sight.

To my mother and father, who I love very much: I am sorry to have missed yet another Christmas with you because of yet another book; sorry, again. I WILL make it up to you. This is meant for my sister Nicole, as well. And lest I forget, if my sister didn't give me her Jem dolls, Barbies, Cabbage Patch Kids, etc., the book you now hold in your hands would be much, much different.

To my mother-in-law Jackie and my father-in-law Walt—and to every other human on the planet who humored me when I talked about entries in this book for the past year or two, "Thank you." And this goes for the lot of you kind people who post comments and feedback and anecdotes on the Inter-webs that say nice things about me and my books. Thanks. Book writing is a heart-wrenching and lonely business sometimes—because with every book you write, you're putting a little bit of yourself OUT THERE to be judged. Your work will essentially be criticized—for good or ill. And anyone who buys this book is entitled to do so.

And finally, to my wife. Who… the second this manuscript is finalized for printing… you will receive a vacation: the first one we've been on since our honeymoon, folks. I love you Jessica; this tome would not have been completed if it weren't for you; you are my LIFE. Honestly, if it weren't for my wife and our two kitties—Pea-Pod and Iggy—I couldn't finish a darned thing in life.

Contents

1987: Child-Like Character Becomes Pop-Culture Icon, 203

1988: Turtle Power and the Future of Law Enforcement, 217

1989: The Dark Knight Rises Again, 233

Introduction

Was there ever a better time to be a kid than in the '80s?

Oh sure, people who grew up in other decades may feel differently, but they are wrong. The '80s were assuredly the greatest. How can a decade that brought us Michael Jackson, MTV, Princess Diana, and John Hughes movies *not* be the best decade of all time?

We lived in an era of Valley Speak and said things like "gag me with a spoon," "grody to the max," and "barf me out" with a straight face. It was a time when Madonna wore eye-threatening bustiers that shook the foundations of conservatism; when the million dollar question on everyone's lips was, Who shot J.R.? A time when every teen-age girl wanted to be Molly Ringwald, while red-blooded boys yearned for the freedom of Ferris Bueller. The '80s was a time of leg warmers, Hawaiian shirts (thanks *Magnum, P.I.*) neon colors, big Aqua Net-teased hair, Members Only jackets with signature neck-strap-snap, colorful and stylish Swatch watches, faux shoulder pads squarer than that of an NFL linebacker's, "preppie" stylings of L.L. Bean and the rise of J. Crew, popular and super-dark Wayfarer sunglasses, and acid-washed jeans with matching jackets. It was a decade that encouraged grown men to wear pastel or fuchsia suit jackets with requisite cuffed sleeves and a solid T-shirt underneath, and combine them with linen pants and slip-on Docksiders *sans* socks, a look that was considered the height of total awesomeness. Affectionately looking back on some of these fashions, it's no wonder Mr. T pitied a lot of fools, myself included.

The '80s are about our youth and the things that shaped it; from the downright silly (Pogo dancing and ruining a perfectly good pair of gloves by cutting the fingers off to be like Madonna or Judd Nelson) to the serious (Reaganomics, the end of the Cold War, and AIDS awareness). Some of the fads of this decade of excess were fleeting (when The Bangles asked us to walk like an Egyptian while we were busy munching away on Gremlins cereal) and some have had a lasting impact (the assassination of John Lennon, and the US Olympic hockey team's "Miracle on Ice").

As a result of one of the most tumultuous decades in American history—and since toys are not created in a vacuum—the '80s has resulted in some of the best toys ever created.

We had a wealth of new toy lines to choose from: Cabbage Patch Kids, He-Man and the Masters of the Universe, She-Ra: Princess of Power, new G.I. Joes, Strawberry Shortcake dolls that smelled good enough to eat, stickers, Atari, GoBots, Transformers, Smurfs, Fraggles, ThunderCats and Silverhawks, Space Invaders and other arcade games, action figures of wrestling superstars including Hulk Hogan and Andre the Giant, toys inspired by *Beetlejuice*, *Ghostbusters*, and *Star Wars Episode V: The Empire Strikes Back* that encouraged us to adopt the identity of an honorable young rebel who could bring down the sinister forces of an entire evil empire.

The decade offered something for "kids" of all ages: from the infamously sophisticated fantasy role-playing game Dungeons & Dragons, to revolutionary new board games that defined the decade: Pictionary, Trivial Pursuit, and the tumbling tower of Jenga. And let's not forget one of the top-selling puzzle games of all time: Rubik's Cube, which is celebrating its 30th anniversary in 2010; a commemoration of the widespread infliction known as "Rubikmania."

As a writer, I feel compelled to immerse myself within each

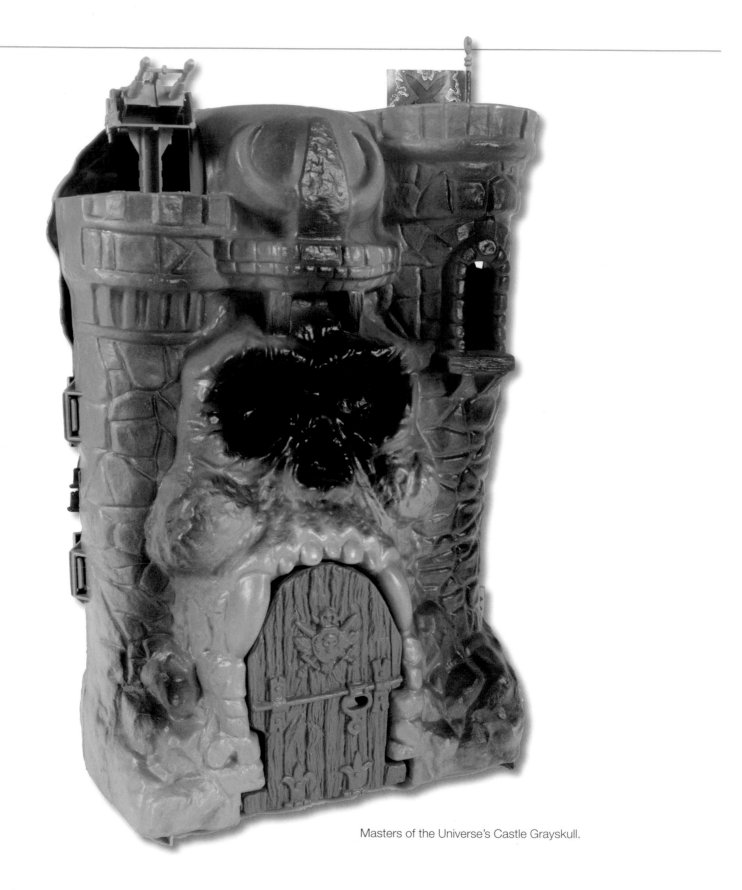

Masters of the Universe's Castle Grayskull.

subject I write about to an advanced—no, *ridiculous*—degree, and if I was going to be describing and documenting an entire decade's worth of artifacts, I suppose I'd have to build myself, well… a time machine. Not an actual time machine, mind you, but the closest possible approximation.

For the last year-and-a-half, I've become engrossed in my subject matter by swimming in an endless ocean of '80s culture. I've screened bubbly '80s movies nonstop, viewed a litany of colorful '80s cartoons, watched a cornucopia of popular television shows from the '80s—from *Three's Company* to *Dynasty* to *Magnum P.I.*—and I have submerged myself within every aspect of the decade. And I mean EVERYTHING. I ate Gummi Bears and Skittles while freeze-framing episodes of *ALF*, Season One; I wore my jeans pinch-cuffed and donned a skinny leather tie when spinning singles of WHAM! and "We Are the World"; I practiced b-boying in parachute pants to Grandmaster Flash's "The Message" and sprained my ankle during a power move.

After this horrifying breakdancing injury that took me out of commission for a few days, I took a break: it was time to slow my "research" down a bit. So for nearly a week, I shuffled out to my garage to root through the hundreds of dusty boxes that contained the premiere pieces of my '80s toy collection. I set up my Super Powers Hall of Justice playset and littered it with DC Comics' Super Powers action figures—Batman and Robin, Green Lantern and The Flash, Superman and Wonder Woman. I gazed lovingly at my mint, loose, and complete Castle Grayskull fortress. I threw open my box of Real Ghostbusters toys, pulled out a few characters, and played with them—triggering their fascinating action features over and over again.

For entertainment's sake—as if hunting through the innumerable toy boxes wasn't enough—I took my portable DVD player out to my garage to accompany me on my quest, and brought with me a box that overflowed with television shows and films from the 1980s. As I examined each box, I was treated to a flood of programming. I watched comedies that triggered fond memories of watching and re-watching Betamax tapes

with friends from long ago (Frankie Woznick and Erin Pierson): *Ferris Bueller's Day Off*, *Trading Places*, *National Lampoon's Christmas Vacation*, *48 Hours*, *Beverly Hills Cop*, *Stripes*, *The Blues Brothers*, *Caddyshack*, *Ghostbusters*, and *Airplane!*

I revisited a syndicated animated universe that was the bread and butter of my formative years: *He-Man and the Masters of the Universe*, *Spider-Man and His Amazing Friends*, *Transformers: More Than Meets The Eye*, *G.I. Joe: A Real American Hero*, *ThunderCats*, and *M.A.S.K.* I gazed upon hours and hours of sitcoms that calmed my nerves and spurred me to take pen to paper: *Night Court*, *Perfect Strangers*, *Taxi*, *Roseanne*, *Pee-wee's Playhouse*, *Bosom Buddies*, *Diff'rent Strokes*, *The Facts of Life*, *Cheers*, *The Cosby Show*, and *Family Ties*.

I viewed '80s films that have most certainly withstood the test of time, such as Barry Levinson's *Rain Man*, Steven Spielberg's *Raiders of the Lost Ark* and *E.T.*, and Stanley Kubrick's *The Shining* and *Full Metal Jacket*. Or how about Michael Mann's *Manhunter*, Ridley Scott's *Blade Runner*, Rob Reiner's *Stand by Me*, Richard Donner's *The Goonies*, or James Cameron's *The Terminator*?

Within the confines of my garage, I also digested films from the 1980s my sister and her friends wore out the analog tapes they were recorded on long ago: *Dirty Dancing*, *Flashdance*, *Can't Buy Me Love*, *Footloose*, *Peggy Sue Got Married*, *Say Anything*, *Mystic Pizza*, and *Adventures in Babysitting*.

So where did I go when my sister and her gaggle of friends obsessed over the color of the late, great Patrick Swayze's eyes (they're blue, by the way)? I headed to the local arcade to plunk some quarters into my favorite video games: Ms. Pac-Man, Galaga, Dragon's Lair (that one ALWAYS drew a crowd), Gauntlet, R-Type, Donkey Kong Jr., and of course…within the cockpit of Star Wars' brilliant "vector-graphic" X-wing fighter simulator.

Ah… it was working. It appeared that my immersion in all things '80s was beginning to percolate within my skull. I was enthralled by the decade's potent charm and endless categorical possibilities for documentation. It struck me all

Panosh Place's Voltron
Castle of Lions.

A 12" Mork with
Talking Spacepack.

Some DC Comics' super-heroes hang out at the Super Powers Hall of Justice.

at once: I'd organize this book by year, from 1980-1989, and recount within its pages not only toys and games, but music, television, and movies as well.

My mother and father showed me that there was a larger world beyond the confines of an insular little town in Western New York. And like so many other kids, I used my toys to construct my own imaginary world(s) to inhabit.

In my mind, I rode a Tauntaun over the frozen crackling tundra of Ice Planet Hoth. I used a space-bridge to visit the techno-organic orb of Cybertron. I flew to Krypton and basked under the scarlet glow of a powerful red sun. I guarded the filthy streets of Gotham City, using a host of devices to assist my mission to fight crime. I swung on my web-line from building-to-building above the populous blocks of New York City even though Manhattan was hours away from my home. I hunted ghosts and spirits in my local cemetery with the assistance of my trusty Proton Pack and P.K.E. Meter. And in retrospect, apparently after all these years, my escapism has served me well.

The long list of '80s toy lines that flashed through my brain when setting out to write this book has been *endless*. It is my hope that the selection of toys included within these pages will reach out, and trigger those all-important imaginative impulses, to everyone who reads this tome. Boys. Girls. Parents. Grandparents.

Even kids growing up *today*.

Various games for the Atari 5200.

1980

More than 300 million Rubik's Cubes have been sold worldwide. If all the cubes were placed on top of each other, it would be enough to reach the North Pole from the South Pole.

The Year of Rubikmania, Pac-Man Fever

NEVER BEFORE HAD A LITTLE HUNK OF PLASTIC caused such pride for people able to solve its perplexing puzzle—and such consternation for those who couldn't.

Invented by famed Hungarian professor Ernõ Rubik in 1974, it took six years for Ideal Toys to mass-produce what became the Rubik's Cube. This Cube was a revolutionary diversion in the U.S. and 1980 was the year a storm of "Rubikmania" hit with great force.

In 1980, another major distraction for children was the invention of the home video game. According to parents, it was one thing for kids to plunk a few quarters in the pockets of their KangaROOS sneakers and walk to the local arcade; it was another situation altogether for a family to drop hundreds of dollars on a video game system that allowed kids to vegetate in front of a television with their friends for hours on end playing *Pac-Man*, *Space Invaders*, or other expensive "wastes of time."

On the movie front, kids headed in droves to see the second installment of the greatest film trilogy of all time—*Star Wars: The Empire Strikes Back*—and then *had* to have the super rad toys that came out soon after.

On TV, two must-see shows included *The Dukes of Hazzard* and the adventures of Bo and Luke Duke, trying to stay one step ahead of the law in their souped-up Dodge Charger, the General Lee; and the primetime soap opera *Dallas,* about a bunch of rich, good-looking people in Texas. *Dallas* dominated television for the first half of the 1980s like no other program.

There were also a wealth of wonderful sitcoms to choose from in 1980. On *The Jeffersons*, George and Louise Jefferson (Sherman Hemsley and Isabel Sanford) moved away from the Bunkers' neighborhood in *All in the Family* and dominated the ratings without their help. *Diff'rent Strokes* was also a favorite of millions who appreciated the spunkiness of Arnold Jackson (Gary Coleman).

Music took a strange turn when a group named Devo donned what can only be dubbed "Energy Dome" headgear and cracked a whip to their hit song, "Whip It!" Blondie and Olivia Newton-John had their share of hits, while Air Supply, Christopher Cross, Diana Ross, and Billy Joel cemented themselves as superstars. The year in music sadly ended with the tragic murder of one of the most famous music superstars in the world: John Lennon, who was gunned down on Dec. 8 by Mark David Chapman.

From the amateur U.S. hockey team's stunning victory against the dreaded professional Russian organization on Feb. 22, 1980, in what would be known as the "Miracle on Ice," American patriotism was at an all-time high. Yet as a country, we were far from unstoppable. The Cold War still loomed around every corner, while natural disaster struck the county with the eruption of Mt. St. Helens on May 8, 1980. Yet we had plenty of distractions.

Still Hip To Be Square

Rubik's Cube continues to be one of the most popular puzzles 30 years later

Millions of people were inflicted with Rubikmania in 1980 after the Rubik's Cube hit toy shelves. Invented by famed Hungarian professor Ernõ Rubik in 1974, it was mass-produced by Ideal Toys.

The 3- x 3- x 3-inch cube is the top-selling puzzle game of all time, shipping over 350 million units worldwide since its inception in 1980.

What once was a mere fad has become an indelible part of pop culture, with modern-day speed cubing tournaments achieving worldwide recognition.

People all over boasted about their skills in solving the puzzle and correctly lining up the blue, green, orange, red, white, and yellow stickers, while the brainteaser was a pain for others who couldn't quite get it.

But there was, of course, the option of simply cheating and peeling the stickers off and then rearranging them to your liking. In fact, Ideal produced a sticker sheet fans could purchase as a quick "fix."

The Rubik's Cube was an unprecedented sensation in a decade chock full of them. In a *Time* article published on December 7, 1981 and titled—of course—"Rubikmania," the magazine stated that even solution manuals were selling in the millions: *"The Simple Solution to Rubik's Cube"*, a 64-page booklet…has become the fastest-selling title in the history of Bantam Books, outpacing *Jaws* and *Valley of the Dolls*…The cube phenomenon is the biggest thing of its kind we have ever experienced."

In 1982, the first annual International Rubik's Championships were held in Budapest. More than 100 million cubes were also sold by then, and Rubik's entered the *Oxford English Dictionary*.

So pervasive was Rubikmania that Ideal rushed to capitalize on the success with a slew of other engaging puzzles. The company offered Rubik's "The Missing Link," a colored, chain-based puzzle that was a bit simpler to solve than the Cube; the uniquely designed and amply creative Rubik's Snake that, with its twenty-four wedges, allowed users to construct a wide variety of different shapes and constructs; and 1981 brought fans Rubik's Revenge, a.k.a. the "Master Cube," which increased the number of cubelets from 26 to 56, and Rubik's Magic (produced by Matchbox in 1986)—a puzzle constructed of eight different tiles arranged in a rectangle, with grooves on the tiles that allow clear wires to attach the tiles to one another; the puzzle must be folded and unfolded over and over again in order to achieve the solution.

Ernõ Rubik, a professor at the College of Applied Science, Budapest University, photographed in December 1981 in London with his famous cube. The small multi-colored puzzle has become known as the "Hungarian horror" among those unsuccessful in rearranging its parts properly. Rubik says he designed the cube to help students relate to three-dimensional problems in architecture. *AP Photo/John Glanvill*

Space Cadets

The Empire Strikes Back one of the most popular chapters in *Star Wars* saga

"In a galaxy far, far away"… the battle to save the cosmos from the evil Darth Vader raged on in the 1980 *Star Wars* sequel, *The Empire Strikes Back*.

While Han Solo, Chewbacca, and Princess Leia busy themselves fending off an attack by the Imperial army and its All Terrain Armored Transport (AT-AT) Walkers, Luke Skywalker seeks out the ancient Jedi Master Yoda to learn the secrets he will need when the dark side of the Force beckons him in a destiny-defining duel with Darth Vader—a duel that ends in a shocking secret that left us moviegoers gasping when we learned who Luke's father really was. How could children of the '80s *not* want to reenact scenes from what many consider to be the most important film they ever witnessed?

A scene from *The Empire Strikes Back* featuring Turret and Probot playset, Rebel Commander, Rebel Soldiers in Hoth Battle Gear, Han Solo in Hoth Outfit, Chewbacca, and a number of Imperial Stormtroopers in Hoth Battle Gear.

Luckily, Kenner knew kids would want to do just that and came out with a line of action figures, vehicles, creatures, playsets, and accessories that included Darth Vader's Star Destroyer, with an opening and closing light-up meditation chamber, an opening escape hatch, and pretend viewing screen so Vader could talk to the "Grand Vizier" (the Emperor wasn't named at the time of the toy's release).

With pegs on its ceiling to "hang" action figures upside down, Vader could interrogate a suspended Star Destroyer Commander, rather than the un-p.c. "Death Squad Commander."

Toys reenact a famous movie scene featuring Darth Vader's Star Destroyer, Imperial Stormtroopers, Darth Vader, Death Squad Commanders, and Imperial Commanders.

Not to trivialize the following analogy in any way, but most Baby Boomers can recount exactly where they were when John F. Kennedy was shot on November 22, 1963. As for the '80s generation—growing up under the auspices of the protective Baby Boomers—was our equivalent moment in pop culture the day we learned who Luke Skywalker's father really is?

I never seemed to have enough money for an AT-AT in spite of my paper route, so I never bought one *or* its command crew until many years later. I truly had to use my imagination to reenact the Imperials' attack on Ice Planet Hoth, miming the many AT-AT Walkers and the flight of the fully loaded Rebel Transports that play out the escape of the Rebels.

The scene pictured below is quite interesting to me, in terms of scale. I never quite realized how large the AT-AT is—and it's my opinion that even if Luke and Han were having a good "Jedi" day, they'd have trouble defeating these Imperials with four Tauntauns and two other soldiers.

Yoda, the Jedi Master.

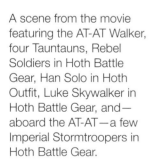

A scene from the movie featuring the AT-AT Walker, four Tauntauns, Rebel Soldiers in Hoth Battle Gear, Han Solo in Hoth Outfit, Luke Skywalker in Hoth Battle Gear, and—aboard the AT-AT—a few Imperial Stormtroopers in Hoth Battle Gear.

Arcade Mania

Pac-Man, Space Invaders, Donkey Kong, Galaga, Asteroids, Super Mario Bros., and more

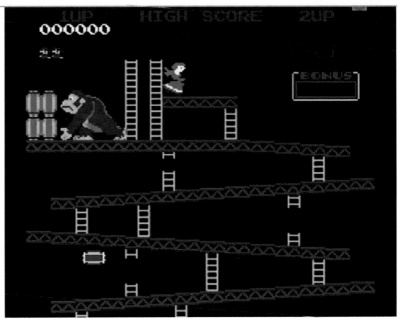

A scene from *Donkey Kong*. *Nintendo/Shigeru Miyamoto*

Video-game icons that established themselves in the 1980s continue to possess a magical hold on those of us who grew up in that decade.

Space-shooter games such as *Asteroids* and *Space Invaders* were the supreme leaders in the confines of the American video game arcade, those pockets of culture that should have had a sign posted above the entrance stating: "Abandon All Hope, Ye Who Enter Here."

Kids everywhere spent hours upon hours maneuvering through mazes trying to eat trails of pac-dots and power pellets as fast as they could, all while trying to dodge four ghosts (Blinky, Inky, Pinky, and Clyde) hot on their tail; furiously moving a laser cannon horizontally to shoot at Space Invader aliens descending upon them; chasing an ape named Donkey Kong in an attempt to rescue a lady he kidnapped (Pauline); destroying insect-like enemies while trying to rack up as many points as possible in *Galaga*; and using a triangular-shaped ship to destroy asteroids and flying saucers.

You entered an arcade with a sole purpose: to obtain a high score. What you'd do is spend a few quarters trying out different games in order to gauge your success at them. When you found the right one, then you "worked at" obtaining a high score.

I recall at the height of arcade culture in the early '80s that if you achieved a high score on a machine, you'd simply run over to a worker at an establishment (in New York, mall arcades were named "time out"), point out the total, and your name would be written on a white slip of paper and placed on the top of the game's cabinet for all to see. You'd also receive *two full dollars* in tokens for the achievement.

Out of this arcade culture sprung a series of characters that appeared larger than life: Donkey Kong, Space Invaders, the "Brothers Mario," and of course…Pac-Man. Due to this character, I was hospitalized on multiple occasions suffering from an advanced and highly contagious form of "Pac-Man Fever" that caused my hand to hurt and my thumb to swell; my eyes became bloodshot and I swore I saw things that weren't there: I was being chased by…ghosts. *Pac-Man*'s popularity in the U.S. was unparalleled, and it became the best-selling video game of all time, selling over 350,000 cabinet-type units.

However, it is the image of *Space Invaders*' pixilated enemy alien that has endured—perhaps even more than *Pac-Man*—the greatest profit margin in the history of video games. Where *Pac-Man* has set a record for total number of machines sold (along with obtaining a starring role in a first-rate '80s Saturday morning cartoon show), *Space Invaders*, as of 2007, has earned Taito $500 million in revenue, ranking it the top arcade game in the *Guinness Book of World's Records*.

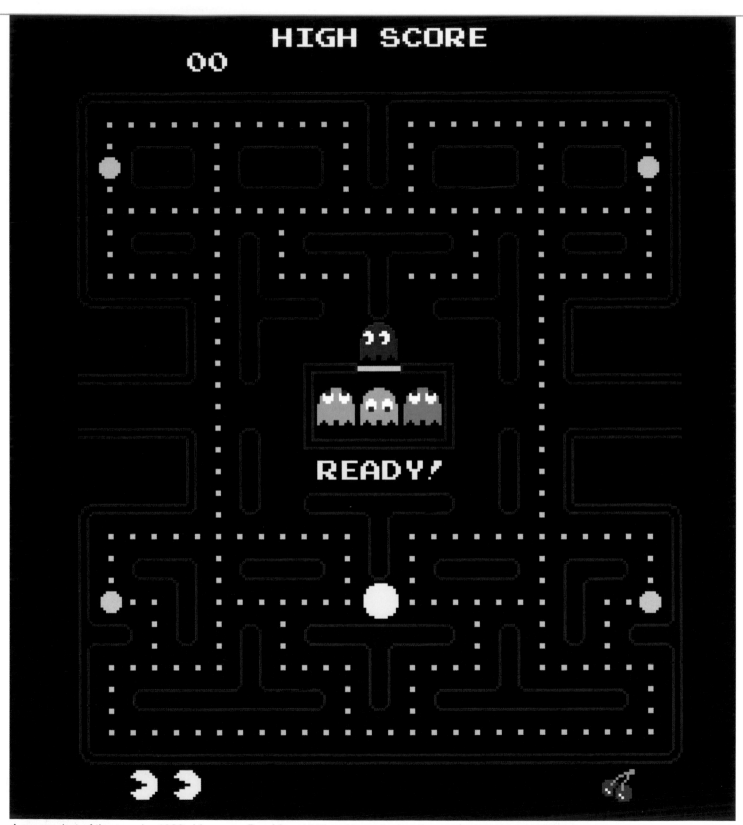

A screenshot of the popular 1980 videogame *Pac-Man*. *AP Photo/Japan Society, Courtesy of NAMCO BANDAI Games America Inc.*

Joystick Revolution

Atari 2600 a pioneer in video gaming

"Let's go play Atari!" was added to pop-culture vernacular in the early '80s after the Atari 2600 hit the market.

Released in October 1977 (until 1982), the Atari 2600, originally solicited as the Atari VCS (Video Computer System), was the best-selling and most revolutionary video game console of the late 1970s/early 1980s, pioneering the use of "cartridge-based" gaming, where you could change your choice of video game in an instant—removing one game cartridge (*Space Invaders*) and replacing it with another (*Pac-Man*).

The 2600 was bundled with two controllers, those iconic black rubber-coated joysticks with a single red firing button. It also came with a pair of paddles that would initially be utilized for Atari's *Combat* cartridge pack-in, yet would become most popular when *Pac-Man* was bundled with the 2600 (post-'82). The Atari 2600 console was so tremendously popular that the system became synonymous with home video gaming in the 1980s.

In recent years, many stores have taken to refurbishing and selling older video game systems such as the 2600. These consoles were built to last and many people still have them in good working condition.

If gamers in the 1980s were looking for a realistic way to play tabletop releases featured in arcades, the Atari 2600 delivered, hands down.

Atari 2600 video game console with two joysticks and a slew of games.

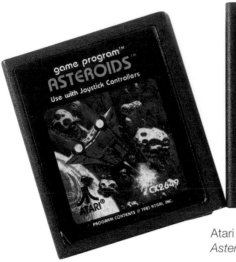

Atari 2600's super-popular cartridges:
Asteroids, *Space Invaders*, and *Pac-Man*.

Atari 2600 Imagic *Demon Attack* and *Star Voyager*.

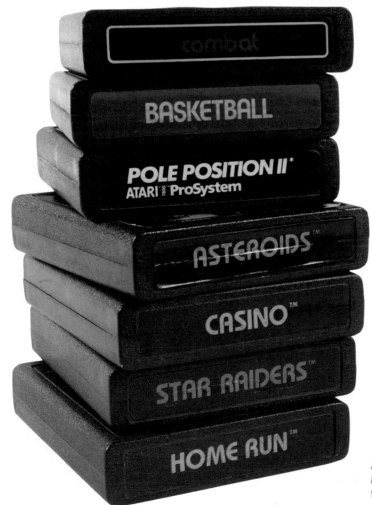

Atari 2600 video game cartridges, stack one: *Combat*, *Basketball*, *Pole Position II*, *Asteroids*, *Casino*, *Star Raiders*, *Home Run*. Stack two: *Target Fun*, *Real Sports Football*, *Football*, *Superbreakout*.

'Intelligent Television'

Mattel develops new console to compete with Atari

To combat the success of the bestselling Atari 2600 and tap into the burgeoning video game culture, Mattel developed the Intellivision and employed a literary patron to help hawk it.

Mattel, which began development of this revolutionary console in 1978, originally retailed the system for $299.99, and a mere four games were offered at its inception. A portmanteau of "intelligent" + "television," Mattel's foray into this market seemed a logical step for the innovative company since it had already pioneered the advent of hand-held sports games under the "Mattel Electronics" banner.

Ingenious commercials appealing to intellectual gamers, as well as die-hard fans featured promotional advertising provided by deep-thinker George Plimpton, editor and founder of *The*

Paris Review. Since Plimpton lambasted the "inferior" graphics and poor playability of the Atari 2600, my parents went the extra mile on a shoestring budget and purchased my sister and me an Intellivision.

When comparing even the console's most basic games, such as the cartridge bundled with the game system itself—*Las Vegas Poker & Blackjack*—Atari's limited graphics, low-quality sound, and the lack of ability to discern between "good guys" and "bad guys" on the court, field, or mission, allowed Mattel to ship 3 million units. With a library of exactly 125 different games developed before the system folded in 1983, Intellivision became known for its superior graphics.

Intellivision video game console with the following cartridges: *NFL Football*, *Armor Battle*, *Las Vegas Poker & Blackjack*, *PBA Bowling*, and *Star Strike*.

Just Desserts

Strawberry Shortcake and her doll friends smell good enough to eat

Orange Blossom and Marmalade in the Oatsmobile, with Mint Tulip riding atop Maple Stirrup.

Children everywhere in the 1980s drifted off to sleep with strawberry-scented dreams: probably because they had a Strawberry Shortcake doll tucked under an arm.

Kenner's Strawberry Shortcake line developed into a massive fad for young girls throughout the United States. My sister Nicole and her gaggle of friends bought them, posed them, and inhaled these figures' aromas as if their fragrance were bottled at $1,000 an ounce. Each doll had its own dessert-themed or fruit/berry name and signature scent. Besides Strawberry Shortcake herself, other dolls in the line shared similar appellations: Apple Dumpling, Huckleberry Pie, Angel Cake, Raspberry Tart, Orange Blossom, Lemon Meringue, and Butter Cookie. These dolls came with cloth outfits, plastic pets (such as Custard, Pupcake and Marza Panda), some minor (yet important) accessories—unique soft plastic or cloth shoes and hats, rooted hair, great toy packaging, and a smattering of vehicles, larger animals, and playsets including a Garden House, Oatsmobile, the super popular Berry Bake Shoppe, and the Big Berry Trolley. All of these characters lived and played under the magical auspices of "Strawberryland."

The line expanded beyond Kenner's dolls, though, and included such items as clothes, sicker albums, and a Parker Brothers Atari 2600 video game called *Strawberry Shortcake Musical Match-Ups*. The characters also starred in several TV specials from 1980-85, produced primarily to sell more toys—the goal of many animated shows in the 1980s.

These dolls possess such a rich history since the 1980s, and so the line was relaunched in 2009 with six main characters: Strawberry Shortcake, Blueberry Muffin, Orange Blossom, Plum Pudding, Lemon Meringue, and Raspberry Tart.

So why not pick up some Strawberry Shortcake figures and prominently display them on your toy shelves? You'll be surprised at how many women, whether aunts, cousins, friends, girlfriends, etc., remember these dolls fondly as you take them on a trip down memory lane.

Raspberry Tart with Rhubarb, Lemon Meringue with Frappe, Angel Cake, Strawberry Shortcake with Custard, Blueberry Muffin with Cheesecake.

Flitterbit with Cherry Cuddler and Crepe Suzette.

Apricot and Hopsalot, Orange Blossom and Marmalade, Purple Pieman and Cackle, Sour Grapes and Dregs the Snake.

Mint Tulip with Marsh Mallard, Crepe Suzette with Éclair, Cherry Cuddler with Gooseberry, Huckleberry Pie with Pupcake, Butter Cookie with Jelly Bear.

Thrillbillies

Good ol' boys stay ahead of the law in *The Dukes of Hazzard*

A couple of good ol' boys fighting against corrupt politicians and self-serving police officials in Hazzard County, Georgia, had millions of people glued to their TVs each week.

The Dukes of Hazzard, with its fabulous theme song and narration provided by country-western music outlaw Waylon Jennings, made my childhood friends and I stop in our tracks every Friday night at 9 to watch the adventures of cousins Bo and Luke Duke. Few casual fans realize that the program, which aired from 1979-1985 on CBS, was created by writer-producer Gy Waldron, was inspired by his 1975 movie *Moonrunners* and shared many identical or similar concepts and character names.

Bo (John Schneider, Jonathan Kent of the WB's *Smallville* fame) was the dashing, impetuous, blond-haired Duke. Bo's cousin Luke (Tom Wopat) portrayed the dark-haired,

level-headed, less-impulsive and more enlightened member of the duo. Through the course of their adventures, they were guided by their wise Uncle Jesse (Denver Pyle).

As the series begins, Bo and Luke are on probation for transporting moonshine, a probation that never seems to disappear thanks to the concerted efforts of their chief adversary, the corpulent, corrupt, cigar-chomping Boss Hogg (Sorrell Booke), an inspired scoundrel. The Duke boys' famed mode of transportation is the iconic General Lee—a souped-up Dodge Charger whose spirit made it a character unto itself. As an ex-stock car driver, Bo's prowess behind the wheel of the General Lee allowed the writers to put the Duke boys in situations where, during a high-speed pursuit, the vehicle would speed over many of their legendary jumps. Bo's exuberance and excitement during these car chases popularized his "rebel yell": a "Yeeee-haaaaw" exclamation featured during the closing seconds of the opening theme song/credits and in nearly every episode.

To capitalize on the show's popularity, Mego came out with a line of toys including action figures and a replica of the General Lee so children could reenact their own Duke boys adventures.

Toy moonshine not included.

Bo and Luke Duke and the General Lee.

Dukes of Hazzard 3-3/4" Daisy Duke, Cooter Davenport, and Daisy's Jeep, "Dixie."

Bo (John Schneider), Luke (Tom Wopat), their cousin, Daisy (Catherine Bach), and the General Lee. Perhaps another reason for the popularity of *The Dukes of Hazzard* was bodacious Daisy Duke. The mere mention of her still stops many red-blooded males in their tracks. Their eyes become wistful and hearts skip a beat as they reminisce about her most pronounced attributes: form-fitting, cutoff jean shorts, now known as "Daisy Dukes." *CBS-TV/The Kobal Collection*

A 3-3/4" Boss Hogg, left, replete with trademark bone-white suit and cowboy hat. Boss Hogg is aided by his nephew, the incompetent and incomparable Roscoe P. Coltrane (portrayed by James Best), who stole the show as the crooked sheriff of Hazzard County.

Loveable Alien

Mork & Mindy makes comic a huge star

Greet any child of the '80s with the expression, "Na-Nu, Na-Nu," and they will know you're talking the special language of a loveable alien named Mork. Broadcast from 1979-1982 for four seasons on ABC, *Mork & Mindy* was improvisational comic Robin Williams' first starring role as Mork from Ork, with Pam Dawber playing Mindy McConnell, Mork's confidant and friend. However, Mork's first appearance was on ABC's *Happy Days*, and Williams' offbeat and inspired performance made Mork a breakout character.

Mork's odd mannerisms endeared him to American adults and children alike: he sat in a chair upside down, drank beverages with his finger (followed by a slight index finger "burp"); he expressed derision with the Orkan profanity of "Shazbot," and agreed in assent with human characters on the show with the mispronounced American colloquial expression, "Kay-o!"

Mattel decided to capitalize upon Williams' popular character, and so a series of figures were produced based upon *Mork & Mindy*. Although the 3-3/4-inch Mork with spaceship egg was the most popular, as it was the least expensive toy in the line, the 12-inch "Robin Williams as Mork with Talking Spacepack" doll was every (odd) child's dream-come-true.

Mork's outfit was a perfect representation of his Orkan fatigues, and although his backpack was bulky and awkward (and filled with hokey late '70s labels), it still impressed kids, who pulled its "talking ring" and eight different sounds would elicit from the pack such as: "Na-Nu, Na-Nu!" and "Shazbot!" Mattel sold thousands of these units…

A 12" Mork waves hello.

Mork (Robin Williams) and Mindy (Pam Dawber). *Paramount/The Kobal Collection*

Sci-Fi Hero Returns

Buck Rogers in the 25th Century

Audiences of the early 1980s were once again treated to an iconic science fiction character who permeated American popular culture and lasted two full seasons on network television: Buck Rogers, a character created in 1928 by Philip Francis Nowlan and previously featured in comic strips, two novellas, and a serial film. Since the 1979 teaser film, *Buck Rogers in the 25th Century* performed phenomenally well with its theatrical premiere on March 30 (grossing $21 million domestically), this success suggested America was once again ready for "Mr. Rogers" to return to the small screen.

NBC quickly green-lit an ongoing series based on the film, starring Gil Gerard as Captain William Anthony "Buck" Rogers, Erin Gray as Colonel Wilma Deering, with the inimitable Mel Blanc providing voice work as Twiki the robot (with his catchphrase "Biddi Biddi Biddi"), and a first-rate supporting cast consisting of Tim O'Connor as Dr. Elias Huer, Pamela Hensley as Princess Ardella, and more expert voice acting by Eric Server as the

sentient computer worn around Twiki's neck: Dr. Theopolis.

The plot revolves around astronaut Buck Rogers assimilating to life in the 25th century following a freak NASA accident; he now has to assist the Earth's Defense Directorate to repel attacks by hostile alien cultures such as Princess Ardella and the Planet Draconia.

Although the show only lasted until 1981, seventies toy giant Mego created a small set of licensed products to let kids create their own space adventures: nine 3-3/4-inch figures, seven 12-inch figures, five vehicles for the 3-3/4-inch line (the Land Rover, Star Fighter, Star Searcher, Laserscope Fighter, and Draconian Marauder), and one Star Fighter Command Center playset.

Unfortunately, sales of these toys were weak. They had limited appeal—only children who watched the television program, as Mego produced the toys merely to support the premiere film, not the ongoing series itself.

Buck Rogers in the 25th Century 3-3/4" action figures: Doctor Huer, Wilma Deering, Twiki, Buck Rogers, Tiger Man, Draconian Guard, Princess Ardella, and Draco.

Myths in Miniature

Clash of the Titans inventive

Released just in the nick of time for the 1980 Christmas season, Mattel's four-figure Clash of the Titans toy line included Perseus' mount, the winged horse Pegasus; and the Kraken, a sea-monster.

Clash of the Titans was a moderately important film. It was the 11th highest-grossing film of the 1981 season; furthermore, it has Ray Harryhausen's beautifully rendered stop-motion monsters that harken back to his *Golden Voyage of Sinbad* (1974) days; a first-rate all-star cast including Harry Hamlin as Perseus, Burgess Meredith as his mentor Ammon, Sir Lawrence Olivier as Zeus, and Dame Maggie Smith of *Harry Potter* fame as Thetis; and the film still resonates with children of the 1980s.

The film recounts, twists, and reinvents the Greek myth of Perseus in dramatic fashion, yet elements of the original tale still exist: Perseus is provided with Hades' helmet of invisibility (Athena's in the movie), Athena's shield, and Hermes' adamantine sword (Aphrodite's in the film). Our hero rescues Andromeda from Medusa of the Gorgons, he encounters the Stygian Witches, he defeats the Kraken, and he must *also* contend with a cluster of fickle and jealous Greek gods and the addition of the goat-footed Calibos as a formidable adversary.

Since *Clash of the Titans* was special-effects master Ray Harryhausen's final film, he spent a full *sixteen months* completing the glorious stop-action animation required to render all the wonderful creatures that supported the actors: Medusa, the Kraken, Pegasus, Bubo the owl, the sinister Calibos, Calibo's pet vulture, and the two-headed Dioskilos.

Charon, the Devil's Boatman, and Calibos, Lord of the Marsh.

Thallo, Captain of the Guard, and Perseus, Hero Son of Zeus.

Comic-Strip King

Garfield loved by millions

Dakin's Garfield stuffed plush Nermal, Odie, Garfield, and Arlene.

What began as creator Jim Davis drawing a small four-panel daily black-and-white strip featuring the adventures of a crudely rendered husky house cat, has boomed into a phenomenon. Since June 19, 1978, *Garfield*, whose title character is an obese, caustic, selfish, self-involved, self-professed sloth of an anthropomorphic tabby, has dominated American newspapers like no other.

Currently, it is the most widely syndicated strip in the world, holding the Guinness World Record for appearing in 2,580 newspapers per day. Set in Muncie, Indiana, *Garfield* is the king of comic strips, and the revenue stream of merchandise staggers the imagination: the franchise garners its creator and his *Garfield* licensing agency (Paws, Inc.), somewhere between $750 million to $1 billion each year.

With a propensity to break the imaginary fourth wall between character and reader, the endearingly goofy characters continue to fascinate: Garfield's owner John Arbuckle, a pathetic nerd desperate for female companionship whose awkwardness is a feature of many of the strip's jokes; Odie the dog, a brown and (mostly) yellow beagle whose lack of intelligence and naiveté mark him as the target for many of Garfield's antics; Garfield's nemesis Nermal, "the cutest kitten in the world," who is lavished with attention which Garfield despises; and Arlene, Garfield's slender, pink-furred and full-lipped love interest. Although she rarely appears in the current strip, during the 1980s, she was one of the only characters who could get away with insulting her beau. Garfield, Odie, Nermal, and Arlene were featured members of the Dakin Corporation's plush Garfield toy released in the 1980s. The accuracy of these stuffed animals is excellent; these toys are surprisingly detailed and were created in-scale with respect to each other.

Fantasy Meets Technology

Dungeons & Dragons takes you on electronic adventures

Although not technically a console video game, Mattel Electronics' Dungeons & Dragons Computer Labyrinth Game was a streamlined follow-up to the complicated and rule-laden Dungeons & Dragons role-playing game.

This computer game of skill was a stunning achievement of technology in 1980. You had to find your way through the labyrinth on a touch-sensitive electronic board and steal the treasure before the dragon captured/destroyed your character. Various electronic sounds helpfully alerted players that the dragon was hot on their trail. Mattel sold tens of thousands of units of this aesthetically pleasing electronic adventure.

Mattel Electronics'
Dungeons & Dragons
Computer Labyrinth Game.

Mass A-Peel

Sticker Craze hits big

The sticker craze of the 1980s was an inexpensive way to produce products, which would go a long way to produce sustenance for a license. Kids didn't care about that part, though; they were only interested in collecting as many stickers as they could.

Throughout the decade, there were individual stickers, sticker sets, hologram stickers (Lazer Blazers), glitter stickers, scratch 'n sniff stickers, puffy stickers, "oily" stickers, fuzzy stickers, Label Makers, trading card sets with bonus stickers (Garbage Pail Kids), movie stickers, stickers with cartoon characters, animal stickers, fruit stickers—you name it.

Kids would swap and collect these various stickers and proudly keep them in collectible "sticker albums," which command ludicrous prices on the secondary market today. We're also sure that more than one parent had to pry a sticker off a living room wall or other unacceptable places.

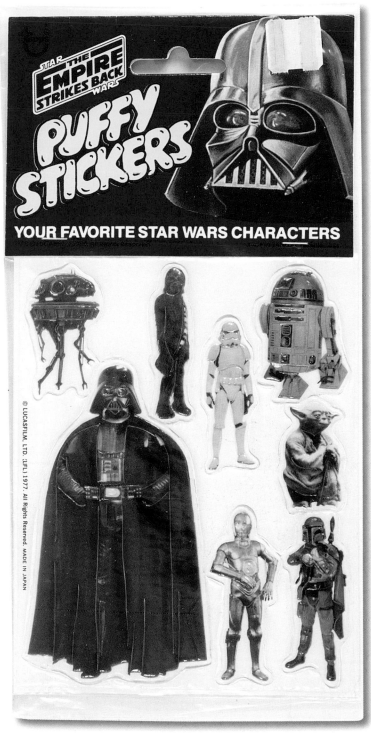

The Empire Strikes Back official puffy stickers.

Pac-Man puffy stickers, google-eye (or wiggle-eye) stickers, and fuzzy stickers.

ENTERTAINMENT-O-RAMA:
1980 MOVIES, MUSIC, TELEVISION

The cast of *Dallas*, back row: Howard Keel, Larry Hagman, and Steve Kanaly; middle row: Priscilla Presley, Barbara Bel Geddes, Linda Gray, and Susan Howard; front row: Victoria Principal and Ken Kercheval. *AP Photo*

Top Ten Television Programs of 1980-81

1 *Dallas* (CBS)

2 *The Dukes of Hazzard* (CBS)

3 *60 Minutes* (CBS)

4 *M*A*S*H* (CBS)

5 *The Love Boat* (ABC)

6 *The Jeffersons* (CBS)

7 *Alice* (CBS)

8 *House Calls* (CBS)

9 *Three's Company* (ABC)

10 *Little House on the Prairie* (NBC)

Sudsy show has lasting influence

Dallas pioneered and codified the concept of a "cliff-hanger." Let's all step into our way-back machines and remember the summer of 1980 when you couldn't walk down an American street without encountering someone wearing a "Who Shot J.R.?" T-shirt.

This March 21, 1980 season two cliffhanger became the highest-rated season finale in U.S. history with a whopping 83 million viewers. How would modern dramatic television function without the use of mind-blowing season finale cliffhangers, as utilized by programs such as ABC's *Lost*, AMC's *Mad Men*, and FOX's *The X-Files*?

Furthermore, if J.R. Ewing was, as many pundits state, television's original man-you-love-to-hate, did Larry Hagman's expert characterization open the door for the development of such complex anti-heroes as *Deadwood*'s Al Swearangen, *The Office*'s Dwight K. Schrute, or misanthropic medic Gregory House, M.D.?

Of course, the show is also infamous because of a number of missteps as well. For instance, dismissing the entire 1985-86 season as a "bad dream"—where Bobby Ewing's death was retracted and the character was "retconned" back into show continuity as a result of actor Patrick Duffy's acceptance of a renegotiated contract.

Top Ten Films of 1980

1 *The Empire Strikes Back* (20th Century Fox)
2 *9 to 5* (20th Century Fox)
3 *Stir Crazy* (Sony/Columbia)
4 *Airplane!* (Paramount)
5 *Any Which Way You Can* (Warner Brothers)
6 *Private Benjamin* (Warner Brothers)
7 *Coal Miner's Daughter* (Universal)
8 *Smokey and the Bandit II* (Universal)
9 *The Blue Lagoon* (Columbia)
10 *The Blues Brothers* (Universal)

Best Picture: *Ordinary People* (Paramount)

In the action-packed hit romp, *The Blues Brothers*, Elwood (Dan Aykroyd) and Jake (John Belushi) are "on a mission from God" to reunite their old band and save the orphanage where they were raised. Along the way, they cause plenty of good-natured havoc, including car chases and the destruction of shopping malls and police cars. *Universal/The Kobal Collection*

Freddie Mercury and Queen enjoyed success with their eighth studio album, *The Game*, and the hit singles, "Crazy Little Thing Called Love," and "Another One Bites the Dust." *AP Photo/Gill Allen*

Top Ten Billboard Singles of 1980

1 "Call Me," Blondie (theme from *American Gigolo*, 1980)
2 "Another Brick in the Wall," Pink Floyd (*The Wall*, 1979)
3 "Magic," Olivia Newton-John (*Xanadu* soundtrack, 1980)
4 "Rock With You," Michael Jackson (*Off the Wall*, 1979)
5 "Do That to Me One More Time," Captain & Tennille (*Make Your Move*, 1979)
6 "Crazy Little Thing Called Love," Queen (*The Game*, 1980)
7 "Coming Up," Paul McCartney (*McCartney II*, 1980)
8 "Funkytown," Lipps, Inc. (*Mouth to Mouth*, 1979)
9 "It's Still Rock And Roll to Me," Billy Joel (*Glass Houses*, 1980)
10 "The Rose," Bette Midler (*The Rose* soundtrack, 1980)

1981

Masters of the Universe line was one of the most successful toy ventures of all time. Here MOTU characters cavort on the Snake Mountain playset.

A Mighty Warrior and Little Blue Creatures

"BY THE POWER OF GRAYSKULL…I HAVE THE POWER!"

To this day, you cannot shout that to any child of the '80s and not watch their facial expression turn to one of glee.

For, in the winter of 1981, Mattel launched its newest toy line, Masters of the Universe, one of the most successful toy ventures of all time.

Television in general was loaded with children's programming, and the expression, "Saturday morning cartoon," began to gain steam, as the adventures of little blue creatures called Smurfs captured our attention and reigned supreme.

Adult audiences were treated to Jack, Chrissy, and Janet in the sitcom *Three's Company*, while *One Day at a Time* featured one of the first working-class mothers, Ann Romano (Bonnie Franklin), raising her daughters. If it was pure entertainment you were after, you could also take a cruise with Captain Stubing, Doc Bricker, and friendly bartender Isaac on *The Love Boat*.

Yet, in spite of the success of programs like ratings giant *Fantasy Island*, escapist fantasy caused a stir when controversy surrounded the fantasy role-playing game Dungeons & Dragons. Although not formally released until 1982, the made-for-TV movie, *Mazes & Monsters*, was test screened at select theaters in 1981 and whipped the general public into an anti-D&D frenzy. As a D&D player myself, I was being accused of all manner of unsavory feats: devil worship, cannibalism, witchcraft, sadism, murder, blasphemy, assassination, prostitution (!), Satanism, suicide, and…animal sacrifice.

Other happenings in pop culture included "Pac-Man Fever," which is still afflicting people by the millions, while a few revolutionary adventure films were released that would have far-reaching effects on the industry, including Steven Spielberg's incomparable *Raiders of the Lost Ark,* the ultimate treasure-hunting adventure.

In music, Lionel Richie and Diana Ross touched our hearts with their duet, "Endless Love," while even in death, nothing could stop John Lennon's accomplishments. Released posthumously, the worldwide success of Lennon's single, "Starting Over," was overshadowed by his omnipresent assassination. 1981 also gave rise to the popularity of "old school" hip hop with The Sugarhill Gang, Spoonie G, Fab 5 Freddie, and Grandmaster Flash and the Furious 5.

Yet the whole music world was rocked to its core when a new network, MTV (Music Television), dedicated to showing (?) music videos premiered on August 1 and eclipsed everything else occurring in the world of popular culture.

In politics, Ronald Reagan won the Presidential election, while the Royal Wedding of Charles, Prince of Wales, and Lady Diana Frances Spencer on July 29 was watched worldwide by 750 million people and labeled the fairytale "wedding of the century."

Prince Charles and his bride Diana, Princess of Wales, march down the aisle of St. Paul's Cathedral at the end of their wedding ceremony on July 29, 1981 in London. *AP Photo*

By the Power of Grayskull!

Masters of the Universe captures children's hearts and minds

Mattel launched its newest toy line in the winter of 1981: the Masters of the Universe. And He-Man, hero of the series, helped make it one of the most revered toy ventures of all time.

Mattel's first MOTU characters found themselves without an animated program on television to support sales when they hit retail stores, and so had to rely on the power of comic books by DC, including the now highly prized mini-comics packaged with the figures.

Although wonderfully written and beautifully illustrated by a stable of stalwart comic book artists—many of whom had contributed in some small way to Marvel's long-running *Conan the Barbarian* series—these charming mini-comics portray an entirely different He-Man universe than what was shown in the Filmation cartoon of the mid-'80s. A slew of mini-comics were written by pop-culture icon Donald F. Glut, who contributed to a long list of children's animated programs in the 1980s. His contribution was quite important, since through these mini-comics, he helped to concoct much of the early back-story for the toy line.

For an entire decade, MOTU truly captured the hearts and minds of children around the world, who made up their own adventures and battles with He-Man and his chief enemy, the blue-skinned, skull-headed Skeletor.

The toy line exploded in popularity when these expertly crafted MOTU figures, vehicles, creatures, playsets, and accessories

The awesome animated series, *He-Man and the Masters of the Universe*, helped the toy line explode in popularity. *Mattel/Filmation Associates*

were paired with the beautifully rendered Filmation cartoon, the *He Man and the Masters of the Universe* animated program which aired from 1983-1985, and throughout syndicated programming for two more years.

Although the bestselling MOTU franchise waned in 1988, for seven strong years Mattel fiercely competed with Hasbro's G.I. Joe and Transformers offerings, as these three toy lines dominated a good deal of the boys' toys market.

The iconic designs of the figures—from Trap Jaw's unique "steampunk" arm configuration to He-Man's exceptionally rendered chest armor (a baldrick with cross-pattée)—allowed the toy line to endure for six full series of releases: 69 total action figures, 12 vehicles, 16 creatures, 6 playsets, and 16 accessories.

Castle Grayskull playset, opened for display, with He-Man, Skeletor, the Sorceress, King Randor, Stratos, Man-at-Arms, and Faker.

He-Man Mini-Comics: *King of Castle Grayskull*, *He-Man and the Power Sword*, and *Battle in the Clouds*.

Snake Mountain playset, back view, with Faker, Terror Claws Skeletor, Trap-Jaw, and Stratos.

Eternia playset, back view.

IMPRESSIVE PLAYSET

Mattel's Eternia playset features three sturdy towers, a working monorail system, and a bevy of wonderful features that would take a child dozens of afternoons to discover. It's the most impressive of all Masters of the Universe-related offerings.

Regarding the name "Eternia," Donald F. Glut, who worked with Mattel on the line, said: "The name Eternia almost instantly sprang to mind when I needed to name this world or dimension… I seem to remember thinking of Disney's *Fantasia* and trying to come up with a similar name."

Masters of the Universe
Horde Trooper.

Masters of the Universe Evil Horde Slime Pit.

Masters of the Universe
Evil Horde Slime Pit, with
Horde Troopers, Fisto,
and Hordak.

Masters of the Universe Wind Raider.

Masters of the Universe Buzz-Saw Hordak.

Masters of the Universe Mosquitor.

Masters of the Universe Extendar.

Masters of the Universe Rokkon.

Masters of the Universe Thunder Punch He-Man.

Totally Smurf-ular

Little Blue Creatures are a huge hit

Smurfette pampers herself in her very own bedroom playset.

Little blue creatures invaded the airwaves on Saturday mornings, much to the delight of children everywhere. Kids loved the *Smurfs* animated series and worshipped these little blue beings for a number of different reasons besides their outwardly adorable appearance.

Was it for their catchy theme song that bordered on lunacy, "Laa, laa, la-la-la-la, la la la-la-la!?" Or was it the Smurfs' rules of syntax? They had an idiosyncratic yet endearing language of omission and replacement, where a slew of nouns, verbs, adjectives, and adverbs were often replaced by a single utterance, "*smurf*": "Have a smurfy day! I hope you smurf the smurfiest smurf smurfer!" Although most can glean the basic meaning from these sentences, you must remember that the omitted words replaced by "smurf" take on different meanings depending on which Smurf actually *states* the greeting/interjection.

Could it have been their fascinating naming process? Since each member of the Smurf clan was named according to the vocation they performed, their appellations were essentially *allusive*—their names functioned as an indirect reference to their skill or occupation. To wit: the Smurf who's the most physically strong is named Hefty, sporting a tattoo of a heart with an arrow through it on his arm; then there's Grouchy, a character who lacks unconditional positive self-regard and possesses little interpersonal or intrapersonal intelligence. Handy is blessed with a high logical/mathematical intelligence, exhibiting an occupational propensity toward becoming mister fixit: a "handy" man. And so on through the ranks of all the rest—Brainy Smurf, Dreamy Smurf, Smurfette, Papa Smurf, Vanity Smurf, *ad nauseam*, *ad infinitum*.

Smurfs were revered the world over and the brainchildren of an aspiring Belgian comic strip artist named Pierre Culliford. As a writer/artist, he was known as Peyo, an eponym stamped onto Smurf products. In 1947, Peyo began chronicling the adventures of a medieval page boy named Johan, and in 1958, the Belgian comics magazine *Le Journal De Spirout* featured one of Johan's many adventures, where he encountered a group of blue-skinned imps, "Schtroumpfs," whose kindness helped him complete his quest.

These characters became an immediate sensation with Belgian children, who began to talk and sing like Schtroumpfs. They were imported to America in the early '80s, where the tales of the Smurfs, their films, and the Hanna-Barbera television cartoon with its classical scores and moral tales (the importance of patience, motivation, friendship, honor, etc.), have been translated into more than 25 languages.

The popularity of characters like Papa Smurf, Smurfette, Gargamel and Azrael, Dreamy, Sleepy, Baby Smurf, Brainy, Hefty, Poet, Clumsy, Harmony, Vanity, Lazy, Jokey, Greedy, Handy, and of course, Johan and Peewit, have endured in global pop culture throughout the past fifty-plus years, and they are still remembered fondly by those of us who grew up with them.

Hanna-Barbera produced 421 episodes of the Smurfs for NBC over the course of nine years, with 91 of them running at a half-hour per clip, and 330 segments running for 15-minute periods.

Smurfs Windmill with the following PVC figures: Vanity, Jokey, Gargamel and Azrael, Brainy, and Papa Smurf

If I ever want to bring back childhood memories, I simply pull out my storage tote full of Smurfs, which includes Mushroom Cottages, hundreds of PVC figures, Smurfette's Bedroom Set, the ingeniously crafted Gargamel's Lab Playset (with a wealth of cool mystical accoutrements), the complicated and fully operational Smurf's Windmill Playset to take a trip down memory lane.

Gargamel's Laboratory playset with Gargamel and Azrael.

Smurf Mushroom Cottages and PVC figures.

Autograph Ma'am?
Dazzling Western Barbie

With *Dallas*' popularity and domination of television for the first half of the '80s, it's odd that no toy company *ever* produced a set of dolls to capitalize on the soapy CBS show that revolved around the Ewings, a wealthy Texas family in the oil and cattle-ranching industries. Maybe they just thought despicable and reprehensible oil baron J.R. Ewing was too larger than life to be reduced to a small action figure?

Although the Mego corporation designed a prototype set of figures, it didn't capture the interest of toy buyers. Other than the company's "Dallas Darts" set and *Dallas* playing card game, the closest a toy company came to capitalizing upon the style of *Dallas*—and the surging interest in country and western music stars such as Dolly Parton, whose height of popularity reached a fever pitch with the smash hit 1980 film, *9 to 5,* was Mattel Toys with its bestselling Western Barbie doll.

This doll was resplendent in her authentic western hat with black-and-silver cord, fancy western boots, and detailed western jumpsuit. She also came with a personal autograph stamp (a two-piece ink pad with pink ink), six head shots of herself to "autograph" for her fans, a comb, brush, perfume bottle, and a hand-held mirror. She also had another special feature: children could press a button on the doll's back to make her wink at fans.

Mattel's Western Barbie, with the tag line, "She gives you her autograph and a wink," was a smash hit for the No. 1 toy company in the world.

Western Barbie with accoutrements.

Dungeons & Dragons role-playing game: Dungeons & Dragons Basic Set, Dungeon Master's Screen, dice (4-sided, 6-sided, 8-sided, two 10-sided dice [a.k.a. "percentiles"] 12-sided, 20-sided), dice bag, map, *Dragon Magazine* supplements, hardcover *Deities & Demigods* book, modules (6), painted lead miniatures (5).

Products of Your Imagination

Dungeons & Dragons escapist fantasy

Although produced since 1974, TSR's Dungeons & Dragons fantasy role-playing game was suddenly made infamous in the early 1980s due to the controversial 1982 *Mazes & Monsters* film that portrayed a group of college students as obsessed with a similar pastime. The protagonist, played by a young Tom Hanks, experiences a psychotic episode because of his depth of immersion in the "Mazes & Monsters" fantasy.

A media circus followed the release of the film, and gamers who played D&D were ostracized by the media as Satanists, outcasts, and demon worshippers. These accusations subsided over time, though, as people recognized D&D for what it actually was: escapist fantasy.

In Tactical Studies Rules Incorporated's infamous game, a participant, known as a "player character," creates an imaginary swords-and-sorcery type of fantasy character by rolling three six-sided dice, and adding the numbers together to create "ability scores" for their character's six attributes: strength, intelligence, wisdom, dexterity, constitution, and charisma.

The role-player's choice of character class is based on these scores. If you have a high strength, you should pick a fighter as your class; a soaring intelligence score and you'd select a Magic User. Role-players can also choose, if their scores are high enough, to become a PC of a different race such as dwarf, elf, or orc. After players have created their characters, these PCs are put through their paces. All of the game's adventures are controlled by a referee-storyteller known as the "dungeon master," whose responsibility is to usher player characters through a series of related imaginary adventures called a "campaign."

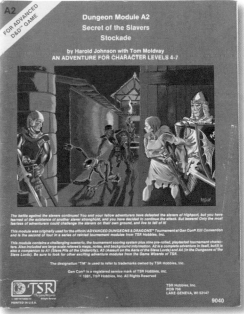

Assorted Dungeons & Dragons modules. Since its inception, more than 20 million people have played this ingenious game, built upon the conventions of timeless myths and (unofficially) the world of J.R.R. Tolkien. Sales have topped $1 billion in rule books, gaming supplies, and pre-constructed adventures.

Stars of the Track and Toy Aisle

Hot Wheels' "gimmick" cars capture imagination

Not one single toy company was immune to implementing gimmicks that permeated toy production in the 1980s—even Mattel's super-popular Hot Wheels line.

Two new retail offerings produced by the long-standing toy automaker in the 1980s were Hot Wheels Crack-Ups and Hot Wheels FlipOuts.

The toys' gimmicks captured the attention of both children and adults alike. Hot Wheels "Crack-Ups" were perhaps my favorite die-cast 1:64 toy line of all time, employing the same technology that Mattel utilized for the "battle damaged" chest pieces of its Masters of the Universe Battle Armor He-Man and Battle Armor Skeletor action figures.

With a tag line that touted, "Crash 'em! Fix 'em! Bash 'em again!" each Crack-Ups automobile featured either a grill, side panel, or rear panel, that—when a plate on the car's frame was pressed—would flip over and reveal body damage: a dent in the car's exterior. The process could be performed over and over again, since all you needed to do was turn the panel back into its starting position, post-crash.

Another impressive "gimmick" car offered by Hot Wheels was its "FlipOuts" series, touting that kids could "Watch 'em flip! Reset for more wrecks!" The instructions for these die-cast metal 1:64 scale automobiles were quite simple: 1) Press button. Rotate lever back to lock position; 2) Vehicle flips on impact! Reset to flip again.

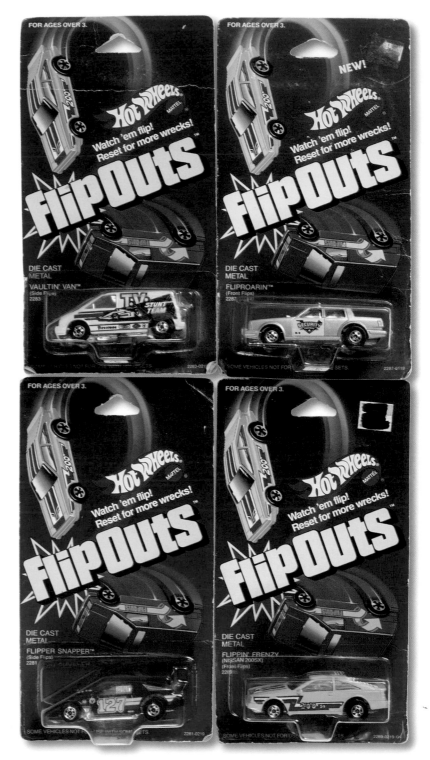

Hot Wheels FlipOuts: Vaultin' Van (side flips); Fliproarin' (front flips); Flipper Snapper (side flips); Flippin' Frenzy (Nissan 200SX; front flips).

Hot Wheels Crack-Ups: Stocker Smasher with undamaged grill, and Sidebanger with undamaged side panel.

Hot Wheels Crack-Ups: Stocker Smasher with smashed grill, and Sidebanger with damaged side panel.

Hot Wheels Crack-Ups: Stocker Smasher, Sidebanger, and Smak Bak.

ENTERTAINMENT-O-RAMA:
1981 MOVIES, MUSIC, TELEVISION

Top Ten Films of 1981

1 *Raiders of the Lost Ark* (Paramount)
2 *On Golden Pond* (Universal)
3 *Superman II* (Warner Brothers)
4 *Arthur* (Warner Brothers)
5 *Stripes* (Sony/Columbia)
6 *The Cannonball Run* (20th Century Fox)
7 *Chariots of Fire* (Sony/Columbia)
8 *For Your Eyes Only* (MGM/United Artists)
9 *The Four Seasons* (Sony/Universal)
10 *Time Bandits* (Embassy)

Best Picture: *Chariots of Fire* (Columbia)

Action-adventure epic *Raiders of the Lost Ark* was the start of an Indiana Jones movie franchise. Jones (Harrison Ford) is an archeology professor who often embarks on perilous adventures to obtain rare artifacts. In *Raiders*, he finds himself battling Nazls for the Ark of the Covenant. *Lucasfilm Ltd/Paramount/The Kobal Collection*

Top Ten Television Programs of 1981-82

1 *Dallas* (CBS)
2 *60 Minutes* (CBS)
3 *The Jeffersons* (CBS)
4 *Three's Company* (ABC)
5 *Alice* (CBS)
6 *The Dukes of Hazzard* (CBS)
7 *Too Close for Comfort* (ABC)
8 *Monday Night Movie* (ABC)
9 *M*A*S*H* (CBS)
10 *One Day at a Time* (CBS)

In 1981, audiences thrilled to the comedy of errors that was *Three's Company*, a program that portrayed three young unmarried roommates who struggle to pay their rent. Featuring aspiring chef Jack Tripper (John Ritter), florist Janet Wood (Joyce DeWitt), and secretary Chrissy "Christmas" Snow (Suzanne Somers), the script was laden with innuendo and broad physical comedy. Whether interacting with their landlords the Ropers—or later, with Mr. Furley (Don Knotts)—you could always count on the three roommates turning a simple misunderstanding into an epic predicament. *DLT Entertainment/NRW Company/The Kobal Collection*

Top Ten Billboard Singles of 1981

1   "Bette Davis Eyes," Kim Carnes (*Mistaken Identity*, 1981)

2   "Endless Love," Diana Ross & Lionel Richie
    (*Endless Love* soundtrack, 1981)

3   "Lady," Kenny Rogers (*Kenny Roger's Greatest Hits*, 1980)

4   "(Just Like) Starting Over," John Lennon (*Double Fantasy*, 1980)

5   "Jessie's Girl," Rick Springfield (*Working Class Dog*, 1981)

6   "Celebration," Kool & The Gang (*Celebrate!*, 1980)

7   "Kiss On My List," Daryl Hall & John Oates (*Voices*, 1980)

8   "I Love A Rainy Night," Eddie Rabbitt (*Horizon*, 1980)

9   "9 To 5," Dolly Parton (*9 to 5 and Odd Jobs*, 1980)

10 "Keep On Loving You," REO Speedwagon (*Hi Infidelity*, 1980)

This is the back cover of the *Double Fantasy* album by John Lennon, featuring his wife Yoko Ono. Behind them is the Dakota apartment building where Lennon was fatally shot. *AP Photo*

The first images shown on MTV were a montage of the Apollo 11 moon landing. *Viacom/MTV*

The Creation of MTV

MTV's first logo/icon would come to be known as the "Moonman," as the fledgling cable station used the iconic image of the 1969 moon landing of Apollo 11 astronaut Buzz Aldrin planting a flag on the moon for its very first commercial on August 1, 1981.

MTV's Moonman image begged the following analogy (whether explicit or implicit): "You thought humankind landing on the MOON was the greatest thing you've ever witnessed on television? I suppose that was correct...until now. Until you watch the revolutionary new television channel called MTV!"

After witnessing the first music video that appeared on MTV that Saturday—the apropos "Video Killed the Radio Star" by English New Wave band the Buggles—television, music, and American society would be forever changed. For although MTV no longer functions (as its initialism once suggested) as "Music Tele-Vision," the channel's original programming continues to impact popular culture.

1982

Trivial Pursuit tests your knowledge about various subjects including geography and history. The inside edge goes to those who have a knack for storing information, useful and otherwise, in their head.

A Pursuit of Trivial Matters
and a Real American Hero
Gets a Re-Launch

G.I. Joe action figure Duke.

ALL OF THOSE ARCANE LITTLE TIDBITS OF INFORMATION stored away in your brain could finally be utilized in a challenging way in 1982, with the advent of the game that defined the "decade of excess": Trivial Pursuit, a revolution in the field of board games.

The realm of collectible action figures also underwent a marked change when Hasbro Inc. decided to re-solicit its most famous toy line as G.I. Joe: A Real American Hero.

On television, America was entranced by the Carrington family in the prime time soap opera *Dynasty*, while many other viewers enjoyed the dynamic between Tom Selleck (as "Thomas Magnum) and John Hillerman (as "Higgins") on the Hawaii-based *Magnum P.I.* I was utterly fascinated by Eddie Murphy and the multiple characters he portrayed on *Saturday Night Live*. His appearances as "Buckwheat," "Gumby," and "Mister Robinson" had me and my friends ending our Saturday evenings in stitches. Murphy simply exploded into American popular culture in 1982.

One of the finest years in American history for film was in 1982, as audiences were treated to Steven Spielberg's *E.T.: The Extra Terrestrial*, *Tootsie* starring a brilliant and re-invented Dustin Hoffman, Sylvester Stallone in *First Blood* and *Rocky III* (also featuring Mr. T as "Clubber Lang"), *48 Hours*, *Poltergeist*, "Anniemania" following the feature film *Annie*, the famous and oft-quoted *Star Trek II: The Wrath of Khan*, Richard Gere and Debra Winger in *An Officer and a Gentleman*, John Carpenter's horrifying cult classic

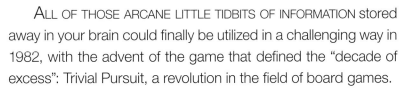

The Thing, Arnold Schwarzenegger's breakthrough film, *Conan the Barbarian*, Ridley Scott's science-fiction masterpiece *Blade Runner*, and the quick-witted *Fast Times at Ridgemont High*.

Thanks to the success of *Rocky III*, Survivor's "Eye of the Tiger" was the victim of over-saturation on the radio; Stevie Wonder and Paul McCartney sang the touching duet "Ebony & Ivory," and A Flock of Seagulls sported the most ludicrous haircuts ever to support their international hit single "I Ran (So Far Away)." John Cougar Mellencamp's eclectic brand of R&B, rock, folk, and country dominated the airwaves in 1982 with his album *American Fool*.

Furthermore, with the release of Frank Zappa's song, "Valley Girl," the lexicon of American English became infused with the influence of "Valspeak"—a dialect borrowed from young girls from the San Fernando Valley in California, whose materialistic lifestyle and focus on their appearance and social status would impact even the most rural communities in the U.S.

Testing Your Inner Genius

Trivial Pursuit gives rebirth to board games

Frustrated when they sat down to play Scrabble, only to find quite a few letter tiles were missing from the game, Scott Abbott and Chris Haney decided to develop their own board game in 1979.

If Mark Twain once said that "necessity is the mother of taking chances," then the creation of Trivial Pursuit was necessitated by the chance to produce a superior board game—one that would challenge people intellectually, of course, yet play to each individual's strength. With question categories in the fields of Arts & Literature (brown), Entertainment (pink), Geography (blue), History (yellow), Science & Nature (green), and Sports & Leisure (orange), the playing field was finally leveled.

Trivial Pursuit indelibly etched itself into pop culture, peaking in popularity in 1984 when 20 million units were sold worldwide. Since then, that total has risen to 90 million games.

The game has also been portrayed on different TV shows. The most memorable appearance is on a fourth-season episode of *Seinfeld*, "The Bubble Boy." In this tale, a misprinted answer card (whose answer "The Moors" is misrepresented as "The Moops") leads George Costanza to engage in fisticuffs with Donald, a bitter boy trapped inside a plastic bubble. Who, indeed, invaded Spain in the 8th century? The Moops, of course…

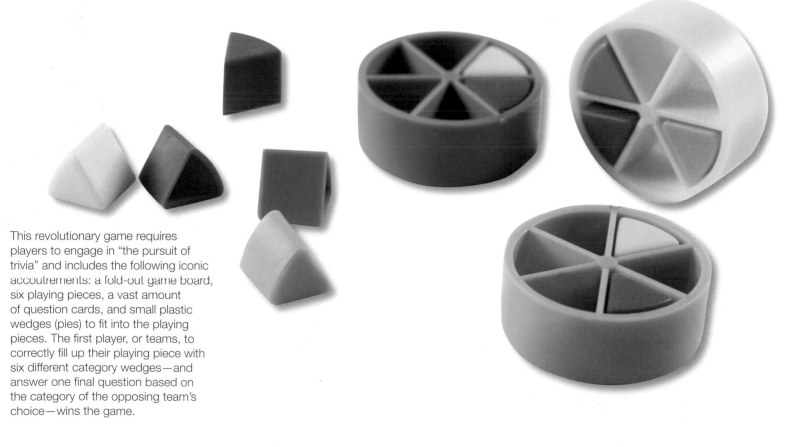

This revolutionary game requires players to engage in "the pursuit of trivia" and includes the following iconic accoutrements: a fold-out game board, six playing pieces, a vast amount of question cards, and small plastic wedges (pies) to fit into the playing pieces. The first player, or teams, to correctly fill up their playing piece with six different category wedges—and answer one final question based on the category of the opposing team's choice—wins the game.

The complete Trivial Pursuit board game.

Standing Small

A relaunch of the G.I. Joe toy line results in massive success

The standard "general issue" soldier of the 1960s and 1970s paved the way for a hugely successful re-launch of America's favorite "movable fighting man," with the release of the 3-3/4-inch G.I. Joe toy line.

Now acting as a team of soldiers and military specialists, the new G.I. Joe Mobile Strike Force Team was the brainchild of Hasbro Industries.

This new line was a smash hit in large thanks to the figures' poseability, a slew of accessories, and low price points: in 1982, you could buy the entire line of sixteen figures (fifteen plus one mail-away character), and seven vehicles and weapons systems for under $100 retail.

With the initial launch of the line, sales were not yet driven by Sunbow's fantastic syndicated daily animated cartoon, *G.I. Joe: A Real American Hero*, but by a clever marketing strategy that let Hasbro sell the toys in concert with a Marvel Comics tie-in. Hasbro and Marvel were allowed to advertise the *G.I. Joe* comic book and toys on television through the use of bombastic 30-second animated commercials, and both literally sold out overnight. Cite whichever influences you want—the rise of a Democratic spirit, the U.S.' triumphant win as underdogs during the 1980s Olympic Games in Lake Placid, or a public oversaturated with fantasy toys—G.I. Joe was a breakout success.

To add to the allure of the line, each Joe came complete with a cut-out "Combat Command File Card"/biographical dossier on the card back, written by über-talented Marvel G.I. Joe scribe and war veteran, Larry Hama. Hama's ability to render G.I. Joe characters to children while still maintaining an adult sensibility established a core principle of the line.

In the 1980s, Hasbro had a knack for suspending our disbelief, allowing us to immerse into a fantasy world (e.g. G.I. Joe, Transformers, Visionaries, etc.) that consumed our imagination and sustained the growth of each line.

Snake Eyes, with Timber.

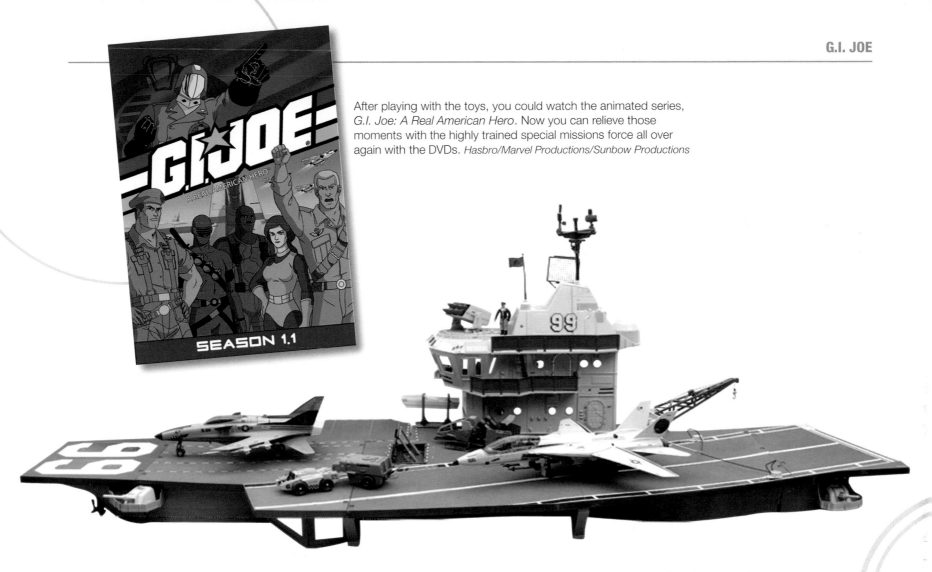

After playing with the toys, you could watch the animated series, *G.I. Joe: A Real American Hero*. Now you can relieve those moments with the highly trained special missions force all over again with the DVDs. *Hasbro/Marvel Productions/Sunbow Productions*

G.I. Joe U.S.S. Flagg Aircraft Carrier with full assortment of vehicles and action figures on its deck and superstation.

H. Kirk Bozigian, Hasbro's vice president of boys' toys, spoke about his role in concocting the reinvention of G.I. Joe. "Plastic was very expensive. Still too expensive to do a 12-inch (action) figure at a reasonable price…we came up with the idea of re-inventing plastic green army men. That is how the 3-3/4-inch line was born."

Bozigian elucidated further upon the origins of G.I. Joe's rebirth: "Also, it is important to note that the line was never positioned as an action figure line. We looked upon it as an action vehicle line. The figures were accessories for the vehicles.

Of course, all of this evolved into an action figure line…"

These G.I. Joe toys were based on "top-secret" military specs. Ronald Rudat, lead designer of the 3-3/4-inch G.I. Joe figures from 1981 through 1987, said Hasbro encouraged its designers to tour military bases to see what it felt like to "be inside" a vehicle, or even to simply gape in awe at a live missile system. Hasbro went the extra mile to obtain the precision and detail that garnered critical acclaim for its toys from even the most astute military miniaturists.

Roadblock, Spirit, Thunder, Baroness, Cobra Commander, Firefly, Copperhead, Wild Weasel.

Zartan, Cobra Stinger Driver, Storm Shadow, Scrap-Iron.

Airtight, Alpine, Barbecue, Bazooka, Flint, Footloose, Lady Jaye, Dusty.

Each of the G.I. Joe action figures had poseability based on Mego's 3-3/4-inch Dukes of Hazzard and CHiPs toy lines: 10 points of articulation. Every character came packaged on a chipboard cardback in a clear bubble, and included "snap-on, stay-on" accessories specific to their Military Occupational Specialty.

For instance, a Ranger came with an M-32 "Pulverizer" submachine gun, a Commando wielded an Uzi pistol, a Mortar Soldier launched shells from his 81mm Medium Mortar. The original line of these figures, vehicles, weapons systems, playsets, and accessories numbered more than 750 total pieces.

Quick Kick, Snake Eyes, Shipwreck, Tollbooth, Crankcase, Heavy Metal, Keel-Haul.

Sgt. Slaughter, Frostbite, Tripwire, Torch, Buzzer, Ripper, Snow Serpent, Eels.

Tele-Viper, Crimson Guard, Lampreys, Tomax, Xamot.

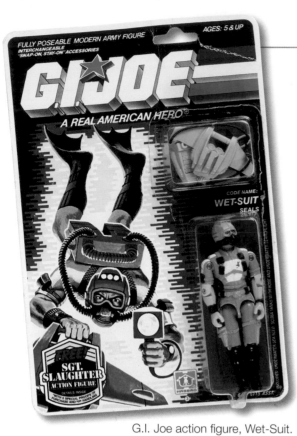

G.I. Joe action figure, Wet-Suit.

Team members and agents of Cobra Command continue to resonate with modern audiences and dominate the toy market with film tie-ins such as the live-action *G.I. Joe: The Rise of Cobra* (2009), which made over $300 million in worldwide ticket sales. It appears that Snake Eyes, Duke, Scarlett, Storm Shadow, Cobra Commander, Destro, and the Baroness will endure for a long time…

G.I. Joe action figure, Lifeline.

G.I. Joe action figure, Sneak Peek.

G.I. Joe action figure, Spirit.

G.I. Joe action figure, Eels.

G.I. Joe action figure, Jinx.

G.I. Joe action figure, Mutt and Junkyard.

G.I. Joe action figure, Shipwreck.

'Everywhere You Go, a Smiling Face'
My Little Pony a beloved toy line

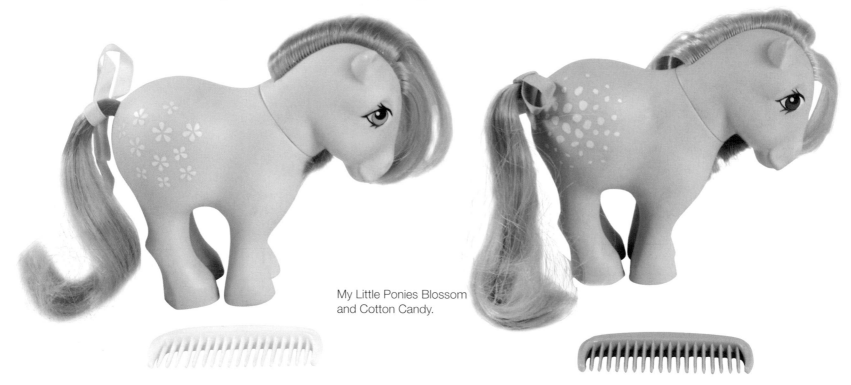

My Little Ponies Blossom and Cotton Candy.

The My Little Pony line easily rivals the "big four" boys action figure lines (Star Wars, G.I. Joe, Transformers, and Masters of the Universe). In terms of breadth and depth of Ponies, the sheer amount of different characters made during the first run of the toy, from 1982-1991, through its modern permutation, is sufficiently overwhelming.

These colorful Ponies were stout, non-articulated, caricatured horses with rooted manes and tails, and each one possessed a group of symbols on their haunches that represented the characters' names. In the first series of My Little Pony offerings, only six Ponies were produced.

These Ponies, nicknamed "Earth Ponies" because of their resemblance to standard horses (as opposed to the later-solicited mythical Pegasi or Unicorns), came with a colored bow tied around the base of their tail, and a matching colored comb as the toy's lone accessory. Of note is that the first series of Ponies are "flat-footed" and do not possess a later characteristic concavity of their hooves.

The first six My Little Ponies were: Blossom, a purple Pony with purple mane and tail, grey-purple eyes, and a symbol on her haunches of a group of tiny white flowers; Blue Belle, light blue with purple mane and tail, blue-grey eyes, and the symbol of a group of small purple stars; Butterscotch, gold with gold mane and tail, brown eyes, and the symbol of a group of small gold butterflies; Cotton Candy, pink with pink mane and tail, purple eyes, and the symbol of multiple white dots; Minty, white-green with white mane and tail, blue eyes, and the symbol of a group of green clovers; and Snuzzle, gray with pink mane and tail, blue eyes, and a group of pink hearts on her haunches.

Originally syndicated by Claster Television and produced by Toei Animation, a cartoon based on the characters titled *My Little Pony 'N Friends*, ran from Sept. 15, 1986 to Sept. 25, 1987. The cartoon chronicles the adventures of various groups of Little Ponies—the Earth Ponies, Pegasus Ponies, and Unicorns.

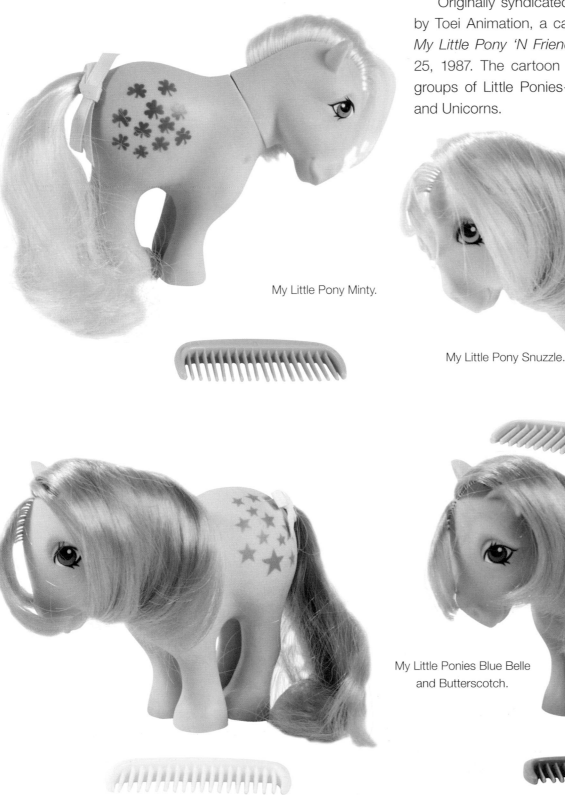

My Little Pony Minty.

My Little Pony Snuzzle.

My Little Ponies Blue Belle and Butterscotch.

Phone Home

E.T.: The Extra-Terrestrial strikes a chord

E.T. the movie made zealots out of American children. Many were revisiting theaters five, ten, sometimes fifteen, times for repeat viewings. Kids simply couldn't get enough of this adorable, waddling, long-necked alien (was he really that cute, though?).

It's no surprise, then, that the toy likeness of everyone's favorite alien flew off the shelves.

LJN Toys capitalized on the E.T. craze and produced a slew of character-related products; E.T. toys, figurines, and action figures released in various sizes and price points to satisfy the voracious demand for all things E.T., from 3-inch solid PVC characters,

to pull-back toys, 3-inch wind-up action toys, to the more detailed 7-inch figures, and even an assortment of plush dolls.

One of the more impressive offerings was the 7-inch tall poseable talking action figure, which was an interesting interpretation of the alien. Dressed in a blue bathrobe, the toy spoke the following phrases when you drew its pull string: "Home," "Elliott," "E.T., E.T., E.T.," and "Ouch!" It also came with the four major accessories that E.T. utilized in the iconic film: a Speak 'N Spell, telephone, can (i.e. beer can), and a flower pot. With decent poseability, the ability to speak, and movie-accurate accessories, it was a standout in the LJN toy line.

Poseable talking E.T. toy with Speak 'N Spell, beer can, telephone receiver, and flower pot.

Poseable talking E.T. toy.

Dynamite Magazine, "A Close Encounter with E.T.," (July 1982).

Advances Were Made

Atari 5200 a step up from 2600 model

The Atari 5200 "SuperSystem" was introduced to the video game marketplace in 1982 as a replacement for the Atari 2600 in order for the company to compete against the more sophisticated Intellivision console.

Approaching its 5th anniversary, Atari's 2600 had not aged well, appearing rudimentary in comparison to both Intellivision and Colecovision. Although the 5200 was, of course, a more sophisticated machine than its predecessor, its lack of backwards compatibility caused it to suffer until an adapter was produced in 1983 (and sold separately).

The greatest detraction was the system's flawed joysticks, which had a tendency to "lock up" or "freeze" at the most inopportune moments. The irony inherent here: each Atari 5200 controller possessed a "pause" button—a novelty not yet enjoyed by any console game.

Combine this poorly received system with the fact Atari greatly overestimated the demand of certain games (such as *The Great E.T.: The Extra-Terrestrial Cartridge Landfill Mountain Burning* of 1983— true story!), and the video game market was riding a thin bubble about to burst.

Enter the video game crash. And it wouldn't be until the production of the Nintendo Entertainment System in 1986 that buyers' faith was restored.

Atari 5200 video game system with two paddle-type controllers, and the following seven games: *Galaxian*, *Pac-Man*, *Super Breakout*, *Centipede*, *Dig Dug*, and *Pole Position II*.

Bringing the Arcade Home

Colecovision a sophisticated marvel in gaming

The Coleco corporation's well-received Colecovision video game console. No longer did gamers have to spend all hours of the evening at the local mall in cramped arcades, pumping an endless stream of quarters into a single machine (as I did with Don Bluth's *Dragon's Lair*). Investing in an expensive Colecovision console allowed you to experience the arcade "flava" of sophisticated gaming at home with *Donkey Kong*, *Donkey Kong Jr.*, *Carnival*, *Mouse Trap*, or *Zaxxon*.

It wasn't until I was invited over to my best friend Frankie Woznick's house on the day after Christmas in 1983 that I actually witnessed the phenomenon that Colecovision had imparted the previous year: allowing home access to coin-operated arcade games.

I always considered the concept of playing an arcade game in the comfort of your own living room to be an impossibility. That technology just didn't exist in the early '80s, until I was handed a Colecovision controller by my friend with a smile on his face. These joysticks (without the "stick") were quite similar to those rectangular keypads with side buttons offered by Intellivision, and so, I tried out Colecovision's *Donkey Kong* myself. Genius. Brilliant. Unparalleled. Atari and Intellivision were infants compared to the sophisticated and authentic graphics of Colecovision.

Fun Franchise
The Adventures of Indiana Jones

Kenner's Streets of Cairo playset, featuring Indiana Jones, Monkey Man, Cairo Swordsman, Belloq, and Toht. Other accessories for this adventure set were a non-poseable Marion Ravenwood molded in a crouching position, so she could easily fit into a basket, a PVC monkey, a knife, a six-piece cart, five-piece table, 13 pieces of fruit (3 watermelons, 10 oranges), and three different baskets—all with lids.

Kenner's The Adventures of Indiana Jones toy line has its origins ingrained in a risky throwback of a film that Steven Spielberg and George Lucas struggled to get made, *Raiders of the Lost Ark*, yet the license ultimately evolved into a three-decade-old franchise whose films' worldwide grosses are just shy of $2 billion.

Thankfully, Kenner "chose wisely" in crafting this magnificent toy line, and provided fans of Dr. Henry Walton Jones, Jr. with some of the most entertaining characters and fascinating play sets ever made.

Building on the enduring triumph of its Star Wars brand, Kenner Toys released these Indiana Jones figures in a 3-3/4-inch format analogous to its Star Wars offerings. There are many similarities between the films that spawned their respective action figure lines, but did Adventures of the Indiana Jones toys sell as well as the contemporary Star Wars line? No, Short Round. It was not in the cards.

Unfortunately, few children were attracted to the toy line and action figures of Indiana Jones, Toht, Marion Ravenwood, the Cairo Swordsman, and the superbly detailed mail-away offer: Belloq in ceremonial robes. It should be noted that a feature was added to some of the action figures called "quick draw action." This allowed you to pull a figure's arm back and then suddenly release it in order to simulate the firing of a weapon.

In 1983, four more action figures were added to the line: Sallah, Indiana Jones in German Uniform, German Mechanic and the standard version of Belloq. Also released for the second series was another playset, the Streets of Cairo, Indy's Arabian Horse, and the Desert Convoy Truck vehicle.

The final piece in the line that deserves a mention is the 12-inch Indiana Jones figure. By today's high standards, the figure is considered a bit inauthentic, yet Kenner did manage to include a revolver, whip, removable hat—albeit one that looks nothing like Indy's trademarked fedora—and removable clothing to cover up the fact that the toy was essentially a re-molded 12-inch Star Wars Han Solo figure released in 1978, with brown hair instead of black.

Kenner manufactured two critically praised adventure sets in this line: the Map Room and Well of the Souls—quite possibly some of the finest playsets ever produced, as they truly capture the essence of the film.

Kenner's 12-inch Indiana Jones figure.

Adventures of Indiana Jones 3-3/4-inch figure.

Well of the Souls playset, featuring Marion Ravenwood and Indiana Jones.

In *Raiders of the Lost Ark*, Indy's discovery of this secret spot leads him to The Well of the Souls, "The Hiding Place for the Ancient Ark" (from the box text). This stunning adventure set included the following delicate components: the gilded three-piece Ark of the Covenant, two poles for carrying the Ark, a crypt-cover for the Ark, a break-apart wall (two pieces), two arches with mounting legs, a mummy, fourteen snakes (nearly impossible to find all of them in loose samples of the playset), a grappling hook, and two torches. This toy—like the other two playsets in the line—is truly a work of art.

Attention: Incoming M*A*S*H Toys

The best care anywhere

At an early age I became addicted to the award-winning TV show *M*A*S*H*, never recalling how much I cared for the fictional characters including Captain "Hawkeye" Pierce, Trapper John,

*M*A*S*H*'s infamous sign-post. Aficionados will note the post-Winchester addition of "Boston" to the top.

Captain B.J. Hunnicut, Colonel Potter, "Radar" O'Reilly, Major Frank Burns, and Major Margaret "Hot Lips" Houlihan until the show ended. *M*A*S*H* had the power to make me quite emotional. I broke down when Radar read the report of Henry Blake's death; and I teared up when Radar left the 4077th, abandoning his lost innocence in the form of his teddy bear.

The only thing better than watching the show would be, you guessed it: playing with the toys. And there were some great—yet little-known—*M*A*S*H* toys.

However, I don't think I would have fully appreciated Tristar International Ltd.'s M*A*S*H toys as a child because the program's doctors were essentially non-combatants; you can't really play "war" with six G.I. Joes and a Hawkeye figure. I suppose I would have had to play "peace"—a much more challenging game to organize. Regardless, it would have been fantastic to have had the 4077th Military Base as a kid, in order to set up Col. Potter's office, the good ol' Medevac landing pad, the P.A. system, tents, hospital beds, and other astonishing accessories to assist my wounded 3-3/4-inch G.I. Joes when recovering from battle.

The eight action figures produced for the line were directly based upon the characters at that time the show was being aired in 1982—for the final two seasons: 10 and 11. Their facial sculpts are fairly accurate to the actors' likenesses, and each toy had a decent amount of poseability. This small selection of figures includes Hawkeye, B.J., Col. Potter, Klinger (with and without ladies' attire), Father Mulcahy, Major Charles Emerson Winchester III, and Margaret Houlihan.

The sixty-piece M*A*S*H Military Base ranks is quite possibly, along with Kenner's The Adventures of Indiana Jones playsets, one of the most superb toys ever made.

"The Swamp" officers' quarters with Winchester, B.J., and Hawkeye.

Colonel Potter's office with Klinger and Colonel Potter action figures.

The playset possesses super-realistic details such as officer's quarters, "The Swamp," an Officer's Mess with benches and tables, Colonel Potter's office with a picture of "Sophie" on his wall, a Pre-Op Ward for emergency surgery, a hospital with beds for the wounded, a basketball hoop, pot-bellied stove, lawn chair, bookcases with martini glasses on them, and a 16-foot-square printed four-color vinyl play surface that shows a helicopter landing pad.

Post-Op Ward with Father Mulcahy and wounded G.I.s.

M*A*S*H Military Base playset, full view, with removable roofs covering the Swamp, Hospital, Mess Tent, and Col. Potter's Office.

Medical Unit ambulance with 3-3/4-inch G.I. action figure.

Medical Unit Jeep with 3-3/4-inch G.I. action figure.

Medical Unit helicopter with 3-3/4-inch G.I. action figure.

The three vehicles produced for the M*A*S*H line by Tristar International Ltd's—the helicopter, jeep, and ambulance—are spot-on likenesses for these transports for the wounded. The Jeep is an accurate depiction of the U.S. Army's M-38A1 jeeps that were sent to Korea, while the design of the helicopter is unbelievable—it truly does look like an OH-13H Sioux light observation helicopter. However, the ambulance is my favorite, as I usually set up Klinger (in drag) as a corpsman along with one of the three regular "generic" enlisted soldiers included with the three vehicles.

Toys of 'Tomorrow'

World of Annie dolls have authentic likeness

I can recall my sister belting out the lyrics to *Annie*'s "It's the Hard Knock Life" while twirling around our living room during the early '80s—over and over and over again like a zealous zombie. She was enraptured with Aileen Quinn's inspiring performance as the title character when singing the hits "Maybe" and "Tomorrow."

Part of my acceptance of my sister's addiction to the tunes was the fact that the Knickerbocker Toy Company released an excellent set of dolls to complement the film's release.

The dolls in the "World of Annie" line had intricate fabric costumes, authentic likenesses, and articulation similar to Barbie dolls, although not in scale since Annie dolls were built to an 8-inch maximum height. The assortment was limited to the major cast members of the film: Annie herself, Daddy Warbucks, Punjab, Miss Hannigan, and Annie's friend, Molly. Along with these five fashion dolls, Knickerbocker also produced a set of outfits for Annie, one vehicle, Daddy Warbuck's Duesenberg Limousine, a Mansion playset/doll house, a larger-scale Annie and Sandy rag doll set, and a series of PVC miniatures.

Annie and Punjab figures.

Ch-Ch-Ch-Chia!

Grow Your Own Pet

Chia Pet, original "Chia Ram."

Produced by Joseph Enterprises, Inc., the original Chia Pet was a terra cotta figurine with enclosed seed packet. Now known as the "Chia Ram," it made its way into American homes through the use of a catchy commercial that was almost viral in its exposure. You couldn't turn the TV on without encountering a maddening tune, played over time-lapse photography, showing the chia seeds sprouting to the tones of the ridiculously sweet and chipper, "Ch-Ch-Ch-Chia!"

Since its debut, there have been many permutations of the figurines: from Homer Simpson to Garfield, from hippopotamuses to alarm clocks, and even a line of patriotic Chias with selections including Abraham Lincoln and President Obama.

This basic formula has never changed since the Chia Pet's introduction, where it was described in the original Chia pet commercial as follows: "Chia Pet: the pottery that grows! It's fun and easy. Soak your Chia, spread the seeds, keep it watered, and watch it grow!"

Electronic Gladiators

The Toys of *Tron*

As the first film to make extensive use of computer graphics, Walt Disney's 1982 innovative science-fiction film *Tron* featured a slew of talented actors who later pursued other starring roles: Bruce Boxleitner (of *Scarecrow & Mrs. King* and *Babylon 5*) as Alan Bradly/Tron; Oscar winner Jeff Bridges as Tron's stalwart chum, Kevin Flynn/Clu (his program counterpart); *Caddyshack's* Cindy Morgan as Dr. Lora Baines/Yori; and award-winning performer David Warner as Ed Dillinger/the evil "Command Program" Sark.

With a unique plot that was quite distinctive in the early 1980s, the story of *Tron* begins when a group of software engineers stumble upon a malevolent computer that has gained sentience and threatens to disable the world's security network. In order to stop the computer, the engineers are essentially downloaded and digitized into a mainframe where their computerized counterparts—humanoids who resemble their human creators—combat the sinister Master Control Program.

The characters' computerized costumes were translated into plastic form by Japanese hit toy-maker Tomy (Takara-Tomy as of 2006) in 1982 when the company released an excellent line of *Tron* action figures and vehicles. This set of 4-1/2-inch tall figures was molded in plastic and, through the use of glow-in-the-dark paint, Tomy expertly rendered the uniforms. Tomy produced four figures: Tron himself with glow-in-the-dark flying disk, an accessory that attached to each figures' back via a peg; Flynn with glow-in-the-dark disk; Sark with glow-in-the-dark disk; and a generic Warrior figure, a nameless member of Sark's army, that came with a unique glow-in-the-dark staff. Tomy also produced one of the most requested vehicles from any action figure line of the 1980s: the Tron Light Cycles. Offered in two different colors, red and yellow, these Light Cycles allowed a Tron figure to sit in the cockpit, while, with the pull of a ripcord on a flat surface, a child could manipulate the vehicle to zoom across a room.

Tron action figures, complete set of four: Warrior (x 3), Sark, Tron, and Flynn.

ENTERTAINMENT-O-RAMA:
1982 MOVIES, MUSIC, TELEVISION

In an iconic scene from *E.T.: The Extra-Terrestrial*, the alien and Elliot fly high. *Universal/The Kobal Collection*

Do you accurately recall E.T.?

Do children of the 1980s remember *E.T.: The Extra-Terrestrial* as it actually occurred?

When questioning dozens of film buffs about the beginning of *E.T.*, nine out of ten respondents couldn't recall the specifics of the opening scene in terms of plot or character. They often begin recounting this movie—one they have seen multiple times—with the following summation: "When Elliott finds E.T. in the forest, the kid leads the little guy back to his house with a trail of Reese's Pieces…"

What really happens at the onset of the film? E.T.'s people arrive on Earth as part of a botanical mission. Their goal: to retrieve samples of indigenous Earth flora and plant-life which they keep in suspension on their spaceship for research purposes. In the midst of this mission, the aliens' "heart-lights" (thanks, Neil Diamond) begin to glow as a signal to return to their

ship. Unfortunately, a single alien is separated from his people. When the spaceship is detected by a group of potentially hostile humans, the ship departs, leaving the lone alien behind. The alien evades his pursuers and hides near the house of a young boy, Elliott (Henry Thomas). After detecting the alien's presence, Elliott leaves a trail of Reese's Pieces to lure the hungry being into his house, where the two form a symbiotic relationship and become fast friends.

Everyone knows the rest. Cue a young, adorable Drew Barrymore, a communication device built to contact the alien's people, sinister scientists, and a close call that leads to the being's safe passage home after a tearful farewell. The motifs of love and friendship are made all the more pronounced by John Williams' brilliant score. What more could you ask for in a film?

Top Ten Films of 1982

1 *E.T.: The Extra-Terrestrial* (Universal)
2 *Tootsie* (Sony/Columbia)
3 *An Officer and a Gentleman* (Paramount)
4 *Rocky III* (MGM/United Artists)
5 *Porky's* (20th Century Fox)
6 *Star Trek II: The Wrath of Khan* (Paramount)
7 *48 HRS.* (Paramount)
8 *Poltergeist* (MGM/United Artists)
9 *The Best Little Whorehouse in Texas* (Universal)
10 *Annie* (Sony/Columbia)

Best Picture: *Gandhi* (Columbia)

Death of John Belushi

John Belushi. *Universal/ The Kobal Collection*

The March 5, 1982 death of comedian John Belushi profoundly affected American popular culture, reverberating through the television and film industry in a way that we will never properly comprehend.

Belushi is one of the few performers to achieve (on his thirtieth birthday, no less; Jan. 24, 1979) the No. 1 album in the country with *The Blues Brothers: Briefcase Full of Blues*, the highest-rated late-night TV program, *Saturday Night Live*, and the No. 1 film in the U.S., John Landis' groundbreaking comedy, *Animal House* (1978).

He left *SNL* in 1979 to pursue a film career, which landed him roles in the successful period-piece *1941* (1979), the hugely influential cult-hit and *SNL* spin-off, *The Blues Brothers* (1980), the poorly received *Continental Divide* (1981), and oft underappreciated *Neighbors* (1981).

Regardless of his professional success, Belushi was frequenting circles where hard drugs were the order of the day. On the night of his death, his relationship with drug dealer Cathy Smith, and former *SNL* writer Nelson Lyon, led the comedian to a heavy night of drinking. Following this, the three began snorting cocaine. Later that evening, Belushi was injected by Smith with a "speedball" a number of times—a combination of heroin and cocaine—and it killed him. Smith was charged with manslaughter, and America would never witness Belushi's genius again.

How different would the entertainment industry be if Belushi had lived? The role of Dr. Peter Venkman in the smash 1984 hit *Ghostbusters* was written by Dan Aykroyd specifically for Belushi.

Top Ten Billboard Singles of 1982

1 "Physical," Olivia Newton-John (*Physical*, 1981)
2 "Eye of the Tiger," Survivor (*Rocky III Original Soundtrack*, 1982)
3 "I Love Rock 'N' Roll," Joan Jett & the Blackhearts (*I Love Rock 'N' Roll*, 1982)
4 "Ebony And Ivory," Paul McCartney & Stevie Wonder (*Tug of War*, 1982)
5 "Centerfold," J. Geils Band (*Freeze Frame*, 1981)
6 "Don't You Want Me," Human League (*Dare*, 1981)
7 "Jack and Diane," John Cougar (*American Fool*, 1982)
8 "Hurts So Good," John Cougar (*American Fool*, 1982)
9 "Abracadabra," Steve Miller Band (*Abracadabra*, 1982)
10 "Hard to Say I'm Sorry," Chicago (*Chicago 16*, 1982)

Top Ten Television Programs of 1982-83

1 *60 Minutes* (CBS)
2 *Dallas* (CBS)
3 *M*A*S*H* (CBS)
4 *Magnum P.I.* (CBS)
5 *Dynasty* (ABC)
6 *Three's Company* (ABC)
7 *Simon & Simon* (CBS)
8 *Falcon Crest* (CBS)
9 *The Love Boat* (ABC)
10 *The A-Team* (NBC)

In the series *Magnum, P.I.*, Tom Selleck plays Hawaii-based private investigator Thomas Magnum. The show was a hit for eight seasons, thanks to deftly blending humor, suspense, and drama, and also the charm of Selleck. *CBS-TV*

1983

A group of
Cabbage
Patch Kids.

A Baby Boom and a Mohawked Icon

Mr. T.
*NBC-TV/
The Kobal
Collection*

CHILDREN WERE ADOPTING THEIR VERY OWN BABIES from the cabbage patch in 1983—*if* they were lucky to get one.

After debuting at New York City's International Toy Fair to great fanfare, Cabbage Patch Kids quickly became THE Christmas toy to have, and had many parents fighting in the aisles of toy stores when there was a mad dash to grab one of the hard-to-find dolls for their children. Unfortunately, there were many crestfallen faces that Christmas morning.

However, there were other huggable dolls and figures to choose from, though, including the plush Fraggles line, inspired by the hugely popular HBO show, *Fraggle Rock.*

In 1983, we bid a sad farewell to the brilliant TV show, *M*A*S*H.* Its final episode, "Goodbye, Farewell and Amen," shattered Nielsen ratings' records.

On a lighter note, Don Adams of *Get Smart* fame provided an all-new generation of viewers with a show about an inept secret agent, *Inspector Gadget,* which garnered a following of fans and adults sustained to this day. David Hasselhoff's career flew to new heights in the formulaic yet technologically fabulous *Knight Rider, a program* about a man and his robotic car (K.I.T.T.): fightin' crime.

Premiering on NBC on January 23, the *A-Team* entertained American audiences with its unique brand of military action, comedy, and super-violence. The show was a sensation and launched the career of Mr. T. With his tough-guy image, distinctive mohawked hair, and bevy of gold jewelry, Mr. T was one of the more colorful personalities of the decade.

The final film in the original *Star Wars* trilogy, *Return of the Jedi,* wowed kids and adults worldwide—simply witnessing Luke Skywalker as a black-robed Jedi Knight sent chills down my spine.

As aerobics and modern dance took hold of American pop culture, a *Flashdance* movie poster was mandatory in girls' bedrooms, while their boyfriends flocked to see the comic pairing of Eddie Murphy and Dan Akroyd in *Trading Places.* The cautionary tale *WarGames* warned us of the ease in which America could enter into a nuclear winter.

Women began to dominate the small screen with programs such as *Kate & Allie* and the award-winning *Cagney & Lacey,* yet the sophisticated films and television productions were undercut by John Hughes' ludicrous trip to the uninhabited Wally World in *National Lampoon's Vacation,* which featured supermodel Christie Brinkley as the girl who drove the red Ferrari.

Although America listened to The Police, 1983 was Michael Jackson's break-out year and "Billie Jean" and "Beat It" from his *Thriller* album obtained the most attention. Pundits credit Jackson for putting the "television" into MTV's acronym: Music Television. David Bowie with "Let's Dance," Annie Lennox and the Eurythmics, Culture Club and Boy George also garnered success, but it was Jackson who Elizabeth Taylor dubbed "the King of Pop."

So Ugly, They're Cute

Cabbage Patch Kids one of the biggest toy fads of the '80s

Preemie size, Caucasian.

Recalling the Christmas of 1983, I remember my sister sitting patiently after each one of our presents was opened, until she broke down in tears when she didn't receive her most treasured gift: a Cabbage Patch Kid.

My mother had tried for months, yet we simply couldn't afford to pay more than retail for the toy. However, my sister had even already constructed a name for her Cabbage Patch Kid—Kimberly Ann Bellomo—but it seemed that she was doomed to be a pariah in her school; the only young girl without a Cabbage Patch doll.

All seemed very grim that cold, winter's morning, until my mother, waiting with a grin on her face, pulled out the package. Never have I seen my sister so excited; never have I witnessed a smile plastered on her face so genuine and pleased.

Cabbage Patch Kids were the brainchildren of Xavier Roberts, who originally sold the hand-crafted "Little People" though his nascent corporation, Original Appalachian Artworks, with the help of four other artists. Roberts sold the license to Coleco in 1982 and when Cabbage Patch Kids made their debut in 1983, they became the most popular toy fad of the year, and one of the most popular in all of the '80s. The dolls made the cover of *Newsweek* before Christmas, and stories of their success were heralded around the world.

But what was it about these now mass-produced characters that set young children's hearts all aflutter? Was it the fact you could actually "adopt" your very own child? Pick your own name, mail it to Babyland General Hospital, where Roberts would sign each set of adoption papers, as he hand-picked each kid out of… well…a Cabbage Patch?

Heck, you could even purchase Cabbage Patch Kid diapers, your own officially licensed "Sticker Baby Book" to record "Baby's Birthday Party," "Dreams for Baby's Future," Baby's [First Day] at the Circus," etc. It was an ingenious combination of marketing and timeliness; one that caused the FIRST Capra-esque "run on the toy stores in Christmastime" of 1983 in recent memory. Although retailing for $25, there were black market sales of Cabbage Patch Kids recorded as high as $2,000 [!]. Tickle me Elmo had *nothing* on Cabbage Patch Kids.

For extra added entertainment, if you get the chance in life, I recommend you take the advice listed on the Birth Certificate packaged with every Cabbage Patch Kid since their inception: "to prove the authenticity of being an official Cabbage Patch Kids Doll…look for the signature birthmark on each baby's bottom."

An assortment of accessories for Cabbage Patch Kids, from adoption papers, to framed "Official Adoption Certificate," to multiple Baby Books, and tags for individual dolls.

A smiling Helen Humphrey, the 1984 National Poster Child for the March of Dimes Birth Defects Foundation, is surrounded by Cabbage Patch Kids in New York in 1984. *AP Photo*

Standard size Caucasian girl
with red hair.

Standard size Caucasian
boy with blond hair.

Preemie size with tooth, African-American.

Pitying Fools and Challenging Jibba-Jabba

Mr. T. emerges as larger-than-life hero on *The A-Team*

In a decade chock full of infamous and dubious icons, one man in a mohawk wearing nearly as much gold as is contained in Fort Knox, stood tall.

A marketable star and one of the most colorful personalities of the decade, Mr. T was uniquely suited to capture the attention of a generation raised on Saturday morning cartoons and pre-sweetened cereal—and rise to fame. He was dangerous but kind, gruff but fair, tough as nails yet conversely sweet as sugar, with an infectious laugh audiences rarely witnessed. Kids loved him and saw him as larger than life: a modern day super-hero.

After a brief stint in the army, Laurence Tureaud became a bouncer, where his intimidating personality and appearance were strong enough to deter even the most persistent troublemakers. After observing a Mandinka warrior donning a mohawk in an issue of *National Geographic*, he adopted the hairstyle for himself.

He also created a larger-than-life persona; at one point, he donned $300,000 worth of gold a day in order to feel the weight of the gold "…as a symbol that reminds me of my great African ancestors, who were brought over here as slaves (in iron chains)."

People simply couldn't get enough of Mr. T, and because of this, Sylvester Stallone handed him the role of "Clubber Lang" in *Rocky III* and Tureaud made the most of it. After a few bit parts on other shows, Mr. T starred in five full seasons of *The A-Team*, playing the character of B.A. Baracus, where the B.A. stood for either "Bad Attitude" or "Bosco Albert Baracus."

The A-Team premiered on NBC on January 23 and lasted until December 30, 1986. The show entertained American audiences with its unique brand of military action, comedy, super-violence, and well… super-non-violence, since both the members of the A-Team itself and their nemeses rarely seemed to get hit by a single bullet. Regardless, the television program was a sensation.

Toy companies took notice and Galoob created a successful 6-inch action figure line of B.A. Baracus, the genius mechanic; John "Hannibal" Smith, the brainy team leader and master of disguise; Templeton "The Face" Peck, who gets by on his looks; and "Howling Mad" Murdock, the slightly wacky ace pilot.

The A-Team: Templeton "The Face" Peck (Dirk Benedict), "Howling Mad" Murdock (Dwight Schultz), B.A. Baracus (Mr. T), and John "Hannibal" Smith (George Peppard).
NBC-TV/The Kobal Collection

Galoob 6-inch A-Team figures, set of four: Templeton "Face" Peck, John "Hannibal" Smith, "Howling Mad" Murdock, and B.A. Baracus.

Mr. T 12-inch action figure.

Galoob also offered a 12-inch tall Mr. T "Real-Life Superhero!" An authentic action figure of the A-Team, he was fully jointed and poseable, dressed with removable clothes, real chains, "Mr. T" medallion, earrings, and bracelets. The package states, "(He is) the most extraordinary man you could ever meet! He's BIG and BOLD! He's the BOSS!"

Galoob 6-inch A-Team "Bad Guy" Python figure.

Humanoid Creatures' Colorful World

Fraggle Rock a worldwide phenomenon

Set of four McDonald's Fraggle Rock Happy Meal with prizes.

The exploits of 18-inch tall fur-covered humanoid Muppets became a worldwide phenomenon when they hit the airwaves in January, entertaining viewers with their antics.

Premiering on HBO, *Fraggle Rock* ran for five seasons (1983-87). The show revolved around the adventures of the Fraggles: 18-inch fur-covered humanoid Muppets that possess a tail with a tuft of fur on the end. Fraggles come in a variety of colors, and they live within a cavernous system of caves inhabited by all manner of interesting creatures: a home they call "Fraggle Rock." Each individual Fraggle has a distinct identity, personality, and a specific function or job within Fraggle society.

The Fraggles engage in a symbiotic relationship with other species in Fraggle Rock. For example, one such relationship is with the diminutive ("knee high to a Fraggle"), green, ant-like Doozers that wear construction hats, work boots, and tool belts who erect detailed buildings for the Fraggles to eat. The Fraggles hungrily devour the Doozer's buildings, and the Doozers view the Fraggles' hunger for their architecture as a testament to the skills; they welcome constructing new buildings for the Fraggles to eat.

Although *Fraggle Rock* functioned essentially as a children's show, it was also a sophisticated allegory for modern human life, as it often dealt with the complex themes of religion, spirituality,

racism (well… "species-ism"), prejudice, tolerance, the concept of identity, environmentalism, and the nature of reality. Since these complicated issues were cleverly cloaked within a children's show about puppets, oftentimes even the characters themselves did not recognize their own individual growth.

In 1983, Tomy became the first company to produce dolls based on *Fraggle Rock*. These dolls were rendered exactly to their fictional counterparts' scale, and seven of these detailed plush toys were made: Gobo, Red, Wembley, Mokey, Boober, Gobo's Uncle Traveling Matt, and Uncle Matt's dog, Sprocket. Tomy also constructed a series of four different poseable Doozer toys with wind-up action, that allowed them to "march." The Doozers were also built in perfect scale with respect to the plush Fraggles.

Always amusing, ridiculously entertaining, sometimes wistful, frequently touching, and on occasion sad, *Fraggle Rock* is a monumental achievement in children's television programming.

As a quiet reminder to those Generation Xers who grew up as kids of the '80s, I wanted to include a set of Fraggle Rock McDonald's Happy Meal boxes and prizes, since those treasured family trips to "Mickey-Dee's" ranked pretty high on my list of memorable events of this decade.

Five Fraggles are cast at the center of the *Fraggle Rock* universe:

Gobo has orange fur, purple hair and tail tuft, and wears a yellow sweater with purple stripes and a brown vest. He's a leader-type who possesses a high level of responsibility; he is practical and prefers to make his own path. He functions as an explorer and adventurer.

Mokey has light purple fur, long turquoise hair and tail tuft, and wears a long gray cardigan. She is the most spiritual of the five main Fraggles and the den mother of the group. She is artistic, reflective, and is an incurable optimist who is a staunch friend; her dangerous job is to pick radishes.

Wembley has green-yellow fur, light yellow hair and tail tuft, and wears a white shirt adorned with banana trees. As the young-est member of the group, he is high-strung and indecisive, yet his indecisiveness is spawned by his concern over not wanting to choose one side over the other so as not to hurt anyone's feel-ings. His job is as the warning siren on the Fraggle fire team.

Boober has blue-green fur, orange hair and tail tuft, and wears a red-brown cap and long brown scarf. A depressed hypochondriac, he is a worrier and superstitious, and often plays the blues when fulfilling his duties as the Fraggle's resident cook and laundryman.

Red has yellow-orange fur, red-orange hair (in pigtails) and tail tuft, and wears a red sweater. She is overtly excited and impulsive and her energetic nature and competitiveness often lead her into trouble. She teaches swimming classes and her job is to clean the swimming pool.

Stuffed Boober plush figure with three Doozer wind-ups.

Mighty Robots... Mighty Vehicles

GoBots on the scene before Transformers

Super GoBot Vamp
(Series 3).

Kids could amass their own robot armies thanks to Tonka's GoBots line of "Mighty Robots...Mighty Vehicles": transforming robot toys that hit the scene before Hasbro's Transformers.

GoBots gave kids the opportunity to either play with them in robot form or transform them into vehicles. Tonka imported molds and ideas from Popy's (soon to be Bandai's) Machine Robo toy line and eschewed allowing pilots and drivers to control the robots. Instead, each GoBot gained life and was granted sentience—these living beings possessed their own unique personality.

Tonka felt it behooved the company to divide its selection of robots into two different factions: good and evil, following the old standard of imaginative play—without conflict, licensed toy properties are doomed to failure.

GoBots were originally divided into two warring factions, regardless of a robot's outward appearance and alternate mode; these two divisions were plainly dubbed "Friendly" or "Enemy."

As the GoBots' reputation rose in popularity due to a first-rate animated program produced by Hanna-Barbera named *Challenge of the GoBots* (1983-87), their faction titles were changed to the "Guardians" versus the "Renegades." The plot of *Challenge of the GoBots* revolved around two warring factions of robots who were fighting for control of their home planet of Gobotron.

There were unfortunately a few disadvantages with these toys: there were no biographies on their packaging to define each GoBot character, there was a lack of a comic book tie-in from a major company, and there was no way to codify, categorize, and organize the standard-sized single-carded GoBots action figures. There is much confusion regarding GoBots' assigned production numbers, since they weren't released in numerical order. Because of this, these excellent robot toys, many with well-made accessories, brilliant die-cast parts, and wonderful molds and sculpts, quickly lost ground to Hasbro's Transformers that came a year later.

There were seventy-two standard-sized GoBots action figures, and Tonka also translated a few select characters into a larger "Super" size. Twenty Super GoBots were release, the third series of which are the most desirable characters.

There were also two unique deluxe armor sets used to protect and complement your GoBots army: two Power Suits were released to act as armor for standard sized GoBots, with all four separate armored pieces (and one jet) combining to form a super robot—one set for the Guardians ("Courageous"), and one for the Renegades ("Grungy"). Also, there were two gestalts unique to the GoBots line—collections of six Guardians and Renegades that merged to form the largest GoBots in the line.

GoBots, assortment of action figures in "robot" mode, from front left to bottom right: Small Foot, Tux, Loco, Cy-Kill, Crasher, Scooter, Leader-1 (blue), Hans-Cuff, Water Walk, Turbo, Geeper Creeper, Fly Trap, Major Mo, Stallion, Block Head, Ace, Vamp, Sparky, Twin Spin, Van Guard, Buggy Man, Slicks, Dive-Dive, Pathfinder, Fitor, Rest-Q, Leader-1 (gray), Turbo, Road Ranger, Screw Head, Night Ranger, Spay-C.

GoBots, assortment of action figures in "alternate" mode, from front left to bottom right: Small Foot, Tux, Loco, Cy-Kill, Crasher, Scooter, Leader-1 (blue), Hans-Cuff, Water Walk, Turbo, Geeper Creeper, Fly Trap, Major Mo, Stallion, Block Head, Ace, Vamp, Sparky, Twin Spin, Van Guard, Buggy Man, Slicks, Dive-Dive, Pathfinder, Fitor, Rest-Q, Leader-1 (gray), Turbo, Road Ranger, Screw Head, Night Ranger, Spay-C.

There is one refreshing and interesting distinction between GoBots and Transformers: Tonka's action figures had quite a few female characters thrown into the canon—the lead role of Crasher for the evil Renegades; the well-designed Pathfinder for the heroic Guardians.

GoBots, selection of four action figures in "robot" mode: Geeper Creeper, Hans-Cuff, Cy-Kill, Scooter.

GoBots, selection of four action figures in "alternate" mode: Geeper Creeper, Hans-Cuff, Cy-Kill, Scooter.

Animated GoBots stars

The GoBots featured most often in the *Challenge of the GoBots* animated series were the following characters, a combination of standard-sized GoBots, Super GoBots, and larger, more deluxe models, such as Scales:

Guardians: Ace, Blaster, Bolt, Dive-Dive, Flip-Top, Hans-Cuff, Heat-Seeker, Leader-1, Major Mo, Mr. Moto, Night Ranger, Path Finder, Rest-Q, Road Ranger, Scooter, Small Foot, Sparky, Treds, Turbo, Twister, Van Guard, and Zeemon.

Renegades: Bug Bite, Buggyman, Bugsy, Cop-Tur, Crasher, Creepy, Cy-Kill, Destroyer, Dr. Go, Fitor, Fly Trap, Geeper-Creeper, Hornet, Loco, Pincher, Scales, Scorp, Screw Head, Slicks, Snoop, Stallion, Stinger, Tank, Tux (Stretch in the cartoon), Vamp, Zero, and the hideous monster known as Zod.

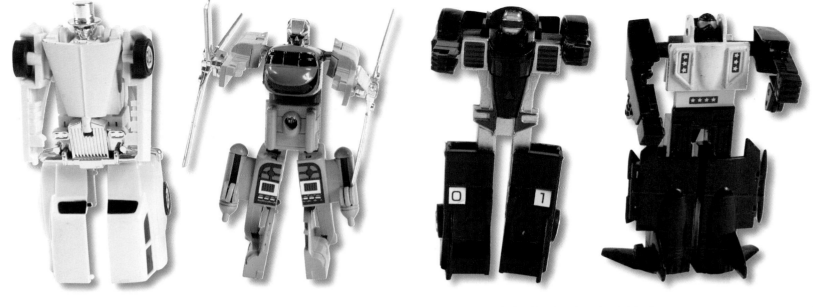

GoBots, selection of four action figures in "robot" mode: Tux, Twin Spin, Crasher, Leader-1 (blue).

GoBots, selection of four action figures in "alternate" mode: Tux, Twin Spin, Crasher, Leader-1 (blue).

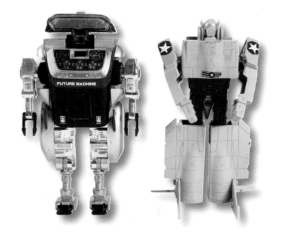

GoBots, Super GoBots: Psycho, Leader-1 (Series 2), Defendor ([sic] Series 2).

Teddies Are Full of Funshine and Love

Care Bears become breakout stars

Grumpy Bear, Love-A-Lot Bear, Share Bear, Birthday Bear, Champ Bear, and Good Luck Bear.

Teddy bears have been around for years, but a new breed of the plush, huggable teddies became breakout stars in 1983.

Named Care Bears, they were created by American Greetings' employee Elena Kucharik, whose painted artwork of the characters was used on many of the company's products. Due to the characters' success and overwhelmingly positive response that children had for them, American Greetings sold the license to Kenner Toys to produce a slew of Care Bears products, from poseable action figures to the most popular permutation of the characters: stuffed animals.

Each Care Bear action figure has what is referred to as a "tummy symbol" (recently changed to "belly badges") located on their stomach. These toys were offered in a few different sizes, but the most popular was the 13-inch scale of stuffed plush, which solicited 12 different characters in the U.S. from 1983-1986: Bedtime Bear (crescent moon tummy symbol), Birthday Bear (cupcake), Champ Bear (trophy), Cheer Bear (rainbow), Friend Bear (two flowers), Funshine Bear (sun), Good Luck Bear (four-leaf cover), Grumpy Bear (cloud), Love-A-Lot Bear (two small hearts), Share Bear (milkshake), Tenderheart Bear

(large heart), and Wish Bear (shooting star). All official Care Bears also came with an informational "tush tag" and had a tiny raised red heart somewhere on the stuffed animal's body with the words "Care Bear" printed lightly in white lettering.

Apart from these standard 13-inch stuffed bears, there were two smaller bears offered at retail, the 11-inch tall Baby Hugs and Baby Tugs, who were watched over by the slightly larger (and wiser) 15-inch "Grams Bear," with removable shawls.

Featured in their own highly successful animated television series, the Care Bears were also featured in five specials and three movies: *The Care Bears Movie* (1985), *Care Bears Movie II: A New Generation* (1986), and *The Care Bears Adventure in Wonderland* (1987).

As a final note, although they are no longer featured in animation, the uniquely designed Care Bear Cousins touched audiences who were simply tired of purchasing standard teddy bears. From their courageous leader, Brave Lion Heart, to the intellectually gifted Bright Heart Raccoon, the Care Bear Cousins remain popular to this day.

Friendship Bear, Funshine Bear, Wish Bear, Tenderheart Bear, Cheer Bear, and Bedtime Bear.

Baby Tugs, Grams Bear (15 inches), and Baby Hugs.

Care Bear Cousins: Cozyheart Penguin, Bright Heart Raccoon, Gentle Heart Lamb, Swift Heart Rabbit, Brave Heart Lion, and Lots-A-Heart Elephant.

Coloring Our World

Rainbow Brite is beloved doll

Mattel's 18-inch Rainbow Brite doll.

The back story of Mattel's Rainbow Brite toy line is simple and straightforward: a young orphan named Wisp is thrust into a place known as "The Colorless World"; there she begins a quest to find an artifact known as the Sphere of Light, befriending a small humanoid, a sprite named Twink. With the assistance of little Twink and an (over)confident steed dubbed Starlite, she rescues a team of young children known as the "Color Kids" from the clutches of the King of Shadows. Each Color Kid represents a single color of the rainbow: Buddy Blue, Canary Yellow, Indigo, Lala Orange, Patty O'Green, Red Butler, and Shy Violet.

At the end of her journey, and with the "Color Belt" in her possession, "Rainbow Brite" returns color to the Colorless World.

The chromatic adventures of Rainbow Brite took America by storm in the early 1980s. The character was created by Woody Kling, scripter and musician for the seminal Golden Age production, *The Texaco Star Theater* starring Milton Berle, and an employee of Hallmark Cards. She was introduced to the general public via a prime-time debut special, *Rainbow Brite: Peril in the Pits*.

In accordance with popular practice, Hallmark continued a marketing scheme established by American Greetings' best-selling stable of characters such as Strawberry Shortcake and the Care Bears. So, beginning as early as 1983, Hallmark licensed Rainbow Brite to toy giant Mattel, which produced a slew of products—plastic and stuffed rag-type dolls.

Offered in both an 18-inch (Rainbow Brite, Patty O'Green, and Shy Violet) and 10-inch scale to satisfy two different levels of price points, Mattel's Rainbow Brite toy line allowed parents to spend an amount they were comfortable with, and products flew off the shelves. With a combination of plastic parts, such as the dolls' heads and other accoutrements, uniquely rooted yarn hair, and intricately detailed fabric costumes, these stuffed dolls were decorated vibrantly and stood out at retail.

The most popular series of dolls were the two series of Mattel's 10-inch Rainbow Brite line, as the toy company packaged each character with their respective sprite companion. Rainbow Brite herself came with the white colored Twink, Buddy Blue was packaged with Champ, Canary Yellow and Spark, Indigo with Hammy, Lala Orange and O.J., Patty O'Green with Lucky, Red Butler and Romeo, and Shy Violet with her sprite, I.Q. Mattel also offered a bevy of stuffed sprites packaged independently of the Color Kids, along with the popular villains, Murky and Lurky.

Still to this day, the full-length feature film, 1985's *Rainbow Brite and the Star Stealer* remains a popular attraction to young children who grew up in the 1980s. Rainbow Brite fans will be pleased to know that the dolls were re-designed and re-released by Playmates Toys as of Christmas 2009.

Call Me K.I.T.T. For Short

Modern-day knight fights crime with the help of smart car

Electronic Knight 2000 Voice Car with Michael Knight action figure.

To capitalize on the sensational new TV show, *Knight Rider*, which debuted on NBC a year prior, Kenner Toys began offering its Electronic Knight 2000 Voice Car with Michael Knight action figure at retail.

The plastic car included in this set was a voice-activated toy (requiring 1 "C" battery) that worked when a child pressed on the car's license plate. Upon activation, the following six phrases would emit: "Engaging infrared tracking scope," "Scanner indicates danger ahead," "I shall activate the turbo boost," "Your reflexes are slow," "Call me K.I.T.T. for short," or "What is our next mission?"

Although the toy did not include a functional pulsing light on the hood similar to the television program (it was a mere "special lens label" [sticker]), the Knight 2000 Voice Car sold well.

The vehicle and figure were also not in scale to other 3-3/4-inch toys offered in 1983 (the Michael Knight figure is 5.8 inches tall), but there is ample detail to make up for this: a realistic computerized dashboard, opening and closing doors, the aforementioned electronic voice, and exceptional free-wheeling action.

Created and produced by Glen A. Larson for NBC, the original *Knight Rider* program ran for four full seasons and launched the career of David Hasselhoff. Hasselhoff's fame had peaks and valleys throughout the decade in the U.S., but he retained his popularity in Germany. His music, including singles such as "Looking for Freedom," especially resonated with the German people during the decline of Communism and the fall of the Berlin Wall, which began on August 23, 1989.

Regardless of Hasselhoff's success, *Knight Rider* revolved around the exploits of Michael Knight, a one-time Las Vegas police detective whose identity is changed in order to save his life and maintain his anonymity in his pursuit for justice, and his extraordinary car, the sentient Knight Industries Two-Thousand (K.I.T.T.): a modified third-generation Pontiac Trans-Am which boasted its own artificial intelligence.

Knight Rider became an instant hit, and the adventures of Knight and K.I.T.T. exploded into American pop culture. With its ability to run automatically on auto-pilot, or while using its famous "turbo boost" during a high speed pursuit, kids and adults couldn't get enough of the intelligent automobile or its dashing driver.

Wowsers!

Inspector and his Go-Go-Gadgets crowning achievement in toys

Inspector Gadget 12-inch action figure, with all accessories on display.

Folks are often left breathless when allowed to play with one of the Galoob toy company's greatest achievements: the stunning 12-inch tall Inspector Gadget doll. To quote Gadget himself, "Wowsers."

With a gorgeous fabric trench coat with fastening buttons, intricate stitching, and a functional belt, Galoob's Inspector Gadget action figure is fully poseable with eleven points-of-articulation, twenty moving parts, spring-loaded ejecting (and jointed) hands, spring-loaded extendable legs, and a pull-up mechanical neck.

The figure also possesses a bevy of amazing features and accessories: a set of real metal chain-linked handcuffs, a large mallet ("Crime Stopper" hammer), a multiple-jointed extension arm, a spinning helicopter hat (which is also head-mounting) with handlebar controls, and a parachute umbrella. With these myriad action features, many industry experts have placed this Inspector Gadget action figure on their lists of "Top Ten Action Figures of All Time."

There couldn't be a better choice of cartoon character to translate into plastic form, as D.I.C. Entertainment/Nelvana's *Inspector Gadget* animated program was a smash-hit during the mid-1980s. With the recognizable voice of Don Adams, of *Tennessee Tuxedo* and *Get Smart* fame, Inspector Gadget was a bumbling, dim-witted detective who was more similar to Inspector Clouseau and Maxwell Smart than to Sherlock Holmes.

As an inspector with the Metro City Police Department, when faced with a mission to investigate the infamous M.A.D. (no acronym is listed in the canon) organization and their leader, Doctor Claw, these cases are almost always solved by Gadget's partner, his niece Penny, and her unusually intelligent dog, Brain.

Although formulaic, the most entertaining aspect of the program was for viewers to witness the various devices Inspector Gadget would utilize throughout the course of an adventure. These items were brought out with the phrase, "Go-go-gadget...," followed by an appearance of the gadget in question, such as: the Gadget Umbrella, Gadget Coat (which inflated in water or air), Gadget 'Copter, Gadget Cuffs, Gadget Hands, Gadget Legs, Gadget Arms, Gadget Neck, or even the Gadget Mallet.

Regardless, the dim-witted detective was made relevant to a new generation of fans when Matthew Broderick starred in the live-action 1999 Disney film, *Inspector Gadget*, yet most die-hards will never forget the appeal and entertainment of the original animated series.

Inspector Gadget 12-inch action figure, with "Go-Go Gadget Cuffs!" and "Go-Go-Gadget Mallet," and whose extendable "Go-Go-Gadget neck" utilizes his "Go-Go-Gadget 'Copter."

Inspector Gadget, 12-inch action figure, utilizing a "Go-Go Gadget hand" to hold his "Go-Go Gadget 'Brella!"

Final Chapter

Return of the Jedi toys capture key moments

Rancor Monster versus Luke Skywalker in Jedi Knight outfit.

In *Return of the Jedi*, the final chapter of the original *Star Wars* trilogy (Episodes IV-VI), children of the 1980s witnessed the conclusion of the most important cultural touchstone of Generation X.

Most importantly, patient *Star Wars* aficionados finally had the chance to observe Darth Vader's true face: that of former Jedi Knight, Anakin Skywalker. Realizing that the Emperor's right-hand man, Darth Vader, was not beyond redemption— thanks to the faith and encouragement of his son, Luke Skywalker—placed an entirely new importance and added depth to the series.

Although a few select "Ewok bashers" crawled out of the woodwork to criticize this tribal community of teddy-bears, essentially affecting others' enjoyment of the film, we must remember that *Return of the Jedi* was released during a time of peace and contentment in Star Wars fans' galaxy; a time

long before George Lucas made some… curious choices that would haunt even the staunchest, most stalwart sci-fi devotees for more than a decade.

Regardless of how pundits and zealots received the new *Star Wars* trilogy of "prequels" (Episodes I-III), it's worth noting the astronomical amount of money that rabid Star Wars collectors dump into "modern" (1995-present) and "vintage" (1978-1985) product. The current market for vintage *Star Wars* toys is truly obscene: high-grade, investment-quality items are selling for five times what they were less than a decade ago.

On a personal note, the reason I began collecting vintage *Star Wars* action figure was not for investment purposes, but because I liked—I still enjoy—playing with the toys. I'm amazed that the Power of the Force Han Solo fits neatly into his Carbonite Block. I enjoy that Artoo-Detoo possesses a "pop-up" light saber in order that kids and collectors can reenact the action-

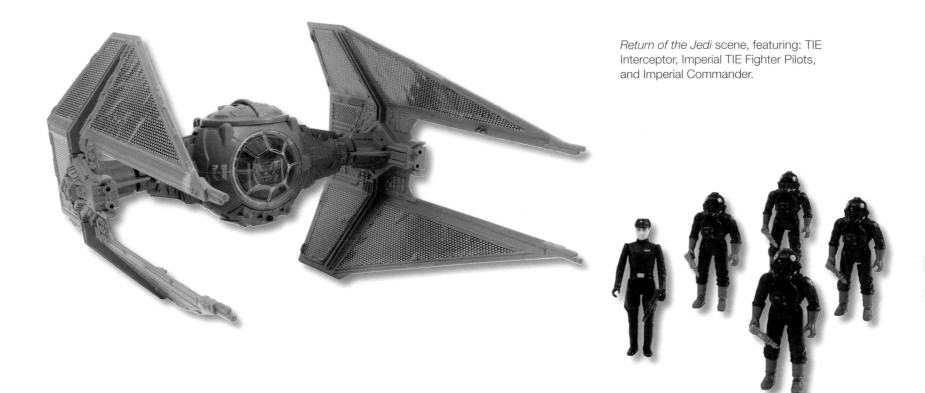

Return of the Jedi scene, featuring: TIE Interceptor, Imperial TIE Fighter Pilots, and Imperial Commander.

packed skiff scene from *Jedi*. I appreciate the fact that Amanaman places shrunken skulls from different galactic species adorning his battle staff. To wit: I initially began collecting Star Wars toys to accompany my appreciation of the original trilogy and re-created my favorite scene from the films, but there are simply so many action figures, creatures, vehicles, playsets, and accessories available to purchase (it seems as if Kenner and Hasbro have developed every single character—regardless of its screen time—into a plastic doll), I don't think I'll ever keep up with the vast amount of new product released each and every year.

But I *want* to recapture these moments again. I'm compelled to nab more vintage toys. I desire to obtain the few pieces I still need in order to complete my entire vintage Star Wars line: from the intricate Imperial Sniper vehicle, to the super-fragile mini-figure collector's cases—preferably with unapplied labels. For sure, I should snatch the few pieces to complete my collection immediately, for if rumors are true, an hour-long, live-action *Star Wars* weekly television show is slated to hit the small screen within the next year; this program will surely increase vintage *Star Wars* prices across the board.

This scene from the movie, *Return of the Jedi*, with Jabba the Hutt, Bib Fortuna, and Salacious Crumb, is what the toys below closely mimic. *Lucasfilm/20th Century Fox/The Kobal Collection*

Return of the Jedi scene, featuring: Sy Snootles and the Rebo Band (Droopy McCool, Max Rebo, and Sy Snootles); Jabba the Hutt, with throne, pipe and bowl, and Salacious Crumb; Bib Fortuna, Princess Leia Organa (Boushh Disguise); R2-D2, with pop-up light saber; C-3PO, with removable limbs; Gammorean Guard; Han Solo, in Carbonite Chamber; Ree-Yees; Squid Head; Lando Calrissian in Skiff Guard disguise; Boba Fett; and Yak Face.

8D8.

B-Wing Pilot.

Kenner released *Star Wars* action figures on, essentially, four different packages: *Star Wars* packaging (1978-1979), *The Empire Strikes Back* (1980-1982), *Return of the Jedi* (late 1982-1984), and *Star Wars: The Power of the Force* (1984-1985). This page shows action figures in their *Return of the Jedi* packaging.

Squid Head.

Logray, Ewok Medicine Man.

Rancor Keeper.

Weequay.

Singing Rodents

Alvin and the Chipmunks still endure

Boxing "Sports Theme" Alvin play figure.

Any fan of Alvin and the Chipmunks believes that these beloved characters originated in their own particular generation—whether the fan grew up in the sixties, seventies, eighties, nineties, or the "Naughts" (the 00s). Although their popularity has peaked within each and every decade since their inception, the concept of the Chipmunks was created by Ross Bagdasarian, Sr. in 1958.

This animated group of singing rodents possesses three members: Alvin, the ringleader and resident troublemaker of the trio; Simon, the bespectacled member who is the tallest and most intellectual; and Theodore, the stocky, innocently naïve member of the group.

Managed by their adoptive father, David Seville, the Chipmunks became a singing sensation in the late fifties and beyond with two popular novelty songs that featured the characters' trademarked high-pitched voices: "The Witch Doctor" (1958) and the infamous Christmas melody, "The Chipmunk Song" (1958).

The Chipmunks' voices were a then-marvel of engineering by Bagdasarian in the late fifties, whose vision allowed the trio to accumulate a Kid's Choice Award, a Golden Reel Award, an American Music Award, five Grammys, and two Emmy nominations.

They are best known by children of the 1980s for their long-running and well-written animated cartoon, *Alvin and the Chipmunks* (1983-1990). However, modern audiences will recall—fondly or spitefully—their recent adventures in 2007's high-grossing ($358 million) CGI/live-action *Alvin and the Chipmunks* film, and the smash hit follow-up, *Alvin and the Chipmunks: The Squeakquel* (2009), which grossed over $380 million. These movies attest to the endurance of the franchise.

More Medieval Action

Advanced Dungeons & Dragons action figures overlooked line

Advanced Dungeons & Dragons basic figures: Warduke, Strongheart, Kelek, Ringlerun, Zarak, and Bowmarc.

To further capitalize on Dungeons & Dragons' popularity, toy producer LJN concocted one of the most overlooked action figure lines in the 1980s—the Advanced Dungeons & Dragons line.

With excellent accessories, brilliant colors, and wonderfully poseable plastic incarnations, nearly all of the "Official Advanced Dungeons & Dragons Fully Articulated Player Characters" were based on pre-constructed heroes and villains contained within the pages of an early edition of a D&D role playing game accessory, *The Shady Dragon Inn*. It is rumored that the special characters contained within the final pages of this booklet were once characters created and role-played by the owner of TSR (Gary Gygax) and his friends, who decided to license these characters to LJN toys for the purpose of translating them into action figures.

TSR created a back-story for these heroes and villains contained within the flavor text of the Special Character section of *the Shady Dragon Inn*, and LJN's action figure line indeed stemmed from the fictional interaction of many of these characters and their relationship to one another. Regardless of this fictional narrative, the first series of LJN's action figures contained the following characters, divided into three distinct groups:

The good action figures: Elkhorn, dwarf fighter; Melf/Peralay, fighter-mage elf; Mercion, cleric female; Ringlerun, wizard; and Strongheart, paladin; the notably larger Battle Masters: Northlord, great barbarian; Orge King, and the Young Male Titan; and the evil action figures: Kelek, sorcerer; Warduke, fighter; and Zarak, half-Orc assassin.

The second series of AD&D action figures are some of the most difficult '80s toys to acquire, with new character classes added to the mix, while an added feature accompanied all new second series figures and those characters re-released and "refreshed" from the first series: LJN's Battle-Matic Action. Battle-Matic Action allowed a child to depress a button on the figure's back, which triggered the figure's arm to move up and down, and sometimes side-to-side, to mimic a weapon's slash.

The second series of action figure releases are delineated as follows: Good battle heroes—Bowmarc, crusader; Deeth, female fighter; Elkhorn, re-release with Battle-Matic Action; Hawkler, ranger; and Strongheart, re-release; Battle Masters: Mandoom, good fighter; Mettaflame, evil fire giant; Northlord, Shield-Shooter re-release; Orge King, re-release (very rare) and Young Male Titan, re-release (very rare); Evil Battle Renegades: Drex, warrior; Grimsword, knight; Warduke, re-release with Battle-Matic Action; Zarak, re-release; Zorgar, barbarian.

Although short-lived, LJN's Advanced Dungeons & Dragons action figure line is worthy to stand alongside any other action figure line of the 1980s with fierce pride. Compare these toys with Hasbro's G.I. Joe, Transformers, or Kenner's Star Wars, and you'll find they hold up quite well.

Advanced Dungeons & Dragons basic figures: Drex, Orge King, Melf/Peralay, Northlord, Elkhorn, Mercion, Mettaflame.

Advanced Dungeons & Dragons adventure figure and monster sets: featuring Hook Horror, Shield-Shooter Ogre King, and Shield Shooter Northlord.

Fortress of Fangs playset.

This toy's got fangs

LJN's Fortress of Fangs Playset was a stunningly well-crafted toy with two full dungeon levels shaped like a large serpent's head, full of big sharp pointy teeth.

There were also numerous action features to add to its remarkable playability: a sliding tunnel, a moving wall of spikes, falling hatchet, stalagmite teeth, trap door, moving monster statue, triggered floor plate, three removable separate lava steps, nine small stalactites that hang from the ceiling, eleven removable stalagmites, a fold out access ladder at the playset's front, a moving tunnel wall, 'steppes' for access to the upper level, a faux lava moat, a flip-down stalagmite bridge (for characters to cross the lava moat), a folding three-part black gate to block the playset's back entrance, an opening gate on the upper level with two skulls mounted on its pikes, and a molded treasure chest full of gold—the goal of traversing the many traps that the Fortress of Fangs presents the adventurers.

ENTERTAINMENT-O-RAMA: 1983 MOVIES, MUSIC, TELEVISION

Top Ten Films of 1983

1. *Return of the Jedi* (20th Century Fox)
2. *Terms of Endearment* (Paramount)
3. *Flashdance* (Paramount)
4. *Trading Places* (Paramount)
5. *WarGames* (MGM/Universal)
6. *Octopussy* (MGM/Universal)
7. *Sudden Impact* (Warner Brothers)
8. *Staying Alive* (Paramount)
9. *Mr. Mom* (20th Century Fox)
10. *Risky Business* (Warner Brothers)

Best Picture: *Terms of Endearment* (Paramount)

All it takes is playing air guitar to a Bob Seeger song while in your underwear, as Tom Cruise does in *Risky Business,* to become a superstar. Cruise's crafty high-schooler Joel decides to have some fun while his parents are out of town and goes into business with prostitute Lana (Rebecca De Mornay), turning his home into a money-making bordello. *Warner Bros./The Kobal Collection*

In the romantic fantasy musical, *Flashdance*, Alex Owens (Jennifer Beals) is a welder by day and erotic dancer by night, waiting for her big break to make it into a prestigious dance school. The soundtrack spawned several hits, including "Maniac" by Michael Sembello. *Paramount/The Kobal Collection*

The cast of *M*A*S*H* bid us farewell in a series finale watched by a record number of viewers worldwide. Cast members shown are David Ogden Stiers, William Christopher, Mike Farrell, Alan Alda, Loretta Swit, Harry Morgan, and Jamie Farr. *20th Century Fox/The Kobal Collection*

Historical TV finale

When reviewing Nielsen ratings and other enlightening statistics regarding the most-watched American television finale in history, one show stands out from the crowd.

The final episode of *Friends* garnered 52.2 million viewers, and it was the most-watched series finale since the final episode of *Seinfeld* with 76.3 million viewers. The series finales of *Cheers* (1993) and ABC's drama *The Fugitive* (1967) beat out both of the previous two sitcoms in terms of viewership, but the decisive winner, the finale that eclipsed and predominated all others in the ratings department, was CBS' aptly titled epic 2-1/2-hour swan song, "Goodbye, Farewell and Amen": the final episode of *M*A*S*H*.

On Monday, February 28, 1983, it was rumored that nearly 125,000,000 people viewed that final episode, and it is likely that this record will never be broken.

Top Ten Television Programs of 1983-84

1 *Dallas* (CBS)
2 *60 Minutes* (CBS)
3 *Dynasty* (ABC)
4 *The A-Team* (NBC)
5 *Simon & Simon* (CBS)
6 *Magnum P.I.* (CBS)
7 *Falcon Crest* (CBS)
8 *Kate & Allie* (CBS)
9 *Hotel* (ABC)
10 *Cagney & Lacey* (CBS)

Top Ten Billboard Singles of 1983

1 "Every Breath You Take," The Police (*Synchronicity*, 1983)
2 "Billie Jean," Michael Jackson (*Thriller*, 1982)
3 "Flashdance...What a Feeling," Irene Cara (*What a Feelin'*, 1983)
4 "Down Under," Men at Work (*Business as Usual*, 1982)
5 "Beat It," Michael Jackson (*Thriller*, 1982)
6 "Total Eclipse of the Heart," Bonnie Tyler (*Faster Than the Speed of Night*, 1983)
7 "Maneater," Daryl Hall & John Oates (*H2O*, 1982)
8 "Baby Come To Me," Patti Austin & James Ingram (*Every Home Should Have One*, 1982)
9 "Maniac," Michael Sembello (*Flashdance* soundtrack, 1983)
10 "Sweet Dreams (Are Made of This)," Eurythmics (*Sweet Dreams [Are Made of This]*, 1983)

1984

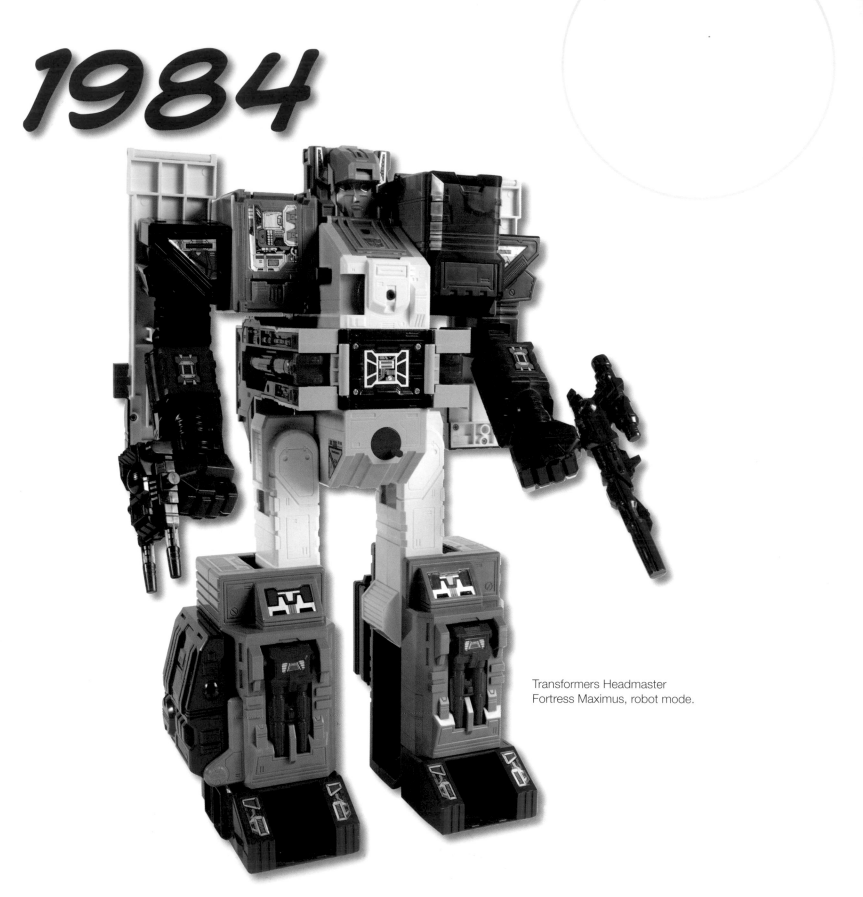

Transformers Headmaster
Fortress Maximus, robot mode.

Transforming Robots
Infiltrate Toy Aisles

Action figures Hulk Hogan and She-Ra.

LIKE HASBRO'S HUGELY SUCCESSFUL G.I. JOE LINE, Transformers were introduced into American homes via a superb television show of the same name.

Also in 1984, another super-robot, Voltron ("The King of Beasts"), became a cultural icon, while the "King of Pop" Michael Jackson was put in doll form. Girls' toys also received some muscle with Mattel's She-Ra: Princess of Power.

For the purpose of this book, the single most important political decision in American history was made by President Ronald Reagan when he directed the FCC to eliminate guidelines for children's television in 1983. This decision came to fruition in 1984, ending the final barriers to companies that wished to produce, in essence, 24-minute toy commercials. The floodgates burst wide open and a slew of animated programs strode onto the airwaves.

Popular culture manifested itself in another curious manner in 1984 as the World Wrestling Federation took hold of children's attention, as the syndicated WWF Superstars of Wrestling with characters such as Andre the Giant, Hulk Hogan, and the Junkyard Dog invaded living rooms across the country.

Films struck a lighter tone in 1984, with *The Karate Kid, Beverly Hills Cop, Ghostbusters*, and *Gremlins* (although this had darker moments that made parents cringe), all making a splash.

Another movie, the slapstick lowbrow *Police Academy*, was so absurdly popular (raking in nearly $250 million total in worldwide ticket sales) that it spawned eight films and a television series.

This was also the year of the musician, as Tina Turner made her comeback, Phil Collins struck out on his own, and Michael Jackson continued to impress and dominate. Van Halen still reaped the success of showcasing the vocal stylings of David Lee Roth. Bruce Springsteen released *Born in the U.S.A.*, while Cyndi Lauper revolutionized how America perceived alternative female artists. Then Madonna hit the charts with "Lucky Star," "Borderline," and "Holiday" from her self-titled 1983/84 release, *Madonna*—yet she is still second compared to Lauper in '84.

Prince followed up his album, *1999*, with the top-selling single of the year, "When Doves Cry," from his album *Purple Rain*. Prince was also the catalyst that led to the formation of the Parents Music Resource Center, co-founded by Tipper Gore, wife of Senator and later Vice President Al Gore.

Finally, '84 was also the year that the cantankerous Clara Peller asked, "Where's the beef?" as part of a Wendy's campaign. It became an instant catchphrase across America and gave Peller cult status.

Rise of the Robots

Transformers: More than meets the eye

Autobot Minicar Huffer, robot mode.

Humanity was thrust into the middle of a great conflict in 1984 between Autobots and Decepticons.

The heroic Autobots, led by Optimus Prime, were in the midst of fighting an age-old war against their cruel nemeses, the Decepticons. Commanded by Megatron, these ruthless war machines were bent on total conquest of the Transformers' home planet, Cybertron. The conflict between the two factions raged for thousands of years and eventually drastically disrupted the orbit of Cybertron, sending the techno-organic orb hurtling though space. To preserve their world's existence, the Autobots assembled a team for a dangerous mission, departing from Cybertron on the Autobot spacecraft known as The Ark. Mid-mission, they were attacked by Megatron and his Decepticons.

Out of desperation, Optimus Prime crashed on the surface of planet Earth during what we consider to be pre-historic times. The impact of the landing disabled its passengers, who would lie damaged and dormant for eons. Four million years later, The Ark awoke and repaired the organic robots contained within indiscriminately: fixing and repairing Autobots and Decepticons alike. Sending out a probe to observe the Earth's native forms circa 1984, the probe transmitted these 'native forms' back to The Ark: thinking that automobiles, jets, and the like were the Earth's life forms. Now Decepticons became jet fighters, weapons, and communications devices, while Autobots became automobiles.

Realizing the gravity of their newfound situation, the Decepticons abandoned The Ark, while the Autobots set up their new base on Earth. Thus began an epic quest for Energon, an energy substance that can be converted into fuel, with the hopes of getting either faction back to far-flung Cybertron. The war between the Autobots and Decepticons still rages on, throughout many ages—past, present, and future—of the Transformers' complicated history.

Autobot Minicars: Brawn, Bumblebee, Windcharger, Cliffjumper, Gears, robot modes.

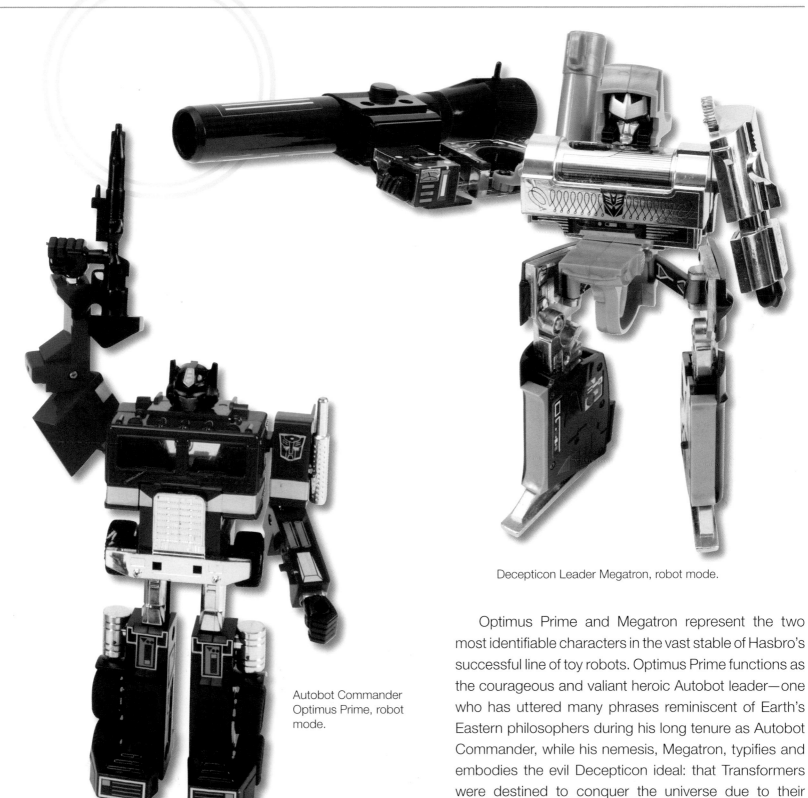

Decepticon Leader Megatron, robot mode.

Autobot Commander Optimus Prime, robot mode.

Optimus Prime and Megatron represent the two most identifiable characters in the vast stable of Hasbro's successful line of toy robots. Optimus Prime functions as the courageous and valiant heroic Autobot leader—one who has uttered many phrases reminiscent of Earth's Eastern philosophers during his long tenure as Autobot Commander, while his nemesis, Megatron, typifies and embodies the evil Decepticon ideal: that Transformers were destined to conquer the universe due to their powerful robot and alternate modes.

Hasbro Bradley infiltrated toy aisles, and pop culture in general, in 1984 with this series of Transformers, based on the designs of Takara's Japanese robots known as Microman and Diaclone. And it's no surprise that kids (and adults) were captivated by them—and in fact still are.

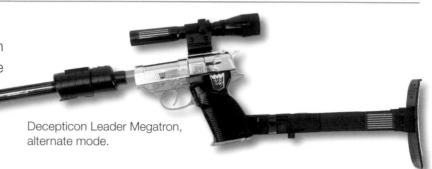

Decepticon Leader Megatron, alternate mode.

With die-cast metal parts, rubber tires, working action features, and only sometimes-firing missiles (not Hasbro's fault, but because of U.S. toy laws), these robots quickly transformed into jets, cars, cassettes, and weapons and constructed a foundation for one of the most successful toy franchises of all time. So successful was Hasbro's Transformers, in fact, that they were imported back to Japan and revitalized the franchise with Cybertrons (good) and Destrons (evil).

Like the hugely successful G.I. Joe line, Transformers were introduced into American homes via a superb television show, *Transformers*, and an excellent comic book by Marvel. The back story of Marvel's *Transformers* was created by Jim Shooter (treatment), Denny O'Neil (plot), and Bob Budiansky (story). It was also Budiansky who generated many of the original, and best, "tech spec" toy biographies. Budiansky has said that he charted graphs for each Transformer according to strength, speed, intelligence, etc., so that he could compare them with each other as he was coming up with their ratings; that way, he was able to avoid making Bumblebee stronger

than Optimus Prime, for example.

Similar to Larry Hama (the "Godfather" of Hasbro's G.I. Joe line), Budiansky said he drew from his knowledge of comic books, science fiction, and his B.S. degree in civil engineering to come up with jargon he hoped would lend a pseudo-scientific, cool-sounding veneer to the characters. "If what I wrote inspired a reader to look a word up in the dictionary, all the better," he said.

Thanks in large part to the most successful grossing films of the past ten years, *Transformers* (2007) and *Transformers: Rise of the Fallen* (2009)—which have reaped more than $1.5 billion in worldwide ticket sales alone—prices for vintage, Generation One Transformers merchandise is currently skyrocketing. Mint, loose, and complete samples are highly desirable and sell out of national auction houses as soon as they are posted on the Internet, and eBay as well is reflecting the Transformers renaissance.

Autobot Commander Optimus Prime, alternate mode.

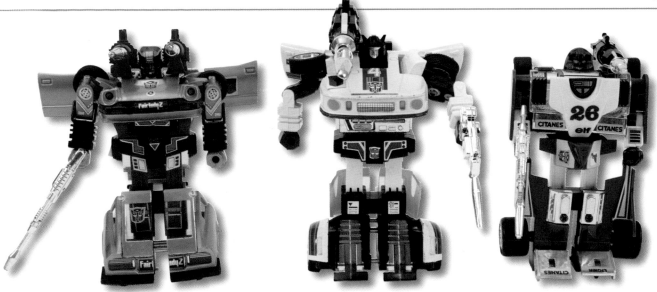

Autobot Cars: Bluestreak, Jazz, Mirage, robot modes.

Autobot Cars: Sideswipe, Wheeljack, Sunstreaker, alternate modes

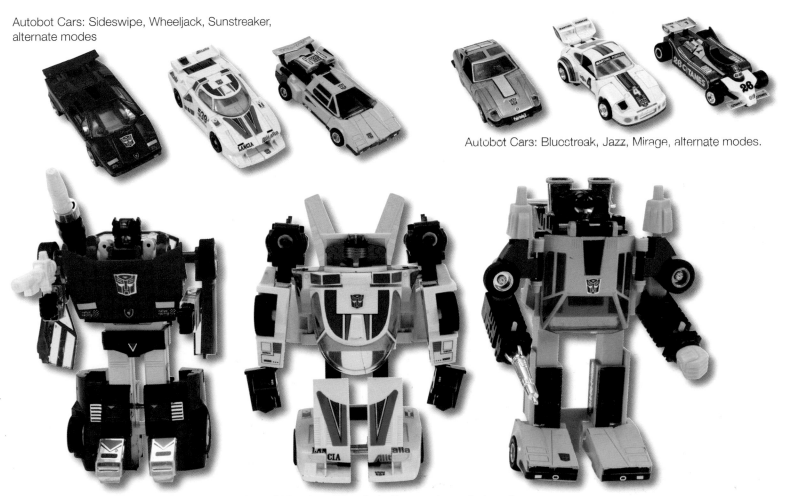

Autobot Cars: Bluestreak, Jazz, Mirage, alternate modes.

Autobot Cars: Sideswipe, Wheeljack, Sunstreaker, robot modes.

Autobot Minicars: Brawn, Bumblebee, Windcharger, Cliffjumper, Gears, Huffer, alternate modes.

In the animated series, *Transformers*, Optimus Prime and the heroic Autobots defend the innocent people of Earth against the Decepticons.
Hasbro/Marvel Productions/Sunbow Production

Soundwave, Decepticon Communications with cassettes: Ravage, Frenzy, Buzzsaw, Laserbeak.

Soundwave, Decepticon Communications with cassettes: Ravage, Frenzy, Buzzsaw (held onto Soundwave), Laserbeak—all transformed.

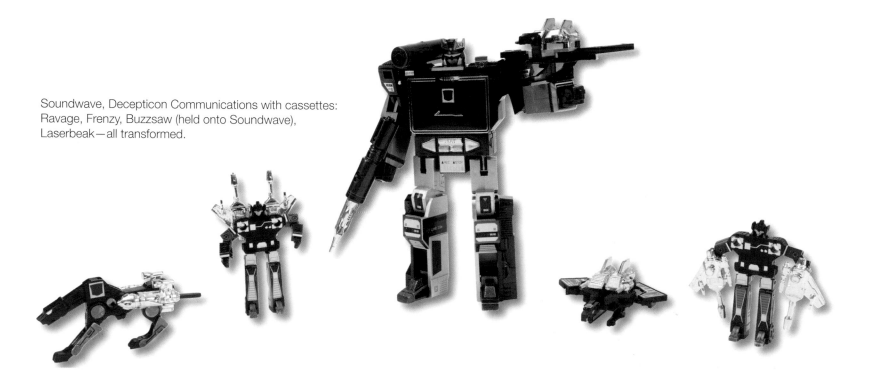

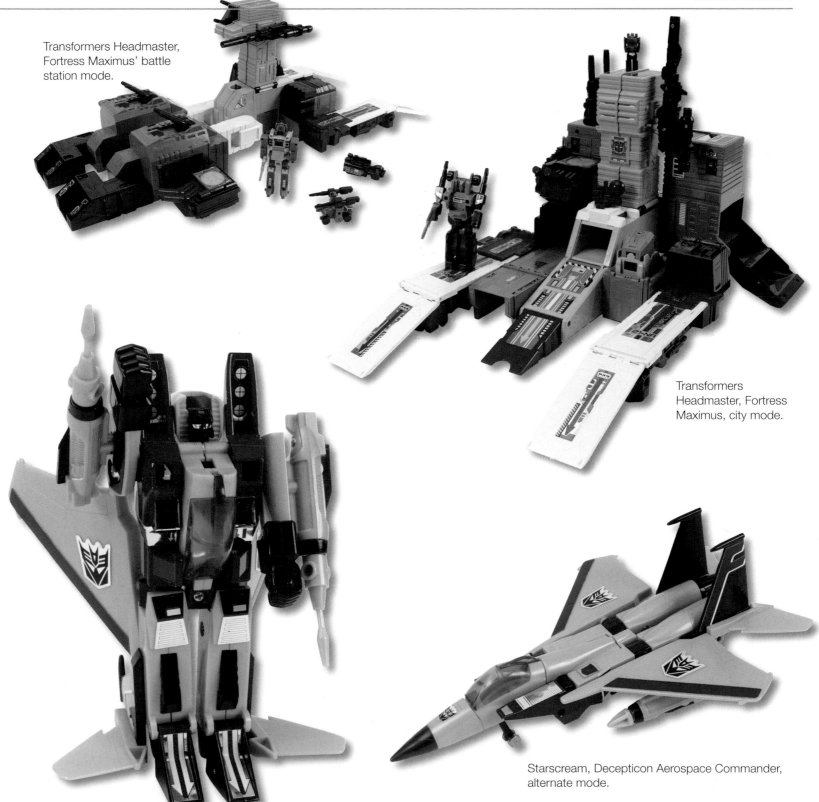

Transformers Headmaster, Fortress Maximus' battle station mode.

Transformers Headmaster, Fortress Maximus, city mode.

Starscream, Decepticon Aerospace Commander, alternate mode.

Starscream, Decepticon Aerospace Commander, robot mode.

Girl Power

She-Ra an empowering character for children

In the 1980s, boys' toys weren't the only ones with muscle. Girls were starting to get some power, too, specifically a princess named Adora and her alter ego She-Ra. But what else would you expect from someone who is the twin sister of He-Man?

She-Ra inhabited the world of Etheria, which was under the tyrannical control of the sinister Hordak. She and her ally rebels united to try and overthrow Hordak, leader of the malevolent Evil Horde empire.

I knew many young boys who eagerly anticipated every episode of the *She-Ra: Princess of Power* cartoon, not only to catch a rare glimpse of He-Man and watch Hordak and his lackeys from the Masters of the Universe canon (Mantenna, Leech, Grizzlor, Modulok, the Horde Troopers), and also not simply because the animation was rendered better and the colors a bit more vibrant than the duller *MOTU* program, but because She-Ra was a subtly more progressive and empowering program for American youth. On *She-Ra: Princess of Power*, other than the prominent male characters on the show (Bow, Hordak, Sea Hawk), most men were portrayed as inept bunglers and doltish idiots, while She-Ra and the other women wielded power responsibly and held the reins of authority in nearly every narrative adventure.

Mattel originally created the She-Ra toy line to merge its two most successful franchises—Barbie and He-Man. Therefore, Princess of Power action figures came with fabric capes and skirts, Barbie-type combs, plastic accoutrements, wonderful poseability, and fabulous weaponry. The She-Ra action figure possessed a shield, sword (with faux gemstone, prone to falling out), plastic headdress/mask (with two delicate "glitter"

Princess of Power She-Ra with Swift Wind.

stickers), a white fabric cape with gold foil belt and snap, a delicate two-sided red and white cape with "wings" that frame her headdress and cape, rooted hair, a comb accessory, and a body with six points of articulation and another fake gemstone lodged in her chest. Besides figures and fashions, there were also creatures, playsets, and other accessories.

With two full seasons of a syndicated animated series and a fairly successful theatrical release, *She-Ra Princess of Power: Secret of the Sword* (1985) to stimulate toy sales, it has been estimated by some experts that the Princess of Power line was produced in roughly the quantity of Mattel's hugely popular Masters of the Universe line.

Princess of Power Crystal Castle playset, with action figures She-Ra and Peekablue (top); and Glimmer and Double Trouble (bottom).

Princess of Power Catra with Clawdeen.

Princess of Power Mermista, Angella, Castaspella.

Princess of Power Sweet Bee, Perfuma, Entrapta.

The vibrantly animated series, *She-Ra: Princess of Power*, follows the adventures of She-Ra and her girl-power friends, as they defeat the Evil Horde and bring peace to Etheria. *Mattel/Filmation Associates*

Princess of Power Frosta and Netossa.

Princess of Power Fantastic Fashions Ready in Red, Fit to Be Tied, Deep Blue Secret, Flower Power, Hold On To Your Hat, Flight of Fancy.

Princess of Power Enchanta, MIB.

A trio of many She-Ra mini-comic books.

King of the Beasts

Voltron defends the universe

One of the most enduring images of the 1980s that has shown up in many pop culture references over the past ten-plus years on such programs as VH-1's *I Love the '80s*, Cartoon Network's *Robot Chicken* and *Sealab 2021*, in Sprite soft drink commercials, and in ditties by the Wu-Tang Clan, is the image of five small lion robots joining forces to form the iconic super-robot Voltron, the "King of Beasts."

Voltron toys were a commanding powerhouse in the mid-1980s, where the daily syndicated cartoon, *Voltron: Defender of the Universe*, produced by World Events Productions, brought the super-robot into homes across America.

To the delight of children everywhere, whenever the danger on the show built to a fever pitch—which was at least once per episode—the five separate lions would join to form the feet, legs, arms, torso, and head of Voltron, who fought evildoers with his powerful Sword of Arus. The five pilots of the lions were Commander Keith, an intellectual strategist who helmed the large and regal Black Lion; Lance Charles McClain, a tall, dashing wisecracker who oversaw the Red Lion; Darell "Pidge" Stoker, the tiny youthful introvert who led the Green Lion; Hunk Garett, the lovable, bulky, "big tough guy" of the group who controlled the Yellow Lion; and Sven Holgersson, pilot of the Blue Lion. Sven was later replaced by Princess Allura of the planet Arus.

Strangely enough, the toys for this animated television show were released by three different companies: Matchbox, Panosh Place, and LJN. The two former companies are of paramount importance, while LJN is of lesser acknowledgment.

Matchbox produced die-cast metal versions of the Voltron robots, with plastic accouterments. They were sold in two different manners: as a "deluxe gift set" containing all the parts

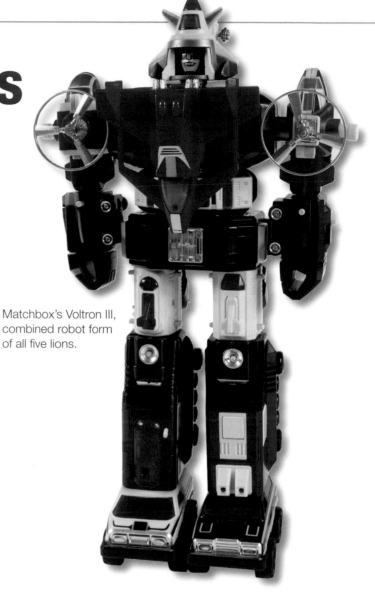

Matchbox's Voltron III, combined robot form of all five lions.

needed to assemble an entire Voltron super robot, or divided into three different separate sets that were exciting to play with individually, encouraging a child to "collect 'em all" to create the deluxe set.

Matchbox's various component pieces of Voltron III (the Lion-Force Voltron) came packaged separately, split into three different "Deluxe Lion" sets: 1) the Giant Black Lion Robot, head and chest of the "King of Beasts"; 2) the Mighty Lion Robots Set with two lions: the larger Yellow, the "massive leg," and the smaller Green, the "powerful arm"; and 3) another Mighty Lion Robots Set with two lions: the larger Blue, the "massive leg," and smaller Red, the "powerful arm."

The second most common Matchbox Voltron offering was the Voltron I robot, which was able to split into three different "Deluxe Warrior" sets. These sets were fascinating components, because these three deluxe vehicle configurations were constructed of five smaller individual vehicles and could combine to form a larger piece of robotics (fifteen pieces total!). Piloted by fifteen individual team members, who were not made into action figures by any company, these three different deluxe vehicle sets were the Space Warrior, Land Warrior, and Air Warrior.

The Space Warrior set had two space probers, two multi-wheeled explorers, and one communications module. The Land Warrior had two all-terrain space vehicles, one armored equipment carrier, one rotating personnel carrier, and one jet radar station. The Air Warrior set had two advanced recon helicopters, a strato-weapons module, a fighter plane, and a command jet explorer.

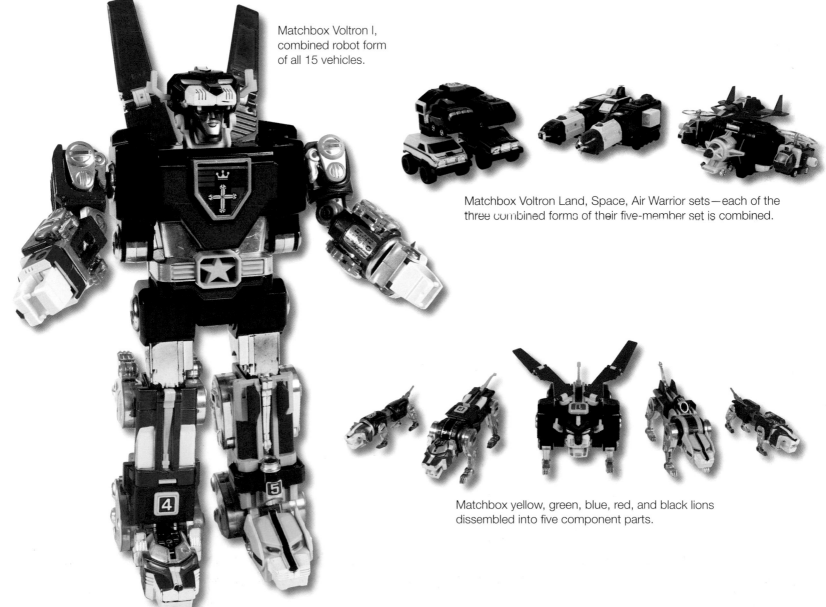

Matchbox Voltron I, combined robot form of all 15 vehicles.

Matchbox Voltron Land, Space, Air Warrior sets—each of the three combined forms of their five-member set is combined.

Matchbox yellow, green, blue, red, and black lions dissembled into five component parts.

The other major producer of detailed Voltron action figures, Panosh Place, limited its toys to only characters from the Voltron III "Lion Robot" series. Geared toward younger fans, the play value of these toys was higher than Matchbox's simply because the Panosh Place Lion Robots had added accessories and opening compartments that would accommodate 3-3/4-inch figures inside the robot lion while forming the larger Voltron III robot.

Heck, the original Matchbox Voltron III Deluxe Set didn't even come with his Sword of Arus—you had to buy it in a separate accessory set! Indeed, compared to Matchbox, the Panosh Place "King of Beasts" was less detailed, yet you could fit action figures into the lions as they combined into the super robot.

The 3-3/4-inch Voltron action figures produced by Panosh

were Doom Commander, Hagar the Witch, Hunk, Keith, King Zarkon, Lance, Pidge, Prince Lotor, Princess Allura, Robeast Mutilor, and Robeast Scorpius. Although most figures were not sculpted very well in comparison to today's standards, they are still fairly iconic: in their basic essence, they effectively represent the characters' likenesses from the *Voltron: The Defender of the Universe* cartoon.

Along with these figures were a few select vehicles and accessories that made the line more special: five Lion Robots combine to form Voltron III, the two Robeast coffins (the Coffin of Doom and Coffin of Darkness), the Skull Tank, the Zarkon Zapper, the Doom Blaster, and the always-impressive Castle of Lions with its many detailed accessories, multiple laser cannons, play value and movable parts.

Panosh Place Voltron yellow, green, blue, red, and black lions dissembled into five component parts.

Panosh Place Voltron, combined robot form of all five lions.

Panosh Place Castle of Lions, front view, opened, with all five GoLion robot pilots, from left: Lance (blue), Hunk (yellow), Keith (red), Pidge (green), and Princess Allura (pink).

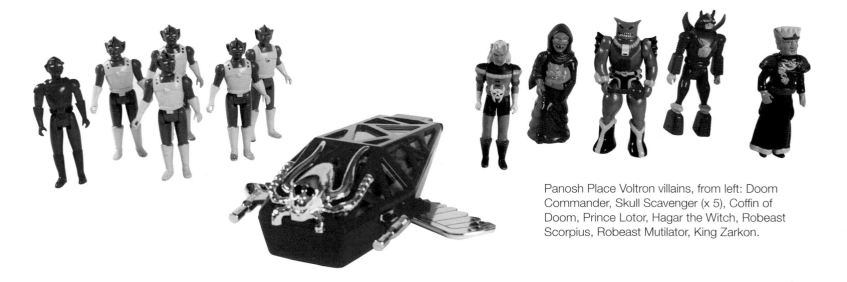

Panosh Place Voltron villains, from left: Doom Commander, Skull Scavenger (x 5), Coffin of Doom, Prince Lotor, Hagar the Witch, Robeast Scorpius, Robeast Mutilator, King Zarkon.

Piledrivers and Choke Slams

Professional wrestling invades pop culture

Wrestling Superstars "Rowdy" Roddy Piper (Series One).

Wrestling Superstars Iron Sheik (Series One).

Wrestling Superstars Jesse "The Body" Ventura (Series 3).

Vince McMahon's vision and business acumen launched the World Wrestling Federation (now World Wrestling Entertainment) into the heights of superstardom in the early 1980s.

With a national touring schedule, the rise of Hulkamania, and fruitful pay-per-view payoffs from smash-hit WrestleManias—those amazing, mind-blowing, über-lucrative events that began in 1985—wrestling had arrived and inhabited tens of millions of living rooms across America. The WWF invaded our backyards, our lexicon and language, our mindset, and the collective consciousness.

In the 1980s, the WWF's loyal and fanatical fans built the sport of wrestling into a colossal industry. Even an untrained observer walking down the halls of any middle school in the U.S. during these years would notice WWF posters hanging inside lockers, WWF Superstars adorning T-shirts, appearing in cartoon shows, plastered on toothbrushes, and printed on candy wrappers: wrestlers were everywhere.

Before he passed away in October of 2009, I had the opportunity to interview WWF legend Captain Lou Albano, wrestling's greatest impresario, rubber band aficionado, and early MTV icon due to his "Rock 'N Wrestling" cameos in some of Cyndi Lauper's music videos. When asked if wrestling was more entertaining back then than it is now, Captain Lou responded: "It was different back then. It just seemed more exciting. Maybe we took more risks. I had two valves replaced

in my heart. I've cracked my back three times. I have no cartilage in my nose. But I guess that's part of the lifestyle that comes with this business. It was a great time back then…(even though) we were making somewhere around $25,000-$30,000 per year. If I could do it all over again, I wouldn't change a thing."

Like the courageous and tough-as-nails Captain Lou Albano, the WWF's original heroes of the 1980s are lauded and heralded by pre-teen WWE fans today. Regardless of a fan's age, wrestling aficionados will never forget the earliest and most famous of all of those "heels" and "babyfaces" who were captured for posterity's sake by the LJN toy company in its 8-inch tall, solid rubber Wrestling Superstars toy line. Nearly impossible to destroy, each figure came with its own bio card for fans to cut out, and a small pin-up poster to display. There were six different series of LJN's Wrestling Superstars.

Wrestling Superstars
Vince McMahon
(Series 5).

Wrestling Superstars Hillbilly Jim (Series One), Brutus "The Barber" Beefcake (Series Two),
Randy "Macho Man" Savage (Series 3).

Wrestling Superstars
Koko B. Ware (Series 4).

Nikolai Volkoff (Series One), The Magnificent Muraco (Series 3), Greg "The Hammer"
Valentine (Series Two).

Wrestling Superstars Mean Gene Okerlund (Series 3), Hulk Hogan (Series 1),
Honkey Tonk Man (Series 6).

Wrestling Superstars Mr. Wonderful (Series 2), Ricky "The Dragon"
Steamboat (Series 3), Sgt. Slaughter (joint LJN/Hasbro mail-away).

King of Pop Immortalized

Michael Jackson in doll form

Advertised on his toy package as "The Superstar of the '80s," LJN decided to add Michael Jackson to its stable of licensed action figures because of the performer's larger-than-life status. Twelve-inch Michael had a fully poseable body (twisting waist, bendable legs, and moveable arms), a glittering "magic" glove, microphone, and a posing stand that allowed you to "make this superstar dance" his famous 'moonwalk'." In order to increase sales, the doll was offered in three different outfits. Apart from his most-popular "Thriller" attire (red and black leather jacket and red leather pants), he could be found wearing his clothes from "Beat It" (red and silver leather jacket and black pants) and "Billie Jean" (black leather suit, white shirt with red bowtie and white shoes).

As a performer in the '80s, Jackson's talent and influence were unparalleled; only Prince would come close for one short year, with 1984's *Purple Rain*. Try as they might, the press simply couldn't turn public opinion against the star and rumors such as his purchasing the bones of the Elephant Man were dismissed. *Time Magazine* in a March 19, 1984 article described Jackson's influence as "[a]… Star of records, radio, rock video. A one-man rescue team for the music business. A songwriter who sets the beat for a decade. A dancer with the fanciest feet on the street. A singer who cuts across all boundaries of taste and style and color, too."

On January 14 this same year, *The New York Times* wrote that, "…in the world of pop music, there is Michael Jackson and there is everybody else."

LJN's "Michael Jackson: Superstar of the '80s" 12" action figure in "Thriller" outfit.

These Rules Are Important to Follow

Gizmo and *Gremlins* a smash hit

Gremlins, three-pack Gremlins figures.

Another film attesting to the Steven Spielberg's producing prowess in the 1980s is Joe Dante's *Gremlins*, an unprecedented smash hit that warranted repeat viewings, and illustrates what happens when you break the rules.

The story of *Gremlins* is now infamous: a father travels to an unusual shop in Manhattan's Chinatown and brings home a unique animal to his son as a Christmas present: a small, brown and white teddy-bear type critter called a mogwai. Named Gizmo, the mogwai comes with a set of three rules that must be followed: Don't ever get them wet. Keep them out of bright light…it will kill them. But most important, no matter how much they cry, how much they beg, never, ever feed them after midnight.

Of course, all three rules are blatantly violated throughout the course of the narrative, and the results are shocking and disastrous: exposure to bright light will destroy a mogwai; allowing water to touch a mogwai causes the creature to asexually reproduce—at the rate of one new mogwai per drop of water; and feeding a mogwai anything after midnight and before dawn causes the adorable being to transform into a hideous, destructive beast known as a "gremlin."

As gremlins, the mogwai are fierce, vicious, murderous creatures with red eyes, fangs, claws, and green snake-like skin. Led by their uniquely mohawked leader, "Stripe" (voiced by the multi-talented Frank Welker of Transformers fame), the gremlins manipulate and terrify the town, yet they are ultimately vanquished by the heroic actions of the un-transformed Gizmo and his owner.

The film was most popular with children and adolescents because of the allure of Gizmo; however, it was criticized by many parents as being too violent to warrant a mere "PG" rating, and so it became one of two movies to lead to the creation of the PG-13 rating by the Motion Picture Association of America.

In the wake of the successful Amblin Entertainment film, LJN released a three-pack of PVC collectible Gremlin action figures: Gizmo, Stripe (as a mogwai), and Stripe (as gremlin). And, of course, the three important rules were posted in bold letters on the packaging.

Musical Button Pushing

Electronic memory game Simon enduring symbol

Although a relatively simple product to understand since it was essentially an electronic, simplified version of the children's game "Simon Says," Milton Bradley's electronic memory game, Simon, sold tens of thousands of units during its lengthy tenure on retail shelves.

This game has enthralled children and adults for an entire generation through simply pressing a combination of red, yellow, blue, and green buttons. An enduring symbol of '80s popular culture, its warm lights and the combination of conforming musical notes and harmonies played are: "A" note (red button), "A" note (green button—one octave higher than red), "D" note (blue button), and "G" note (yellow button).

So popular was the game that Milton Bradley followed up with new releases such as the eight-button Super Simon (a game I could never, ever master), and the portable Pocket Simon. The Simon craze also spawned a host of knock-offs, clones, and imitators hoping to capitalize on the popularity of the revolutionary game.

Milton Bradley's Simon and Super Simon.

Wax On…Wax Off

The Karate Kid with karate-kickin' (tri-) action

Every time I return to *The Karate Kid*, I feel there's a little bit of Rocky Balboa in young Daniel Laruso (well… not so young; Ralph Macchio was 23): he's an underdog that no one believes in—particularly those arrogant members of a local dojo, the Cobra Kai, maintained by merciless ex-Special Forces soldier John Kreese. Yet Daniel's skill in his chosen profession, karate, is a wonder to behold.

Daniel is taught the precepts of the martial art by his famous wizened instructor, Mr. Miyagi, portrayed by the late, great Pat Morita of *Happy Days* fame. Mr. Miyagi's manner of instruction is so subtle, that Daniel can hardly believe he's being trained at all ("Show me…wax on…wax off," "Show me…paint the fence…"). That is, until his "crane kick" stance wins Daniel the All Valley Karate Tournament, after learning from his sensei that "…the secret to karate lies in the mind and the heart. Not in the hands…"

Ahh…how many of us as young children imitated this kata and fell on our faces? Perhaps it would have been easier to manage this martial art if we just went to the local department store and picked up Remco's Karate Kid/Daniel-San figure or a Mr. Miyagi action figure which possessed auto-release TRI-ACTION features: "Karate Cop," "Karate Twist," and "Karate Kick" motions.

Daniel and Mr. Miyagi.

Daniel (Ralph Macchio) practices the crane kick that eventually wins him the big tournament in *The Karate Kid*. *Columbia/The Kobal Collection*

It All Begins With 'Power Action'

DC's greatest characters translated into plastic form

Second only to Mego's Official World's Greatest Super-Heroes (1972-1983), Kenner's Super Powers line is frequently hailed as the greatest DC super-hero characters ever translated into plastic form.

The Super Powers action figures' biographies were based directly on the characters in DC comics, and each figure possessed a distinct "power action feature"; for instance, Superman's "Power Action Punch," Flash's "Power Action Lightning Legs," Plastic Man's "Power Action Stretching Neck," and Wonder Woman's "Power Action Deflecting Bracelets." These paragons of DC Comics lore looked exactly like specific renderings of their characters from the pages of their respective comic books–the Hal Jordan Green Lantern smacked of Gil Kane, while Desaad, the Parademon, Kalibak, and Darkseid were crafted out of the magic of Jack Kirby's war-torn world of Apokolips.

The first two waves of Super Powers figures came with a mini-comic book packaged within the figures' bubbles, and also included a collector's card that a child could cut off the back of the toy package. Series One showcased DC's heavy hitters—the main members of the Justice League of America, and the primary focus of Hanna Barbera's cartoons *Superfriends* (1973) and *Challenge of the Superfriends* (1978): Batman and Robin, Superman, Wonder Woman, and Aquaman. However, they also offered up characters who might be new to both children and casual fans—those 'other characters' portrayed on Hanna-Barbera's show: the speedy-legged Flash, ring-toting Green Lantern, and the winged warrior, Hawkman.

Series Two introduced some gambles on Kenner's part: Dr. Fate, Firestorm, Green Arrow, Red Tornado, and an excellent Martian Manhunter figure, complete with his blue cape. To further the problem, the villains offered in Series Two switched from the rogues galleries of Batman and Superman offered in Series One (the Joker, Penguin, Lex Luthor, and Brainiac) to more Apokolips-themed villains: Darkseid (with "glowing" eyes), Desaad, Kalibak, Mantis, and a Parademon as a troop-builder. Nevertheless, these figures sold fairly well, supported of course, by action figures of the original Superfriends members, a DC comic book, and a new cartoon.

The action figure accessories for the Super Powers line were highly appropriate: from the trademarked "S" stamped onto Superman's red cape, to Green Lantern's power battery to aid him in "the brightest day...the blackest night." Hawkman's huge museum-absconded mace was spiked to the hilt. Aquaman's trident reflected his royal status. Lex Luthor wore his power suit out of the pages of *Action Comics*. And, of course, Wonder Woman possessed her Magic Lasso of Truth.

Yet, in Series Three, the Super Powers line introduced some fairly obscure second-tier characters into playrooms across America: Samurai (from the Superfriends cartoon; with sword and removable tunic), Shazam! (with removable cape), Cyborg (the rarest of all Super Powers figures, with chrome features and three arm attachments), Orion (with power action arms and changing faces), Mr. Miracle (the second rarest figure in the line, with manacles and cape), and Plastic Man (with stretching neck). Due to consumers' lack of familiarity with these characters and others, this revolutionary toy line was doomed to cancellation; but that's okay, because at the very least we have the three spectacular series of Kenner's Super Powers—perhaps the greatest small-scale super-hero action figures ever made.

Super Powers Hall of Justice playset.

Super Powers Batmobile with Batman and Robin.

Super Powers action figures, Series One, villains: Brainiac, Lex Luthor, Joker, Penguin.

Super Powers action figures, Series One, heroes: Superman, Wonder Woman, Green Lantern, Hawkman, Flash, Aquaman.

Super Powers action figures, Series Two, heroes: Martian Manhunter, Dr. Fate, Firestorm, Green Arrow, Red Tornado, Clark Kent.

Super Powers action figures, Series Two, villains: Steppenwolf, Kalibak, Parademon, Darkseid, Desaad, Mantis.

Super Powers action figures, Series Three, villains: Mr. Freeze, Cyclotron, Tyr;
heroes: Orion, Plastic Man, Golden Pharaoh, Mr. Miracle, Cyborg, Shazam, Samurai.

Unmasking the Enemy

V pits humans against aliens

V: Enemy Visitor action figure in human disguise.

"They're not what they appear to be," toy company LJN stated on the package front of its 12-inch tall V: Enemy Visitor action figure.

This fully poseable toy with extendable tongue (triggered by the push of a hidden button) perfectly mimicked the carnivorous race of alien villains known as "The Visitors" on NBC's 1983-85 television series, simply titled *V*.

With instructions that directed you to "unmask the Visitor to reveal his lizard face," this action figure, whose poseability was reminiscent of Mattel's Ken doll, included an authentic removable outfit, a "Laser Weapon," and removable black sunglasses.

Conceived by producer-writer-director Kenneth Johnson, also responsible for NBC's cult hit *The Incredible Hulk* (1978-1982) and the character of Jaime Sommers in *The Bionic Woman* (1976-78), the plot of the *V* franchise began in 1983 with the advent of a two-part mini-series where a race of aliens land on earth.

Upon exiting their spacecrafts, these friendly alien Visitors welcome humanity with open arms, pleading with the governments of Earth to help them as their home world is depleted of its natural resources. Strangely enough, these Visitors appear human in appearance, yet are required to wear sunglasses to protect their eyes from earth's harsh sunlight.

During this brief period of friendship between the Visitors

V: Enemy Visitor action figure, original alien form.

and humans, scientists begin to disappear, as well as politicians, world leaders, and any other humans wishing to research the nature and physiology of the Visitors more closely. So then, we learn that the Visitors are sinister, carnivorous, reptilian aliens who wish to conquer earth and enslave the human race, keeping humanity as a type of chattel.

The re-imagined *V* franchise was resurrected in 2009 to critical acclaim.

Mega Crossover a Milestone

Uncovering Marvel's Secret War

Captain America in the Turbo Cycle.

In a strategically planned, editorial driven, epic comic event, Marvel launched one of the first major crossovers, *Marvel Super Heroes Secret Wars* (May 1984-April 1985), published as a twelve-issue limited series.

MSHSW has often been criticized by some fans, though, as an editorial stunt, while others remember the ambitious project quite fondly due to 1) the high stakes determined by the plot, and 2) the vast array of important characters featured in the narrative. The story is a simple one with subtle complexities: an omnipotent being from beyond Earth (appropriately dubbed "The Beyonder") kidnaps the greatest heroes and deadliest villains in the Marvel Universe and whisks them to the far side of the universe, on a place called "Battleworld." On Battleworld, these powerful characters repeatedly clash with each other in order to obtain the ultimate prize of unlimited cosmic power.

The pages of *MSHSW* exhibit stunning artwork, particularly for the 1980s, penciled by Mike Zeck. Although the artwork and story were powerful to me at thirteen, the twelve-issue comic book series was a methodically conceived piece of toy-selling propaganda fueled by Mattel Inc., as revealed in an interview conducted by Tim Hartnett for the defunct Silver Bullet Comics. Within the context of the interview, Marvel's then-editor in chief, Jim Shooter, reminisced about the impetus for the *MSHSW* toy line: "Kenner had licensed the DC Heroes. Mattel had He-Man, but wanted to hedge in case super-heroes became the next big fad. They were interested in Marvel's characters, but only if we staged a publishing event that would get a lot of attention, and they could build a theme around. Fans, especially young fans, often suggested to me 'one big story with all the heroes and all the villains in it,' so I proposed that. It flew. Mattel thought that kids responded well to the word, 'secret' so after a couple of working names bit the dust, we called the story '*Marvel Super Heroes Secret Wars*'."

Furthermore, even the most casual of comic book collectors in the 1980s will recognize that issue #8 of *MSHSW* (titled "Invasion!", December 1984) contains the first appearance of Spider-Man's controversial "black costume"—an outfit later revealed to be an alien symbiote who would eventually bond with Eddie Brock, ultimately becoming one of the wall-crawler's deadliest enemies: Venom.

Marvel Super Heroes Secret Wars Series One villains: Dr. Doom, Dr. Octopus, Magneto, and Kang.

Marvel Super Heroes Secret Wars Series One and Two heroes: Series One: Iron Man, Spider-Man; Series Two: the Falcon and Wolverine (black claw variation).

Marvel Super Heroes Secret Wars Series Two heroes and villains: villains: Hobgoblin, Baron Zemo; heroes: Spider-Man (black costume) and Daredevil.

Marvel Super Heroes Secret Wars Doom Cycle.

Marvel Super Heroes Secret Wars Series One hero Captain America.

The figures in the *Marvel Super Heroes Secret War* toy line possess limited poseability (a mere five points), yet, like Kenner's Super Powers line, designers somehow tapped into the romantic representation and essence of each of the thirteen domestically produced characters: Captain America finally received an updated figure that modified his Mego incarnation's all-blue arms and lack of red gloves; longtime fans of the X-Men got their wish for a figure realized in the form of a comic-accurate Wolverine with prominent and pointy claws—"Wolvie" was the first X-Man to be immortalized as a toy; fans of Spider-Man in the early '80s were treated to a fully tentacled Doctor Octopus figure, and a Spider-Man action figure in his new black-and-white threads.

Sectaurs warrior Pinsor and his loyal insect steed Battle Beetle. This duo also came with gun, shield, sword, weapons belt/bandolier, and battle axe.

Sectaurs warrior Skulk and and his loyal insect steed Trancula. This duo came with gun, shield, weapons belt/bandolier, dart, and dagger.

New Insect Overlords

Sectaurs: Warriors of Symbion elaborate toys

Sectaurs action figures: Mantor with Raplor, Zak with Bitaur, Skito with Toxid, General Waspax with Wingid; Prince Dargon with Dragonflyer hovers above.

One of the most elaborate toy lines of the 1980s is Coleco's line of Sectaurs: Warriors of Symbion action figures. A play on the word "insect," the imaginary world of the 'Sectaurs took place on the planet of Symbion (another play on words, here—symbiosis, i.e. "a mutually beneficial relationship between two organisms"), where insects have grown to tremendous proportions due to an experiment performed long ago on the planet's inhabitants.

Furthermore, many Sectaur soldiers—humanoids who share characteristics with insect and arachnids—have telepathically bonded to their insect companions via a process called "binary-bonding" (in some instances called "tele-bonding") that benefits both creatures when engaging in combat.

With an eight-issue comic book tie-in produced by Marvel Comics (June 1985 to September 1986) and a five-episode animated mini-series produced by Ruby-Spears, Sectaurs was an underappreciated and short-lived toy line that included nine action figures and one playset, the Hyve.

Each action figure came with a host of weapons and accessories, such as bandoliers, belts, pistols, rifles, swords, and shields, and a unique insect companion that possessed some type of action feature.

The most revolutionary of all Sectaurs toys were Coleco's four deluxe action figure sets, which included a humanoid Sectaurs figure accompanied by an oversized insect companion which was fundamentally a hand-puppet. When manipulating the toy, a humanoid figure would be attached to a saddle that rested on top of the insect companion, then a child would insert their hand into the underside of one of these hand-puppet steeds which fit like a glove (dubbed "Hands-In Action"); a child's fingers would then function as the insect's legs, an effect that was interesting to behold. Furthermore, attached to two of the deluxe-sized insects—Price Dargon's Dragonflyer and General Spidrax's Spiderflyer—were a pair of thin, twin, translucent, battery-powered wings that would flap when you flipped a switch.

These motorized wings, combined with the movement of the child's hands as an insect's legs and appendages, were a marvel of toy engineering.

ENTERTAINMENT-O-RAMA:
1984 MOVIES, MUSIC, TELEVISION

Top Ten Films of 1984

1 *Beverly Hills Cop* (Paramount)
2 *Ghostbusters* (Sony/Columbia)
3 *Indiana Jones and the Temple of Doom* (Paramount)
4 *Gremlins* (Warner Brothers)
5 *The Karate Kid* (Columbia)
6 *Police Academy* (Warner Brothers)
7 *Footloose* (Paramount)
8 *Romancing the Stone* (20th Century Fox)
9 *Star Trek III: The Search for Spock* (Paramount)
10 *Splash* (Buena Vista)

Best Picture: *Amedeus* (Orion)

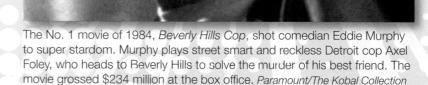

The No. 1 movie of 1984, *Beverly Hills Cop*, shot comedian Eddie Murphy to super stardom. Murphy plays street smart and reckless Detroit cop Axel Foley, who heads to Beverly Hills to solve the murder of his best friend. The movie grossed $234 million at the box office. *Paramount/The Kobal Collection*

One of the biggest phenomenons of the '80s was the movie *Ghostbusters*, about three unemployed and eccentric parapsychologists who set up shop as ghost exterminators: Dr. Venkman (Bill Murray), Dr. Stantz (Dan Aykroyd), and Dr. Spengler (Harold Ramis). They are later joined in fighting ghosts by Winston Zeddemore (Ernie Hudson). The film would have had a distinctly different sensibility had Venkman been portrayed by John Belushi instead of Murray. Regardless, in order to keep his best friend's spirit alive, Aykroyd based the obnoxious green ghost encountered early on in the Sedgewick Hotel Ballroom, known as "Slimer," on Belushi. With a supporting cast that also includes Rick Moranis and Sigourney Weaver, *Ghostbusters* was unprecedented hit. The popularity of this movie resulted in an animated series and a toy line, featured in the 1986 chapter. *Columbia/The Kobal Collection*

Top Ten Television Programs of 1984-85

1 *Dynasty* (ABC)

2 *Dallas* (CBS)

3 *The Cosby Show* (NBC)

4 *60 Minutes* (CBS)

5 *Family Ties* (NBC)

6 *The A-Team* (NBC))

7 *Simon & Simon* (CBS)

8 *Murder, She Wrote* (CBS)

9 *Knots Landing* (CBS)

10 *Falcon Crest* (CBS)

Although Bill Cosby's offbeat humor has spanned more than four decades, to many Americans his most memorable role was that of Dr. Heathcliff Huxtable, the patriarch of NBC's smash-hit *The Cosby Show*. Starring opposite Phylicia Rashad (as his wife, Claire Huxtable), *The Cosby Show* was one of the first programs on network television to chronicle the adventures of an upper-middle class African-American family, and did so for eight full seasons (and 197 episodes) from 1984-1992. Cliff Huxtable's children were often the source of both comedy and tragedy throughout the show's tenure, and these roles were deftly filled by Malcolm-Jamal Warner (as Theo Huxtable), Tempestt Bledsoe (Vanessa Huxtable), Kesiha Knight Pulliam (Rudy Huxtable), Lisa Bonet (Denise Huxtable), and Sabrina Le Beauf (Sonrda Huxtable Tibideaux). *NBC-TV/The Kobal Collection*

Top Ten Billboard Singles of 1984

1 "When Doves Cry," Prince (*Purple Rain*, 1984)

2 "What's Love Got To Do With It," Tina Turner (*Private Dancer*, 1984)

3 "Say Say Say," Paul McCartney & Michael Jackson (*Pipes of Peace*, 1983)

4 "Footloose," Kenny Loggins (*Footloose* soundtrack, 1984)

5 "Against All Odds (Take a Look at Me Now)," Phil Collins (*Against All Odds* soundtrack, 1984)

6 "Jump," Van Halen (*1984*, 1984)

7 "Hello," Lionel Richie (*Can't Slow Down*, 1984)

8 "Owner of A Lonely Heart," Yes (*90125*, 1984)

9 "Ghostbusters," Ray Parker Jr. (*Ghostbusters* soundtrack, 1984)

10 "Karma Chameleon," Culture Club (*Colour By Numbers*, 1983)

Rock star Prince was riding high in 1984 with his movie, *Purple Rain*, and album of the same name, which included the top single of the year. *AP Photo/F. Carter Smith*

1985

ThunderCats Mumm-Ra with Ravage, and Lion-O with Snarf.

Cats of Thunder and Female Rockers

With the likes of Rankin/Bass' brilliant *Thunder-Cats* cartoon, *Disney's Adventures of the Gummi Bears*, *Jim Henson's Muppet Babies*, and female rockers *Jem and the Holograms*, it was a challenge to pry kids off of the great "idiot box," except when they played with the tie-in toys of these and other cartoons.

Over the next few years, two shows that have recently entered popular syndication have been Angela Landsbury's *Murder, She Wrote*, and *Miami Vice*, with the charismatic Don Johnson and Philip Michael Thomas. Crockett, Tubbs, and Jessica Fletcher were not made into action figures to America's dismay; even a lone MacGyver toy would have been a fine addition to retail pegs.

There were a few films that fans begged for action figure treatment, including *Back to the Future* featuring Michael J. Fox of *Family Ties* fame; 1985 was Mr. Fox's *year*.

However, it was Sylvester Stallone who was awarded the glory of an action figure. *Rambo: First Blood Part II* featured a super-violent portrayal of John Rambo, was a financial windfall that led to the *Rambo and the Forces of Freedom* toy line (featured in the 1986 chapter). Even Steven Spielberg and Richard Donner's smash-hit *The Goonies* and Fox's teen comedy *Teen Wolf* missed out. And fashion doll fans still anticipate a set to represent each of the informal members of the "Brat Pack": Demi Moore, Andrew McCarthy, Rob Lowe, Emilio Estevez, Judd Nelson, Anthony Michael Hall, Molly Ringwald, and Ally Sheedy.

Jem/Jerrica, "with flashing Jemstar earrings."

As for music, WHAM! (George Michael and Andrew Ridgeley) produced two singles in the Billboard Top 20 in one year, while Madonna finally arrived on heavy rotation with "Like a Virgin," "Material Girl," "Crazy for You," and "Dress You Up."

The biggest surprise of 1985 was the myriad group of stars dedicated to sing "We Are the World": Al Jarreau, Bette Midler, Billy Joel, Bob Dylan, Bob Geldof, Bruce Springsteen, Cyndi Lauper, Dan Aykroyd, David Paich (of Toto), Diana Ross, Dionne Warwick, Hall & Oates, Harry Belafonte, Huey Lewis and the News, Jackie Jackson, James Ingram, Jeffrey Osborne, Jermaine Jackson, Kenny Loggins, Kenny Rogers, Kim Carnes, LaToya Jackson, Lindsey Buckingham, Lionel Richie, Marlon Jackson, Michael Jackson, Paul Simon, Randy Jackson, Ray Charles, Sheila E., Smokey Robinson, Steve Perry, Steve Porcaro (of Toto), Stevie Wonder, The Pointer Sisters, Tina Turner, Tito Jackson, Waylon Jennings, and Willie Nelson.

Feel the Magic, Hear the Roar

Thunder...Thunder... ThunderCats Hooooo!

Mumified Mumm-Ra.

One of my favorite animated programs of all time is Rankin/Bass Productions' *ThunderCats*.

Making a name for themselves as the producer of the most iconic stop-motion animated specials of all time—*The Little Drummer Boy* (1968), *Santa Claus in Comin' to Town* (1970), *Here Comes Peter Cottontail* (1971), *The Year Without a Santa Claus* (1974), and *Rudolph the Red-Nosed Reindeer* (1964)—Arthur Rankin Jr. and Jules Bass have provided quality entertainment to children for forty years.

The *ThunderCats* animated series is lauded as one of the crowning accomplishments of mass-produced animation in the 1980s, and most action figure and toy aficionados compare the quality of its programming quite favorably to other popular cartoons of the time that were natural competitors for children's attention: *G.I. Joe: A Real American Hero*, *Transformers*, and *He-Man and the Masters of the Universe*.

ThunderCats follows the adventures of a cat-like race of heroes from the planet of Thundera. When we first meet them, they are busily escaping the total destruction of their home world. Due to their elevated status as the ruling elite, the ThunderCats (Jaga, Tygra, Panthro, Cheetara, Lion-O, Wilykat, Wilykit, and Snarf) are entrusted to protect the mystic "Eye of Thundera"—an artifact which retains the ThunderCats' main source of power, which has been embedded in the super-powerful Sword of Omens. While fleeing their planet with the Sword of Omens, the ThunderCats' ship is attacked by their age-old foes, the evil Mutants of the planet Plun-Darr, who are determined to obtain the sword and the all-powerful Eye.

The Mutants are comprised of four different species that have fought the ThunderCats for eons: Reptilians, large humanoid reptile-men; Simians, a race of ape-men; the dog-like Jackalmen; and the Vulturemen, who typify carrion birds of prey.

Similar to the Mutants, when Tobin "Ted" Wolf, ingenious creator of the ThunderCats' fictional universe, concocted the idea of a team of super-heroes, he deigned that each ThunderCats character was based in some way on a real-life cat: Lion-O is, of course, modeled after a lion; Jaga's likeness is that of a jaguar; Tygra is, well...a tiger; Panthro is designed in the manner of a "gray" panther; Cheetara is a cheetah; and the twins, WilyKit and WilyKat, are based upon wildcats.

The ominous entity that manipulates the Mutants and becomes the heroes' primary foe is the infamous undead magician known as Mumm-Ra. His transition from tattered and putrefied demon-priest—a self-touted "ever-living source of evil," into the more powerful and frightening "Ever-Living" incarnation (replete with grinning maw, blackened skin, and further suggestion of his undead Egyptian nature)—is terribly frightening.

Rumors about a *ThunderCats* film have been swirling on the Internet for the past five years. Although a movie was slated for a summer 2010 release, the project has been placed on hold, as reported on the premiere Web site for ThunderCats information, www.thundercatslair.org, citing speculation that the weak economy and poor returns by the latest CGI-animated toy licensed film, *Star Wars: The Clone Wars*, had left the production of a *ThunderCats* movie in limbo.

Thanks to the LJN toy company, kids received fairly accurate representations of the ThunderCats in action-figure form. With an average of five points of articulation and a few character-specific accessories per figure, the package back of each ThunderCat toy stated: "Lion-O leads the band of ThunderCats against Mumm-Ra and his evil army of mutants. The battle for the Sword of Omens is on!" Most of the action figures also possess LJN's trademarked "Battle-Matic Action", which allowed a child to move a lever on the figure's back to make its arm move up and down.

ThunderCats assorted "Berserkers" action figures: Hammerhand, Ram Bam, and Top Spinner.

The *ThunderCats* animated series, which follows the adventures of a cat-like race of heroes from the planet Thundera, is lauded as one of the crowning accomplishments of mass-produced animation in the 1980s. Characters shown are WilyKit and WilyKat, Cheetara, Snarf, Tygra, Lion-O, and Panthro. *AP Photo/HO/Courtesy of Warner Home Video*

ThunderCats action figures: Panthro, Tygra with PVC WilyKat, and Cheetara with PVC WilyKit.

ThunderCats' "Evil Mutants" action figures: Monkian, Jackalman, Vultureman, S-s-slithe.

ThunderCats assorted action figures: Tuska Warrior, Hachiman,
Grune the Destroyer, Ratar-O.

Baby Kermit, Piggy and Company

Jim Henson's Muppet Babies

Muppet Babies, full set of Hasbro Softies stuffed plush: Baby Piggy (Miss Piggy), Baby Kermy (Kermit the Frog), Baby Fozzie (Fozzie the Bear), and Baby Rowlf (Rowlf the Dog).

Who knew that a brief dream/fantasy sequence from *Muppets Take Manhattan* (1984) would spin off into one of the most endearing and popular of all of Jim Henson's many different Muppet productions?

From this sequence, an animated program about the exploits of the "Muppet Babies" charmed a generation of viewers, as the Muppet Nursery provided Babies Kermit the Frog, Miss Piggy, Fozzie Bear, Animal, Scooter, Skeeter, Rowlf the Dog, and Gonzo (and let's not forget Dr. Bunsen Honeydew and Beaker) with a vast array of touching adventures—always under the watchful eye of the omnipresent and omniscient "Nanny." Even though I was a teen when the program aired, I found something oddly calming and transcendent about the show—about most Jim Henson productions, really.

Jim Hensons' Muppet Babies (September 15, 1984-December 29, 1990) was a certified hit with American children and soon, a truckload of merchandise would follow. Perhaps the best translation of Henson's charming animated characters into toy form would be the four plush Muppet Babies dolls produced by Hasbro for its 'Hasbro Softies' line. Of particular interest in these dolls are Baby Piggy's soulful eyes, Baby Fozzie's playful attire, Baby Rowlf's charmingly innocent smile, and Baby Kermy's cheerful optimistic wide-armed ebullience. Although their outfits are a bit inauthentic—substituting Baby Piggy's standard pink bow for a bonnet; Baby Kermit is not attired in his sailor suit; Baby Fozzie's cap is propeller-less and is now monogrammed with the letter "F"; Baby Rowlf appears fully clothed in overalls instead of a simple white bib and diaper—these peccadilloes were forgivable in order for Hasbro to achieve a consumer's elicitation of…well… "Aww…isn't that DARLING!" Any Muppet Babies fan's life is simply not complete without these beautiful toys.

Contagious, Outrageous Rockers

Jem and the Holograms

Jem/Jerrica, first issue.

"Jem...Jem is excitement!/O-o-o Jem...Jem is adventure!/ O-o-ooh...Glamour and glitter/Fashion and fame!/Jem...Jem is truly outrageous/Truly, truly, truly outrageous/Whoah-oh-oh Jem.../Jem the music's contagious, outrageous/Jem is my name/No one else is the same/Jem is my name..."

Any young girl growing up in the mid-'80s would recognize the above lyrics as the famous theme song for the fictional super-group Jem and the Holograms, a band of talented female rock stars. The brainchild of designer Christy Marx and concocted by Hasbro, Marvel Comics, and Sunbow Productions, the *Jem and the Holograms* animated program entranced a generation and converted devout acolytes of Mattel's Barbie line of fashion dolls to something completely different and "truly outrageous"— and Jem became a pop-culture icon who has endured to this day. With the rise of female rock 'n' rollers in the '80s such as Blondie, Madonna, Cyndi Lauper, the Bangles, and Joan Jett and the Blackhearts, the time was rife for a toy line to capitalize upon this phenomenon, and so Jem and the Holograms were born.

Jem and her band—Aja, lead guitarist and backup vocals; Kimber, keyboards and backup vocals; Raya, drummer and backup vocals; Shana, drummer/bass guitarist—often were pitted against their sworn enemies, the sinister and greedy Misfits: Pizzazz, lead vocals, guitar; Stormer, keytarist and backup vocals; Roxy, bassist and backup vocals; and Jetta, saxophone.

Produced through 1987, Hasbro crafted a slew of well-sculpted Jem products, combining fashion, adventure, and music that afforded an attractive end product: nearly every figure came with a full performance outfit, a musical instrument, a poster, and cassette tape full of well-produced, original rock songs.

Since Hasbro's Jem brand fashion dolls stood a bit taller than Mattel's Barbie toys, clothing and shoes were not interchangeable between the two lines. Jem figures boasted more impressive articulation and included a considerable amount of accessories. One standout in particular is the original 1985 Jem/Jerrica figure, which came with a microphone, Jem's stage dress, tights, shoes, hair comb, bracelet, a reversible belt, and a fashion doll stand. She even had a "secret outfit" for her daytime identity, Jerrica Benton, that consisted of a hat, dress, shoes, and sunglasses, and utilized the other side of her reversible belt. Each first-issue Jem/Jerrica doll also possessed built-in "flashing Jemstar" earrings that, with the touch of a button on the doll's back, would light up and flicker on and off in a strobing pink color.

Rumor has it that Hasbro will be registering Jem and the Holograms' domain names for a re-release of the line sometime within the next few years. Many thousands of young women who grew up in the '80s wait with bated breath...

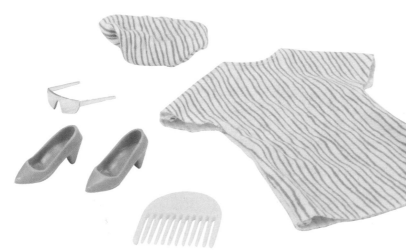

Jem/Jerrica's "secret outfit."

Kimber, of the Holograms.

Teddy Ruxpin: Storytelling Bear

Instant babysitter, just add cassette

Teddy Ruxpin, complete with all clothing, paperwork, and storybook and cassette combo ("The Airship").

An animatronic bear known as Teddy Ruxpin became an immediate sensation in 1985 when the plush doll was released by Worlds of Wonder, an innovative toy company founded by former Atari employees.

Essentially a battery-operated teddy bear that functioned on four alkaline "Cs," Teddy Ruxpin possessed technology that allowed the toy to narrate a story to children when a cassette tape was placed into a slot in its back. After pressing play, Teddy would become lively and animated, moving his mouth and eyes up and down while relating an adventure. Worlds of Wonder also provided a picture book for children to follow while Teddy Ruxpin read the tale aloud. Some snippets overheard during a story session include, "Hi. I'm Teddy Ruxpin. Come with me and I will sing songs and tell you wonderful stories that will make you laugh and smile."

Advertised as "The World's First Animated Talking Toy" and retailing for a whopping $69.99 (let's recall that Intellivision and Atari video games sold for $59.99), Teddy Ruxpin was praised by many parents for encouraging children to read. Teddy was a considerable feat of marketing and promotion.

Worlds of Wonder also offered sets of picture books and "animated cassettes" to supplement its talking bear. Since the actual Teddy Ruxpin doll came with a single cassette tape adventure (*The Airship*), and the entire recorded program was duplicated on both sides of the cassette, children would repeatedly listen to one short story that topped out at twenty-five minutes over and over again. The brevity of this tale encouraged

children to plead to their parents to buy more accessories such as the Teddy Ruxpin Christmas set that featured a storybook/cassette combo along with a deluxe outfit. The Christmas set was a sales bonanza, as it was packaged with the picture storybook, *Teddy Ruxpin's Christmas: A Musical Celebration*, a cassette tape of the same name, and an elegant Santa Claus ensemble which consisted of a pair of black boots, black belt, a red velvet jacket elaborately trimmed with faux fur, a pair of red velvet pants, and cozy trimmed Santa hat.

Worlds of Wonder produced twenty-four storybook/cassette combos, so there was no need for a child to become bored ever again. With titles such as "The Day Teddy Met Grubby," "Tweeg and the Bounders," "Lost in Boggley Woods," and the inexplicable "Grunge Music" (you just can't make this stuff up, folks…), this endearing toy is fondly remembered by children of the '80s to this day.

Worlds of Wonder Teddy Ruxpin.

Teddy Ruxpin's Christmas set came with a picture storybook (*Teddy Ruxpin's Christmas: A Musical Celebration*), a cassette tape, and a detailed Santa Claus outfit.

Quick Draw

Pictionary fast-paced

One of the most popular party games of the 1980s, Hasbro/Milton Bradley's Pictionary divides four or more people into opposing teams, where, after rolling a dice, one member of the team draws an image onto a piece of paper. This player may not speak, gesture, gesticulate, or prompt the other team members, who must guess what the sketch represents.

Pictionary is a high-energy, fun, fast-paced, and wonderfully frustrating game—"HOW could you not see that THAT was a PUPPY? HOW did you NOT know!?!"

"Well…because it had wings."

""THOSE aren't WINGS!!!"

And on it went; an ingenious idea for a game that sells well to this very day.

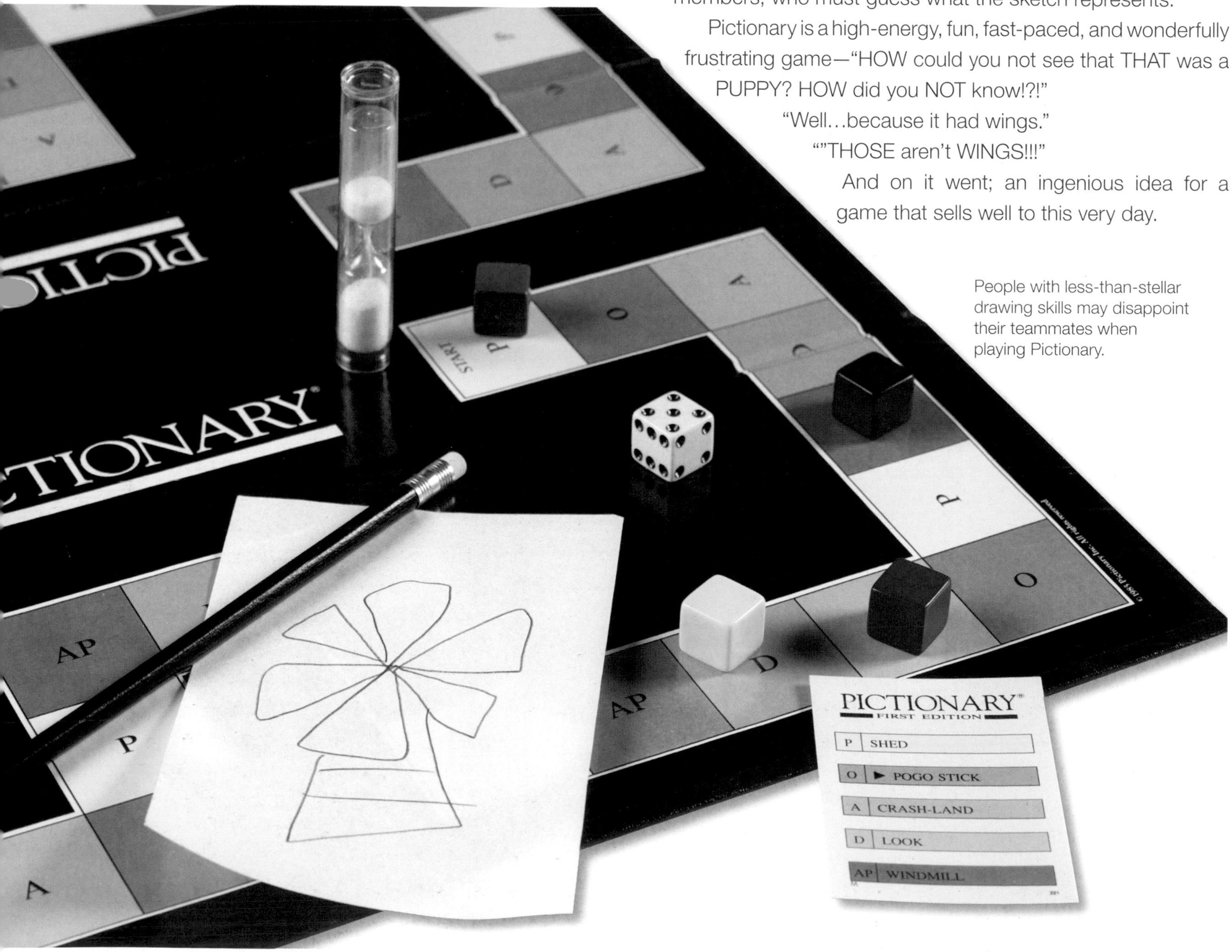

People with less-than-stellar drawing skills may disappoint their teammates when playing Pictionary.

Loveable Adopt-a-Toys

Pound Puppies: almost like the real thing

Large brown-and-white Pound Puppy in carrier kennel with adoption papers.

Although released in Canada by Irwin Toys in 1984 as the brainchild of Ford auto employee Mike Bowling, it was Tonka that introduced Pound Puppies to the American market. Perhaps in recognizing the popularity of Coleco's Cabbage Patch Kids, Tonka sought to capitalize on this "adopt-a-toy" concept with its famously adorable line of stuffed animals, the "lovable, huggable" Pound Puppies.

Tonka explained its conception of the toy line in great detail on the packaging of each Pound Puppy toy: "Hi! I'm a Pound Puppy…and I'm looking for a warm, loving home. I've been waiting for someone like you to choose me as their very own pet…You can give me a name and play with me! Won't you take me home with you? I'll love you very much!" These words and the endearing faces of each Puppy tugged on the heartstrings of every small child who walked past them in a department store. To compound the folly, each one was ingeniously packaged in its own cardboard "carrier kennel" box.

A major selling point of the toy was that Pound Puppies afforded consumers the opportunity to allow their child to "own" and name a stuffed puppy without having the responsibility of a live animal running around the house. Pound Puppies were manufactured in many different varieties of colors and styles (similar to Cabbage Patch Kids), so children lucky enough to "adopt" one felt that their toy was singularly unique and one-of-a-kind.

Upon bringing home this machine-washable (!) toy and removing it from its box, the package also contained a few other items: a collar embossed with the Pound Puppies logo,

and a "Puppy Care" sheet that outlined, in great detail, the rules for owning and caring for a Pound Puppy. This interesting care page instructed children on how to rear their Pound Puppy as if it were a living, breathing pet with rules such as: "… please be gentle with them. Just like other puppies, they don't like to be treated roughly," and "[they] like to play and need exercise to keep fit… lots of short walks with you will keep Pound Puppies exercised and safe." The final item included in the box was a mail-in form for a Pound Puppies "Tender Loving Care Package." For $3.50, a child would receive an official 8" x 10" Ownership Certificate mailed to their home in 6-8 weeks (similar to a Cabbage Patch Kid's set of adoption papers), a Personalized Puppy Tag which was stamped with the animal's name and the child's name as well, a set of Pound Puppies stickers, and a $1.50 refund offer coupon for the purchase of Pound Puppies' outfits.

Pound Puppies were a runaway hit for Tonka, grossing $300 million in sales worldwide (distributed to 35 different countries) for the first five years of production.

Gross-Out Cards

Controversial Garbage Pail Kids modeled after Cabbage Patch Kids

The head-exploding Adam Bomb has become the mascot for the entire series of Garbage Pail Kids.

Beginning in 1985, the Topps trading card company, inspired by the success of Coleco's mass-produced Cabbage Patch Kids created a collectible set of sticker/trading cards known as the Garbage Pail Kids.

Essentially, Garbage Pail Kids were patterned after Xavier Roberts' lucrative creations, except these characters possessed a disgusting or shocking flaw and a name usually rich with wordplay. The most well-known and iconic card was named "Adam Bomb" and featured a small Cabbage Patch-type character with its finger depressing a red-buttoned trigger which caused the character's head to explode similar to an atomic blast with telltale mushroom cloud. This violent image was quite controversial: parents groups went ballistic; children scooped them up by the dozens: Topps sold millions of packs.

The irony inherent in the public backlash against Garbage Pail Kids rests in the fact that the creator of the line, revolutionary underground comic artist Art Spiegelman (Topps' staff member for Product Development), would go on to contribute another bit of genius that was lauded by both the mainstream media and educators worldwide: the 1986 Pulitzer Prize winning Holocaust memoir, *Maus*. Spiegelman was a brilliant designer whose contribution to Topps also included "Garbage Candy" (1970-77) and long-running "Wacky Packages" cards (1967-intermittently to present), which were essentially the forerunner of Garbage Pail Kids.

Garbage Pail Kids stickers were solicited in a manner similar to baseball cards, with each packet consisting of five Garbage Pail Kids stickers along with one stale stick of pink bubble gum for a mere twenty-five cents. The cards were a runaway hit and kids couldn't get enough of these comically singular stickers to the extent that Topps would produce fifteen different sets of standard stickers, two large-format ("giant-sized") sets, and a slew of posters, even resurrecting the line for seven new series of stickers in 2003.

Garbage Pail Kids stickers ushered in a new era of acceptance for "gross-out" toys and ephemera for kids in the 1980s; it seemed that everything paled in comparison when set against these insidious cards. The gross-out theme allowed such eccentric materials as Mattel's once-bestselling toy, its green "Slime" compound of the 1970s, to become popular once again and so a similar substance was offered with '80s toy lines, such as Kenner's The Real Ghostbusters' Ecto-Plazm, Mattel's Masters of the Universe's Slime Pit playset, and the Retro-Mutagen Slime found in Playmates' Teenage Mutant Ninja Turtles action figure collection.

Another major "gross-out" toy worth mentioning—one that would experience a re-production and resurgence in recent years—is AmToy's Madballs collection. These were initially offered in an assortment of eight different models/characters

With these tips, you, too, can be a
Garbage Pail Kid.

Madball Skull Face.

in 1985: Aargh, a Frankenstein's Monster-themed Madball; Crack Head, with fractured skull and exposed brain (eventually changed to Bash Brain due to the words "crack head" attaining a new meaning in the 1980s); Dustbrain, patterned after a mummy; Hornhead, a Cyclops with a single horn; Oculus Orbus, an enormous eyeball; Screamin' Meemie, modeled after a baseball—with prominent tongue and frightening face; Slobulus, a disgusting face with one eyeball drooping; and Skull Face, which is self-explanatory. The first series of Madballs sold so well that a second series of eight was commissioned, along with three "Super Madballs" and a set of eight highly-prized Madballs "Head Poppin' Action Figures."

Illusion is the Ultimate Weapon

Mobile Armored Strike Kommand

M.A.S.K. Series One, conventional modes for, from left, front to back: Rhino, Gator, Piranha, Firecracker, Jackhammer, Switchblade, Boulder Hill playset, T-Bob, Thundercracker, Condor.

After the decline in sales and eventual cancellation of Kenner's Star Wars toy line in 1984-85, the company's income and revenue from male action figure manufacturing began to wane until there was resurgence in the boys' toys division in 1985. During this time, Kenner launched two fantastic toy lines that were far removed from a space opera: its Super Powers Collection (1984), based on DC Comic's most famous super-heroes, and a curious figure/vehicle line dubbed "M.A.S.K."

The epigraph from the frontispiece of the 1985 M.A.S.K. catalog reads: "Join M.A.S.K—Mobile Armored Strike Kommand—where ordinary vehicles and men become an awe-some fighting team to wage battle against Venom: the Vicious, Evil Network of Mayhem. M.A.S.K. …Where illusion is the ultimate weapon."

There were fascinating appellatives for the character's masks, those super-powered helmets that possessed a unique ability for their owner: Brad Turner's mask Hocus Pocus, Hondo MacLean's Blaster, Matt Trakker's Spectrum, or even Miles Mayhem's Viper. These masks suggested that something was distinctly different with each character—that each member of M.A.S.K. or V.E.N.O.M. possessed an exceptional ability. Their masks had a special power, whether it a beam of light, a flame

M.A.S.K. Series One 1985, action modes: Rhino, Gator, Piranha, Firecracker, Jackhammer, Switchblade, Boulder Hill playset, T-Bob, Thundercracker, Condor.

torch, a burst of lava, or even a razor-sharp buzz saw.

With the clever use of masks and illusion, kids could really suspend their disbelief with this action figure line and buy into the fantasy. From the very first series of vehicles and playsets, Kenner captured the imagination of children everywhere. In Series One, a service station transformed into an armored bunker (Boulder Hill); a simple green motorcycle changed into a helicopter (Condor); and a large trailer rig metamorphosed into a mobile defense unit (Rhino). In the world of M.A.S.K., off road vehicles became hydroplanes, while Camaro sports cars switch to fighter jets.

To support the line, Kenner licensed a DC comic book as a tie-in, they packaged brochures within their toys, and launched a successful animated series that lasted two full seasons for a total of 75 episodes—and directed by several un-credited Japanese studios.

M.A.S.K. Series Two action modes 1986: Hurricane, Firecracker, Vampire, Raven, Stinger, Outlaw, Slingshot, Volcano.

M.A.S.K. Series Three ("Racing Series"), conventional modes for, from left front row to back: Manta, Buzzard, Bullet, Bulldog, Razorback, Meteor, Pit Stop Catapult, Iguana, Wildcat, Goliath, Billboard Blast, the Collector.

M.A.S.K. Series Three ("Racing Series"), action modes, 1987: Manta, Buzzard, Bullet, Bulldog, Razorback, Meteor, Pit Stop Catapult, Iguana, the Collector, Wildcat, Goliath, Billboard Blast.

M.A.S.K. Series Five ("Laser Command"), conventional modes and alternate modes, 1988: Hornet (packing crate) & Ratfang (ORV [Off-Road Vehicle] Truck).

M.A.S.K. adventure packs (1986): Coast Patrol with Matt Trakker, Jungle Challenge with Matt Trakker, Rescue Mission with Bruce Sato, Venom's Revenge with Miles Mayhem, and (European Issue) Glider Strike with Jaques LaFleur.

Small Creatures Lurk Everywhere

Action figures M.U.S.C.L.E in

M.U.S.C.L.E "Battlin' Belt" and ten PVC figures.

Approximately 2 inches tall and constructed out of a bubblegum-colored PVC plastic (Polyvinyl Chloride), Mattel produced these M.U.S.C.L.E. (Millions of Unusual Small Creatures Lurking Everywhere) action figures through 1988. With a total of 236 domestic figures made in a wide variety of colors—their original bubblegum pink ("flesh" colored), followed by dark blue, red, purple, magenta, salmon, lime green, neon orange, light blue, grape and light purple—the back story for the toy line remained the same. Originally dubbed Kinnikuman (for the manga that featured these characters), the M.U.S.C.L.E. toy line is a perfect example of the Japanese hobby of amassing collectible erasers known as kinkeshi. Capitalizing on the action figure craze of the 1980s, Mattel produced a line of figures that were relatively inexpensive to purchase and easy to amass in great numbers.

These toys were offered in a variety of different price points: blister-carded 4-packs (with randomly inserted figures), small semi-opaque garbage can 10-packs, and a set of four fixed-sculpt 28-pack assortments (the "Thug Busters" set, "Cosmic Crunchers" set, "Mighty Maulers" set, and "Cosmic Showdown" set). The "M.U.S.C.L.E. Mega-Match" board game (with ten included figures), championship-type "Battlin' Belt" and a "Hard Knockin' Rockin'" wrestling ring (with two exclusive figures) were also solicited at retail.

Candy Inspires Sweet Cartoon

Disney's Adventures of the Gummi Bears

Applause's PVC Cubbi Gummi Bear with trumpet.

Haribo, the long-standing German confectionery corporation, targeted the American market in 1982 with its famously tasty gelatin-based treats, the Haribo Gold-Bears gummi candy. Demand for gummi candy (or alternatively, "gummy" candy) was so strong during the first year of production in America that the company couldn't produce its sweets fast enough—and the floodgates opened for other European corporations to export gummi products and nab a percent of the market (e.g. Black Forest, Trolli, etc.).

The '80s is a decade that was famous for new additions to the standard lineup of children's candy—candy that was created in a decade of excess and has endured to this very day. Confectioneries such as Skittles, Nerds, Runts, and, of course, those tasty and chewy gummi bears, have all cemented their space in children's hearts. One child in particular would affect the course of pop culture history and the means by which gummi bears would be remembered fondly by an entire generation: the son of (former) Disney C.E.O. Michael Eisner. A request for the candy by his son sprouted a germ of an idea in Eisner's mind: why not create a television program based on his son's favorite treat? Why not construct a cartoon about gummi bears?

So, in 1985, Disney Studios concocted the long-running and engaging animated program, *Disney's Adventures of the Gummi Bears*, featuring a slew of endearing characters: Gruffi Gummi, the stubborn leader of the Gummi Bears who inhabit "Gummi Glen"; Zummi Gummi, the old, absent-minded wizard of the Gummis, often shouting "spoonerisms" under duress; Grammi Gummi, the strong-willed matriarch of the clan and the preparer of the bears' infamous "gummiberry juice"; Tummi Gummy, the slow-witted but courageous adolescent of the group; Sunni Gummi, the rebellious, trendy youngster of the clan who yearns to one day become a princess; and Cubbi Gummi, the youngest of the group who longs for adventure and desires to be taken seriously by his elders.

The exploits of these anthropomorphic bears entranced young viewers, and so *Disney's Adventures of the Gummi Bears* became the corporation's first attempt at sustaining an ongoing serialized animated program. The series' success would launch Disney into the competitive realm of weekday animation, which would help the company become the forerunner of the genre in the late '80s and early '90s with such successful programs as *The Wuzzles*, *DuckTales*, *Chip 'n Dale Rescue Rangers*, *TaleSpin*, *Darkwing Duck, Gargoyles*, and the *Who Framed Roger Rabbit*-inspired *Bonkers*.

For fans who don't wish to break the bank when purchasing Walt Disney's ridiculously expensive 1985 Gummi Bears plush dolls, which can sell for more than $100 each on the collector's market, a solid alternative is the Applause toy company's authentic Gummi Bear PVC figurines with enclosed mini story booklet which can be purchased for a mere $5 in most collectible shops.

Most Popular Anime Import of '80s

Robotech a revolutionary cartoon

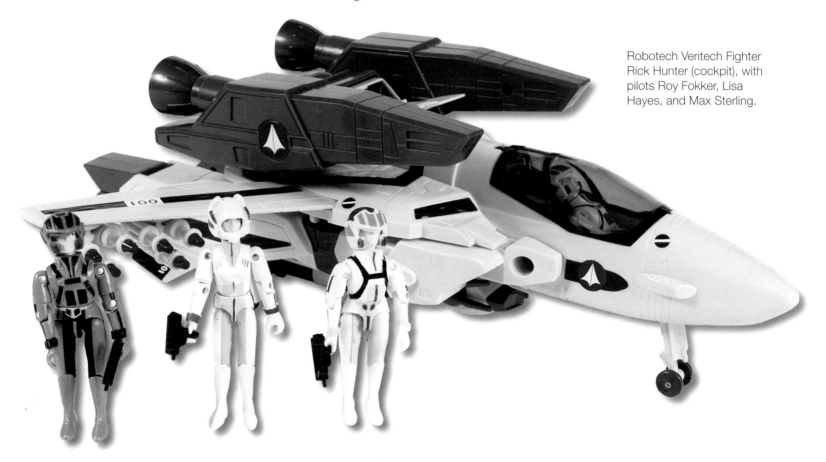

Robotech Veritech Fighter Rick Hunter (cockpit), with pilots Roy Fokker, Lisa Hayes, and Max Sterling.

Americans credit the Matchbox toy company and Tatsunoko Production Co. Ltd.—the famous Japanese anime (cartoon/animation) studio—for importing Harmony Gold's brilliant and sophisticated animated program known as *Robotech* to our shores. With its catchy slogan and song, the revolutionary *Robotech* cartoon was a much different animated program than any other offered in the 1980s.

Robotech was an 85-episode animated science-fiction franchise that was an adapted combination of three different Japanese anime series: *The Super Dimension Fortress Macross* (U.S. title: *Robotech: The Macross Saga*), *Super Dimension Cavalry Southern Cross* (in the U.S., *Robotech: The Robotech Masters*), and *Genesis Climber Mospeada* (U.S. designation: *Robotech: The New Generation*). These three different U.S. animated series were kept as close to the original Japanese anime's complex and sophisticated source material as possible.

The Third Robotech War (The New Generation) featured a new set of villains—the alien Invid, a series of bipedal crab-like beings attached together via a hive-mind. Attracted to

Earth by the planet's invasion of the Zentraedi, the Robotech Expeditionary Force encounters these alien beings, which sets in motion the Third Robotech War.

Although Matchbox's toys were produced in 1986, Harmony Gold would concoct similar figures and accessories six years later, in 1992. Made of an inferior quality plastic, some characters in their assortments were markedly different than their Matchbox counterparts.

Matchbox's stellar Robotech line included 3-3/4-inch and 6-inch figures, vehicles, robots, mecha, weapons, accessories, and playsets. The "holy grail" of all Robotech toys is the SDF-1 playset. The one pictured here is one of only a handful of complete, existing samples, as its many loose pieces and delicate nature make it extremely rare.

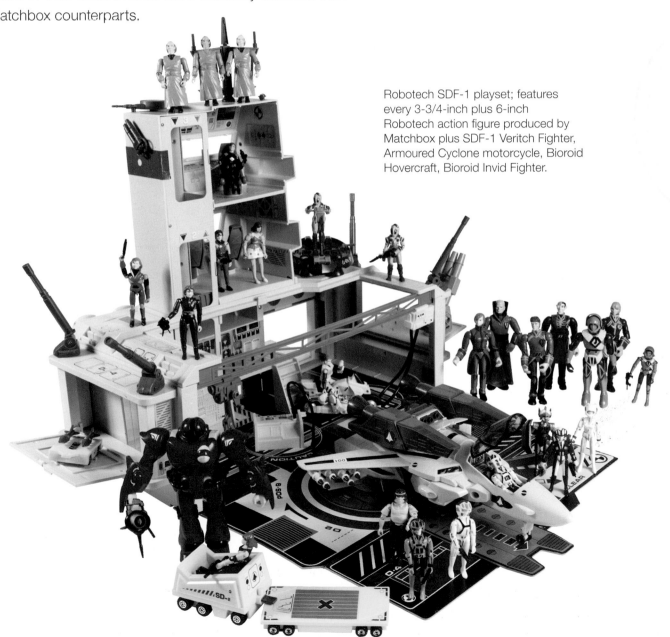

Robotech SDF-1 playset; features every 3-3/4-inch plus 6-inch Robotech action figure produced by Matchbox plus SDF-1 Veritch Fighter, Armoured Cyclone motorcycle, Bioroid Hovercraft, Bioroid Invid Fighter.

The Saga Continues
Star Wars Power of the Force

Star Wars *Return of the Jedi* scene, featuring Luke Skywalker (X-Wing Pilot), A-Wing Pilot, Nien Nunb, Lando Calrissian (General Pilot), and the Y-Wing Fighter, with R2-D2 inside the ship's "astromech socket."

In 1985, the original Star Wars trilogy was phasing out of the collective consciousness, and a slew of new toy and action figure offerings began crowding Star Wars product off retail shelves—such as Hasbro's better-articulated G.I. Joe and Transformers, and Mattel's Masters of the Universe—and so, Star Wars action figures had one last gasp in late 1984/ early 1985 when Kenner produced the final assortment of the vintage Star Wars line: Star Wars, Power of the Force ("POTF"). Although hailed by Star Wars aficionados as some of the best-sculpted and well-rendered of all the vintage Star Wars action figures, due to waning interest the line, these toys (packaged with a special silver colored foil-embossed collector's coin) did not sell well and were often discounted at retail.

It should be noted that although fifteen all-new action figures were sculpted under the Star Wars Power of the Force banner (one figure, Yak Face, was only available outside of the domestic United States), many older figures (Ben Obi-Wan Kenobi, Luke Skywalker: Jedi Knight, C-3PO, etc.) were re-released on POTF cards with newly created POTF collector's coins. Many of these coins (and other coins that were only available as mail-aways) are worth their weight in gold—quite literally—on the secondary market. Twenty-seven coins were available only through a Kenner mail-away offer; these are the most difficult-to-find of all POTF coins.

The fifteen all-new Star Wars film characters which were released on Power of the Force card backs were: A-Wing Pilot,

Star Wars Power of the Force Amanaman, Han Solo (in Carbonite Chamber), Barada, Yak Face.

Star Wars Power of the Force R2-D2 (with pop-up light saber), Luke Skywalker (in Battle Poncho), A-Wing Pilot, Imperial Dignitary.

Amanaman, Anakin Skywalker, Artoo-Detoo (R2-D2) with pop-up light saber, Barada, EV-9D9, Han Solo (in Carbonite Chamber), Imperial Dignitary, Imperial Gunner, Lando Calrissian (General Pilot), Luke Skywalker (Imperial Stormtrooper Outfit), Luke Skywalker (in Battle Poncho), Romba (Ewok), Warok (Ewok), and the hard-to-find Yak Face.

To capitalize on the poor sales of the POTF assortment and diminishing popularity of the Star Wars toy franchise, Kenner decided to tap into the emerging children's programming market by constructing two disparate toy lines with Saturday morning cartoon tie-ins: the *Droids* and *Ewoks* collections. Both toy lines continued the procedure established with Kenner's Star Wars: Power of the Force assortment, packaging a foil-stamped collector's coin unique to each figure within the toy's blister card: Droids coins were minted in gold; Ewoks coins produced in bronze.

Star Wars Power of the Force, EV-9D9, Anakin Skywalker, Lando Calrissian (General Pilot), Luke Skywalker (Imperial Stormtrooper Outfit).

Star Wars Power of the Force trio: Imperial Gunner, Romba, Warok.

Star Wars Power of the Force Luke Skywalker, Jedi Knight Outfit.

In Trouble Again

Star Wars Droids: The Adventures of R2-D2 and C-3PO

Star Wars Droids scene, Droids A-Wing Fighter with A Wing Pilot.

The *Star Wars Droids: The Adventures of R2-D2 and C-3PO* animated program recounted events which took place during the nineteen-year span between *Star Wars Episode III: Revenge of the Sith* and *Star Wars Episode IV: A New Hope*. The *Droids* cartoon, which ran from September 7, 1985-June 7, 1986 on ABC, follows the exploits of the two most popular droids in the *Star Wars* galaxy: the loquacious C-3PO, voiced by Anthony Daniels, and his determined companion, R2-D2, as the two robots serve a series of four different masters over the course of thirteen episodes and one television special. With its catchy theme song ("Trouble Again") provided by Stewart Copeland of the hit '80s rock band The Police, the Droids' toy line was the closest of the two to the vintage Star Wars line.

The toy line translated the most prominent animated characters into plastic form. In addition to C-3PO and R2-D2, these included Thall Joben, a teen-ager from the planet Ingo with a passion for speeder racing; Jord Dusat, Thall Joben's best friend, a "tough" guy who wants to become a speeder racer champion; Kea Moll, brave and beautiful teenager from the planet Annoo who can handle any challenge; Tig Fromm, the leader of an underworld gang of thugs and cutthroats who prey on the weak and helpless of Ingo; Sise Fromm, one of the most notorious gang leaders in the galaxy whose secret desire is to run The Empire; Kez-Iban, a lost prince named Mon-Julpa, who was left to wander from planet to planet after his memory was stripped by an evil vizier; Uncle Gundy, an old fortune hunter whose hard luck never discourages him from seeking the "pot of gold" on every planet; Jann Tosh, a teen-ager who was orphaned in the Clone Wars and now travels with the adventurous Uncle Gundy; Boba Fett, the most notorious bounty hunter in the galaxy; and the A-Wing Pilot, daring and fearless pilot of the speedy A-Wing Fighter.

Kenner also produced three outstanding vehicles for the Droids toy line: the ATL-Interceptor, the Side Gunner, and the beautifully constructed, highly prized, and VERY expensive A-Wing Fighter.

Star Wars Droids action figure line: Jord Dusat,
Tigg Fromm, Sise Fromm, R2-D2, Jann Tosh,
Thall Joben, Kea Moll, and Kez-Iban.

Cute, Quirky Furry Fun

Star Wars: Ewoks

Star Wars Ewoks action figure line: King Gorneesh, Dulok Shaman, Urgah Lady Gorneesh, Dulok Scout, Wicket W. Warrick, Logray.

Hoping to capture the imagination of the horde of young children who worshipped the furry, quirky, cute, teddy bear-esque Ewoks—those adorable hunter-gatherers who inhabited the forest moon of Endor in *Star Wars Episode VI: Return of the Jedi*—the *Ewoks* animated series was broadcast from September 7, 1985-December 13, 1986.

Created by George Lucas and his faithful team, the *Ewoks* cartoon revolved around the antics of Wicket W. Warrick, Princess Kneesaa, and their tribe of Ewoks as they fight against another clan, the sinister Duloks—distant cousins to the Ewoks. Lasting one season longer than *Droids*, ABC's *Ewoks* ran for two full seasons (*Ewoks*, and *All-New Ewoks*) of thirteen episodes each.

The Kenner Ewoks toy line was targeted for younger children, as the figures' lack of poseability and bright colors suggest. Of the two spin-off cartoons—*Droids* and *Ewoks*—the Ewoks line is least similar to the original vintage Star Wars action figures. Although only six characters from the cartoon were released

at retail (more were planned), no vehicles or playsets accompanied these toys. Rather than engage in the costly process of repackaging older Star Wars vehicles and playsets under the Ewoks banner, Kenner simply re-solicited Ewok-themed toys from Star Wars' Power of the Force and Return of the Jedi assortments and offered them on Ewoks packaging.

The six characters released as action figures for Kenner's Ewoks toy line were: Wicket W. Warrick, a friendly and inquisitive young Ewok who loves adventure; Logray, wise old medicine man who aids the Ewoks with magic spells and potions; King Gorneesh, the conniving king of the Duloks who hopes to enslave the Ewoks; Urgah Lady Gorneesh, sly mate of King Gorneesh who aids him in his devious plans; Dulok Scout, a loathsome, villainous, swamp-dwelling creature who spies on the Ewoks; and finally, the Dulok Shaman, an inept "witch doctor" who uses nasty tricks to attempt to frighten or outwit the Ewoks.

Part Boy Scout. Part Hero. All Genius

Action figure memorializes man of action

Although Brazil was the only country in the world that received a full-fledged MacGyver toy line, which consisted of a single figure and multiple vehicles, America would receive one lone action figure toy to memorialize a television program that permeated pop culture for seven full seasons (1985-92) on ABC.

Produced by "rack toy" company JA-RU Toys, the MacGyver multi-colored motorcycle was a low-quality toy that featured a removable, non-poseable driver rendered solely in black. This toy surely didn't capture the spirit of Angus MacGyver, an ex-scientist and Vietnam vet who specialized in Explosives Ordnance Disposal, and who was also a former agent for the fictional United States Department of External Services. When the show begins, MacGyver functions as a current employee of the Phoenix Foundation; his background and training allows him to solve problems with an intelligent, non-violent approach that was appreciated by parents around the world. Why blow up a terrorist cell, killing its members in cold blood, when you can defeat them—without bloodshed—with a Swiss Army Knife, a champagne cork, and a small bit of bird droppings?

Portrayed by veteran actor Richard Dean Anderson, the character of MacGyver became so popular with Americans that jury-rigging a device—or finding a simple, elegant solution to a crisis—from the late 1980s until modern day is unofficially known as "MacGyver-ing": therefore, the consummate pacifistic action hero has now become an action verb.

JA-RU Toys' MacGyver motorcycle and rider.

Original Scale Miniatures

If it doesn't say 'Micro Machines,' it's not the real thing

Television commercials for Galoob's "Micro Machines: The Original Scale Miniatures" toy line in the 1980s were made memorable due to the narration of these advertisements by Guinness World Record holder John Moschitta Jr.

Thanks to Moschitta's ability to articulate 586 words a minute, his voice was featured in over 100+ Micro Machines commercials worldwide, ending these adverts with the catchphrase: "Remember: if it doesn't say Micro Machines, it's not the real thing."

These myriad catchy commercials ensured the toys were catching the public's eye, but were the toys attractive enough to warrant such a quality sales pitch? The answer: a resounding "yes." With a variety of different styles to choose from—and offering the popular contemporary and classic automobile and truck models—sales were excellent. A point of pride with Micro Machines was Galoob's ability to expertly translate detail down to a "micro" scale: this included paint applications, decaling, tires, logos, etc. Micro Machines eventually would encapsulate some popular licenses such as Indiana Jones, Star Wars, and Star Trek, and launch playsets with micro-sized figures as well, but production would cease before the turn of a new century. Micro Machines would return to retail in 2003.

Assortment of eight Galoob Micro Machines.

ENTERTAINMENT-O-RAMA: 1985 MOVIES, MUSIC, TELEVISION

Top Ten Films of 1985

1 *Back to the Future* (MGM/Universal)
2 *Rambo: First Blood Part II* (Sony/Columbia)
3 *Rocky IV* (United Artists)
4 *The Color Purple (Warner Brothers)*
5 *Out of Africa* (MGM/Universal)
6 *Cocoon* (20th Century Fox)
7 *The Jewel of the Nile* (20th Century Fox)
8 *Witness* (Paramount)
9 *The Goonies* (Warner Brothers)
10 *Spies Like Us* (Warner Brothers)

Best Picture: *Out of Africa* (MGM/Universal)

During the height of his *Family Ties* fame, Michael J. Fox took on the role of Marty McFly in the most successful film of 1985: *Back to the Future*, which grossed more than $380 million worldwide. In Robert Zemeckis' rousing comedy, high schooler Marty is catapulted back to the 1950s, where he meets his teen-age parents and accidentally changes the history of how they met. Laughs abound as the 1950s' ideology is filtered through the smarts of an '80s teen. The movie is filled with great special effects and also stars Christopher Lloyd as the crazy scientist who builds the time machine (a DeLorean luxury car) and Crispin Glover as Marty's supremely nerdy dad.
Amblin/Universal/The Kobal Collection

It may not have cracked the Top 10 movies for 1985, but John Hughes' popular coming-of-age comedy, *The Breakfast Club*, really struck a chord with children of the '80s. Five stereotypical high school students, a princess (Molly Ringwald), nerd (Anthony Michael Hall), weird girl (Ally Sheedy), jock (Emilio Estavez) and bad boy (Judd Nelson) share a Saturday in detention. Over the course of the day, they pour their hearts out to each other and discover how they have a lot more in common than they thought. The movie's great theme song, Simple Minds' "Don't You (Forget About Me)," was Billboard's No. 16 song for the year.
Universal/The Kobal Collection

The new light-hearted CBS drama, *Murder, She Wrote*, was quickly becoming a show not to be missed. Jessica Fletcher (Angela Lansbury) is a widowed teacher from a small Maine coastal town, who writes a best-seller which leads her into the business of sleuthing. *CBS-TV*

Top Ten Television Programs of 1985-86

1 *The Cosby Show* (NBC)
2 *Family Ties* (NBC)
3 *Murder, She Wrote* (CBS)
4 *60 Minutes* (CBS)
5 *Cheers* (NBC)
6 *Dallas* (CBS)
7 *Dynasty* (ABC)
8 *The Golden Girls* (NBC)
9 *Miami Vice* (NBC)
10 *Who's the Boss* (ABC)

Madonna's second album, *Like a Virgin*, was her breakthrough, thanks to hits "Like a Virgin," which she crooned while wearing a bustier and Boy Toy belt buckle of course, and "Material Girl." *AP Photo*

Known for her flamboyant style and distinctive vocals, singer-songwriter Cyndi Lauper had many hits in the '80s including "Girls Just Want to Have Fun" and "Time After Time." Here she picks up an MTV Award for Best Female Video for "Girls." *AP Photo/G Paul Burnett*

Top Ten Billboard Singles of 1985

1 "Careless Whisper," Wham! (*Make It Big*, 1985)
2 "Like A Virgin," Madonna (*Like A Virgin*, 1984)
3 "Wake Me Up Before You Go-Go," Wham! (*Make It Big*, 1985)
4 "I Want to Know What Love Is," Foreigner (*Agent Provocateur*, 1984)
5 "I Feel for You," Chaka Khan (*I Feel for You*, 1984)
6 "Out Of Touch" Daryl Hall & John Oates (*Big Bam Boom*, 1984)
7 "Everybody Wants to Rule the World," Tears For Fears (*Songs from the Big Chair*, 1985)
8 "Money for Nothing," Dire Straits (*Brothers in Arms*, 1985)
9 "Crazy For You," Madonna (*Vision Quest* soundtrack, 1985)
10 "Take On Me," a-ha (*Hunting High and Low*, 1985)

1986

Wisecracking ALF: The Outspoken Talking Alien Doll.

Kids Start Ghost Busting and a Furry Alien Becomes Breakout Star

Ghostbusters' Stay-Puft Marshmallow Man.

A COUPLE OF '80S ACTION *MOVIE* SUPERSTARS, Sylvester Stallone and Chuck Norris, were turned into action *figures* in 1986. While Barbie went into space, Jenga had millions of people playing with blocks, and we embraced console gaming again with the Nintendo Entertainment System.

In an era when the live-action *ALF* and cartoons such as *The Real Ghostbusters* dominated TVs nationwide, it was obvious that Americans were looking for escapism, and that's what they received every Thursday night on NBC with *The Cosby Show, Family Ties, Cheers*, and *Night Court*.

One show in particular that has often been overlooked is *Moonlighting,* which paired a rugged Bruce Willis (pre-*Die Hard*) and the sophisticated Cybil Shepherd running a detective agency. Yet comedies still remained supreme in the Nielsen's, from my sister's favorite program that we never, ever missed, *Who's the Boss?*, to the oft-syndicated *Golden Girls*. The format and function of the standard television talk show was also changed forever with the premiere of *The Oprah Winfrey Show* on September 8.

A new television channel appeared in 1986. Created by Cable/Fox Broadcasting, FOX—the *fourth* television network station—was launched on October 9 with very little fanfare. Its programming began with any show that resonated with viewers: *The Late Show, Married...with Children, The Tracey Ullman Show, 21 Jump Street,* and in 1989, a mid-season replacement called *The Simpsons*.

There were a couple of issues that struck me as "off" about the year 1986 in entertainment: why was Vanna White so popular, simply for turning over letters on *Wheel of Fortune*; and how did the Mets win the World's Series over my beloved Red Sox?

Beyond the small screen, Tom Cruise entered the ranks of superstardom with *Top Gun, Crocodile Dundee* taught us all how to act like an Aussie, and my personal hero for the past thirty years, Matthew Broderick, showed us how to skip school to our supreme advantage in John Hughes' *Ferris Bueller's Day Off*. Molly Ringwald's acting chops stunned me in *Pretty in Pink*.

In the music industry, Whitney Houston hit the peak of her career with two top twenty Billboard hits in 1986, Robert Palmer and his dancers for the video "Addicted to Love" reflected the excesses of the 1980s. Aerosmith and RUN DMC showed us how to "Walk This Way," the first rock 'n' roll and hip hop collaboration. Furthermore, it appeared as if Janet Jackson hit the big time, while the Bangles taught us how to "Walk Like an Egyptian."

Yet 1986 was not without tragedy: the Chernobyl disaster, a nuclear reactor accident followed by radiation poisoning and fallout, forced the evacuation and resettlement of 336,000 people on April 26; Sean Penn's "camera-punching" antics on Aug. 12; Clint Eastwood elected mayor of Carmel, CA; and "Baby Jessica" McClure falling into a well.

Don't Fear...Dr. Venkman and Staff Are Here!

The Real Ghostbusters

As the result of the phenomenally successful 1984 movie, *Ghostbusters*, Columbia Pictures Television produced an animated series that continued the exploits of the four paranormal investigators from the movie: Dr. Peter Venkman, Dr. Egon Spengler, Dr. Ray Stantz, and Winston Zeddemore, who are joined by secretary Janine Melnitz, and their ghostly mascot Slimer. As Ray Stantz says in the film, they are still out to "...bust some heads—in a spiritual sense, of course."

The ABC show, produced in conjunction with Coca-Cola Productions and D.I.C. Entertainment, was titled *The Real Ghostbusters* due to a conflict with Filmation Productions' proposed (and totally unrelated) more juvenile cartoon, *Ghost Busters* (1986). It lasted for six full seasons.

The Ghostbusters featured in this cartoon are a bit different from the film, as each Ghostbuster's outfit is slightly different than that of their compatriot's. Egon's hair is also inexplicably colored white instead of brown, and Slimer is a mascot instead of a villain. Yet the core conventions remain: the Ghostbusters' headquarters is still a firehouse in New York City (Tribeca), they drive the "Ecto-1" ambulance as their primary mode of transportation, and fight a slew of different spirits and villains, many of whom are exceptionally creepy and chilling (thanks to the mythic research tome, Tobin's Spirit Guide).

Kenner was poised to capitalize upon the popularity of *The Real Ghostbusters* animated phenomenon, and from 1986-1991, pumped out as many Ghostbusters toys as the market would allow.

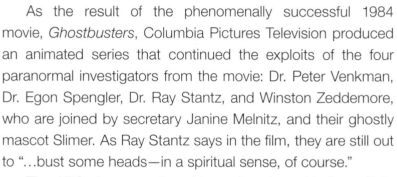

Real Ghostbusters: Egon Spengler with Gulper Ghost, Peter Venkman with Grabber Ghost.

Real Ghostbusters Firehouse playset with Egon Spengler, Peter Venkman, Winston Zeddmore, Ray Stantz, Ecto-1 vehicle, Slimer (Green Ghost), Boo-Zooka boo-lets, and Mini-Trap ghosts.

Real Ghostbusters Ecto-1 vehicle with the Ghostbusters team.

Real Ghostbusters Monsters: Dracula, Frankenstein, Zombie, Quasimodo, Mummy, Wolfman.

Real Ghostbusters ghost figures: Fearsome Flush, Mini-Traps—orange and purple, Gooper Ghost: Squisher, Stay-Puft Mashmallow Man, H2O Ghost, Mini Shooter with Boo-Zooka Boo-lets, Green Ghost (Slimer) with accessories, Bad-to-the-Bone Ghost, and Bug-Eye Ghost.

Real Ghostbusters ghosts, "haunted mode": Granny Gross Ghost, Mail Fraud Ghost, Tombstone Tackle Ghost, Highway Haunter vehicle, X-Cop Ghost, Haunted Vehicles Air Sickness, Terror Trash Ghost.

Furry Wiseguy

An Alien Life Form charms everyone

Close-up of eight Topps ALF "Bouillabaisseball Cards."

ALF, the nickname of Gordon Shumway from the planet Melmac, is a friendly "Alien Life Form," who crash lands in the garage of the suburban middle class Tanner family.

The Tanners try to adjust to their new guest, but it's not easy: the sarcastic and caustic ALF causes trouble, has a massive appetite with a special fondness for cats, and risks being discovered. He of course has a benevolent side, too, and he made his way into our hearts through four seasons of the NBC show.

The plot of nearly every *ALF* episode revolves around the alien's lack of understanding of Earth customs and his longing for life back on Melmac (playing "Bouillabaisseball," etc.), and the program's popularity was directly related to ALF's humorous yet abrasive personality. Production of the program was both costly and taxing for the human actors on set, since each scene shot with ALF—nearly every scene of the show—required either a master puppeteer (the show's creator, Paul Fusco) to intricately portray the actions of the alien, or the production team was obliged to hire an actor (Michu Mezaros) to fit inside a faux fur-covered suit for longer, full-camera shots.

Coleco produced an 18-inch plush battery-operated Wisecracking ALF: The Outspoken Talking Alien. This toy utters the following famous phrases when you push a button on his belly: "No problem," "Here, kitty, kitty, kitty...," "Hey gimme four," "Hey just kidding," "A whisker for your thoughts," "Be there or be square," "I'm a people alien," "Let's go check out the fridge," and "How about a hug for the ol' ALFer?"

Beyond the live-action NBC program, fans were treated to *Alf: The Animated Series* (NBC, 1987), two sets of Topps trading cards, a Marvel Comic book (1987-1991) containing more than sixty issues, a television movie, *Project ALF* (1996), and most recently, seven episodes of *ALF's Hit Talk Show* on TV Land.

Fun for Blockheads

Strategic Jenga breaks out

Although debuting three years prior, 1986 was the breakout year for a game that involves strategically stacking wooden blocks: Jenga.

Although many Jenga aficionados take great pride in building the highest, most unique, unstable tower known to man—using one finger at a time to carefully push out piece by piece—I don't know of any Jenga game that has ended in any manner but absolute failure.

Concocted by Leslie Scott and marketed by Parker Brothers, Jenga is one of those unique games where failure is all but guaranteed; all 54 blocks MUST fall in order for a winner declared.

One of the more clever aspects of Jenga is its outer package that allows players to align and set up the game in a matter of minutes if the pieces are placed within the case correctly.

The Jenga blocks neatly set up.

One wrong push and the tower can go falling down.

The Game That Moves at the Speed of Light

Lazer Tag merges old-school war combat with electronic wizardry

Laser Tag set: pistol, sensor, belt, holster, chest straps.

Many red-blooded American boys playing soldier would argue for minutes and sometimes hours about who was "hit" first, oftentimes these digressions ended an entertaining afternoon.

That all changed once World of Wonder's Lazer Tag hit the market. One of the many sensations to come out of a decade chock full of them, Lazer Tag was a fad that allowed children and adults to "play war" electronically, without aiming archaic plastic guns at one another and shouting a simple "Bang" to fire a faux weapon and record imaginary hits.

With the use of electronic sounds and sensors, Lazer Tag was mass-produced and arrived at retail the same time that the game's forerunner, Photon (1984-89), issued a "home version" of its set and the game permeated popular culture. However, distribution and marketing of Lazer Tag was larger and more extensive than Photon, even though the latter had already set up sophisticated leagues and extensive arenas across the United States (45-plus free-standing arenas). Regardless of the similarities between the two, the dynamics for each game were quite similar. A minimum of two opponents are equipped with laser guns to fire at one another via infrared signaling tracking, and these shots are measured and tracked on sensors worn by the player in order to record shots: the first player who is "hit" a predetermined number of times is determined by the sensor to be "dead."

In order to participate in Lazer Tag, a player must own the following equipment: a laser tag rifle or pistol and a sensor at the bare minimum, yet other accoutrements could be purchased for aesthetic appeal, including a form-fitting helmet, a variety of belts and shoulder strap, and an intricate vest.

Demand for original Lazer Tag sets continue to soar on the secondary market. People who once participated in paintball and airsoft (the modern-day equivalent of laser tag), are recognizing the terrific expense of their contemporary hobby, and so they turn to Lazer Tag: what is essentially old school war combat merged with a three-dimensional video game. And you don't have to purchase bags and bags of paintballs each week.

Fire, Wood, Water

Battle Beasts capitalize on century-old game

Battle Beasts Shocking Shark playset.

Produced by Japanese toy company Takara and distributed to the U.S. in 1987 by Hasbro Inc., the Battle Beasts (dubbed "Beast Formers" in Japan) were a line of 2-inch anthropomorphized animal action figures, with each one possessing a unique character sculpt and hand-held melee weapon.

The sales pitch revolved around the childhood game, "rock, paper, scissors." The Battle Beast toy line was a clever attempt at Takara to sell a product that capitalized on this century-old game. Many children simply couldn't resist the lure of these tiny colorful figures whose key selling point featured a heat-sensitive chest label (new technology for the time) that when rubbed by a child's thumb, would reveal one of the following three symbols: fire, wood, or water. Based on an elementary concept, it was effortless for a child to learn that when their Battle Beasts toys fought one another, "fire" beats (burns) "wood," "wood" beats (floats on) "water," and "water" (douses) "fire."

In the U.S., Battle Beasts action figures were sold in two-packs, and part of the mystery that drove the sales was the use of randomly inserted rub signs, as the package front of Battle Beasts stated: "Fire! Wood! Or Water! You'll never know until you own them!"

A lone departure from the standard "fire, wood, water" (and the unsubstantiated "sunburst") symbols established in

Series One through Three occurs in Series Four, with a set of thirty-six figures that were formally named Battle Beasts' "Shadow Warriors" in the U.S. (and "Laser Beasts" in Japan). Instead of a heat-sensitive rub sign revealing one of the four standard symbols, in Series Four, each Shadow Warrior Battle Beast action figure two-pack reads: "Fire! Wood! Water! Only the crystal shield will reveal their strength!" This crystal shield the package alluded to was part of a novel feature incorporated within the new series of figures; now each figure's heat-sensitive label that was applied to each character's chest was replaced by a translucent circular orb that filled the chest and torso of each character. When a child looked through this circular orb, the figure's "faction" (fire, water, or wood) would become apparent.

To accompany the 112 domestically produced Battle Beasts action figures, Hasbro distributed four Battle Chariots that all also possessed an anthropomorphic animal theme. The company also sold three Battle Beasts Transport Station playsets which were intricate, expansive, and at the same time surprisingly compact. These Transport Station playsets reflected the three major symbols of the line: Blazing Eagle represented the earth, Shocking Shark the water, and Wood Beetle, was, of course, wood.

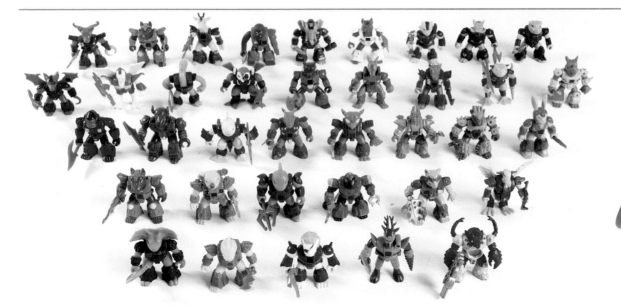

Roamin' Buffalo.

Battle Beasts, assortment of figures complete with accessories: Series 1-3.

Pirate Lion, Sledgehammer Elephant, Sawtooth Shark.

Blitzkrieg Bat.

Horny Toad, Rubberneck Giraffe, Leapin' Lizard, Fleet-Footed Ante-lope.

PowerXtreme!

Centurions fuse man with machine

Centurion Max Ray, resident sea operations expert.

Playing off the ages-old conceit in literature of Man vs. Machine, what would the result be if you combined and fused the two together?

Kenner examined this relationship between humanity and technology and the result was its first-rate Centurions toy line of seven action figures/robot drones and 10 assault weapon sets. Naturally, it helps to have an animated program tie-in, and Ruby-Spears produced *Centurions* to support the toy line, which was much beloved by fans and a modest success for the company.

With the tag-line "PowerXtreme," and toy designs based on sketches provided by Jack "King" Kirby and Gil Kane (two celebrated Silver Age comic book artists), Centurions

action figures have an intricate design, ludicrous amounts of accessories that refused to fall off during play, and first-rate poseability—10 total points of articulation.

The three main protagonists are: Ace McCloud, the team's air operations expert with skyknight assault weapons; Jake Rockwell, the unit's land operations expert with fireforce assault weapons system; and Max Ray, the resident sea operations expert with cruiser assault weapon system. Each of the Centurions' names alludes to their specialty in some way: Ace "McCloud" defends the sky; Jake "Rock-well" patrols the ground; Max "Ray" safeguards the oceans. Each Centurion toy/animated character can swap their parts and accessories, combining assault weapons systems to construct an endless amount of new combinations and play.

The two major villains in the toy line and cartoon are the menacing Doctor Terror and his lunk-headed assistant, Hacker. These two characters are a more sinister combination of man and machine than the Centurions team members, who are mere humans in strength-amplifying armored suits (exo-frames). As they possess fully cybernetic body halves, Doc Terror and Hacker can change up their weapons, but furthermore, their construction allows the cybernetic halves of their bodies ("Syntax" and "Lesion," respectfully) to be removed and swapped between the two.

Although we never saw figures for the second series characters Rex Charger and John Thunder (or recurring cartoon characters such as Crystal Kane, Shadow, or Lucy), we can still re-visit this first-rate line of fully-articulated action figures and revel in a decade when toy makers were at the top of their game.

Centurions heroes Ace McCloud and Jake Rockwell.

Centurions villains Doc Terror and Hacker.

Chuck Norris and the Karate Kommandos, action figure assortment: Ninja Warrior, Super Ninja, Reed Smith, Kimo, Chuck Norris Kung-Fu Training Gi, Tabe.

Action Hero Gets Plasticized

Chuck Norris and the Karate Kommandos

As one of the most marketable action heroes of the 1980s, with films such as *Silent Rage* (1982), *Missing in Action* (1984), *Code of Silence* (1985), *Missing in Action II: The Beginning* (1985), *The Delta Force* (1986), *Firewalker* (1986), *Braddock: Missing in Action III* (1988), and the '90s television program, *Walker: Texas Ranger* (1993-2001), Chuck Norris was the Cannon Group's leading star—launched into the ranks of the action elite by Bruce Lee as the legend's nemesis in *Way of the Dragon* (1972).

In 1986, capitalizing on Norris' burgeoning popularity with children, Ruby-Spears produced a five-episode animated mini-series recounting the adventures of a U.S. government operative named Chuck Norris, played by the actor himself, and his team of martial-arts experts. *Chuck Norris and the Karate Kommandos* chronicles the exploits of Chuck Norris and his commando agents as they fight against the Claw and his group of evil ninjas (capitalizing on the "ninja craze" of the mid-'80s).

In conjunction with the cartoon, Kenner released a series of nine action figures: Norris, available in either Battle Gear outfit, Kung-Fu Training Gi, or as an Undercover Agent; Kimo, the samurai; Reed Smith, Chuck's apprentice; Ninja Serpent, Ninja Warrior, Super Ninja, Claw's right-hand man; and Tabe, a champion sumo wrestler. There was also one vehicle, the Karate Corvette. Oddly enough, there was no Claw figure released

Chuck Norris and the Karate Kommandos, Chuck Norris Undercover Agent.

in the assortment of figures—perhaps Kenner had decided to offer him in Series Two if a full season of the animated program was ordered.

Since 2005, Norris has become one of the Internet's leading searches. There are myriad Web sites that contain what are known as "Chuck Norris Facts," humorous exaggerations of Norris' legendary toughness and fighting skills. Some of the most famous samples of these facts, taken from chucknorrisfacts.com, include: "Chuck Norris destroyed the periodic table, because Chuck Norris only recognizes the element of surprise," "Some people wear Superman pajamas. Superman wears Chuck Norris pajamas," "Chuck Norris can divide by zero," "Chuck Norris doesn't wear a watch. HE decides what time it is," and the inimitable, "If at first you don't succeed, then you're not Chuck Norris."

Toys Pack a Lot of Heat

Rambo and the Forces of Freedom

Rambo in the Forces of Freedom Skywolf Assault Jet.

Rambo and the Forces of Freedom was an animated program produced by Ruby-Spears from September 15 to December 26 for 65 episodes. The cartoon was created due to the popularity of psychologically troubled Vietnam veteran and former prisoner of war John James Rambo, as portrayed by Sylvester Stallone in *First Blood* (1982) and *Rambo: First Blood Part II* (1985).

Both fans of the cartoon and of the *Rambo* films were surprised that an animated program was created utilizing Rambo as its main character, for, although he's a sympathetic character, the film canon describes him as a hyper-violent commando whose psychopathic tendencies as a result of his lack of integration into American society results in an extreme body count in both films.

The plot of *Rambo and the Forces of Freedom* revolves around the adventures of John Rambo and his allies, as trained by Colonel Trautman: K.A.T., Sgt. Havoc, Turbo, the White Ninja, etc. Here, they battle the evil agents of S.A.V.A.G.E. (Secret Administrators of Vengeance, Anarchy and Global Extortion), a gaggle of over-the-top villains and terrorists led by General Warhawk: the Black Ninja (the White Ninja's brother), Nomad, Gripper, and Mad Dog. The program was—in all respects—a 24-minute toy advertisement riddled with abhorrent clichés, such as monocled Aryan antagonists and Middle-Eastern, turban-wearing terrorists, weak dialogue, and tropes and conventions utilized in most '80s cartoons. But there are a few aspects of the show that are worth noting: 1) where the *Rambo* films show a multitude of murders and homicides, this "family oriented" cartoon never explicitly showed the death of any character; 2) many episodes reflected and satirized current social or political events that were "hot-button" issues in popular culture (e.g. arms dealing); and 3) oftentimes, military hardware portrayed on the show would reflect armaments and vehicles used by the U.S. armed forces (i.e. the Battleship Yamamoto and the Lockheed AC-130 "Spectre" gunship).

Many G.I. Joe fans enjoyed *Rambo and the Forces of Freedom* when it was released in 1986, and the 6-1/2-inch tall Colcco toy line garnered a loyal following. Since these figures, accessories, and vehicles often came with a huge assortment of extra weapons and armaments, they were a quick impulse buy.

Furthermore, most Rambo figures possessed a single "firing" (spring-loaded) weapon or motorized accessory that added play value to the toy; along with a multitude of other accoutrements. Heck, Coleco provided its Colonel Trautman figure with so many different accessories, the toy was not able to effectively hold them all at one time.

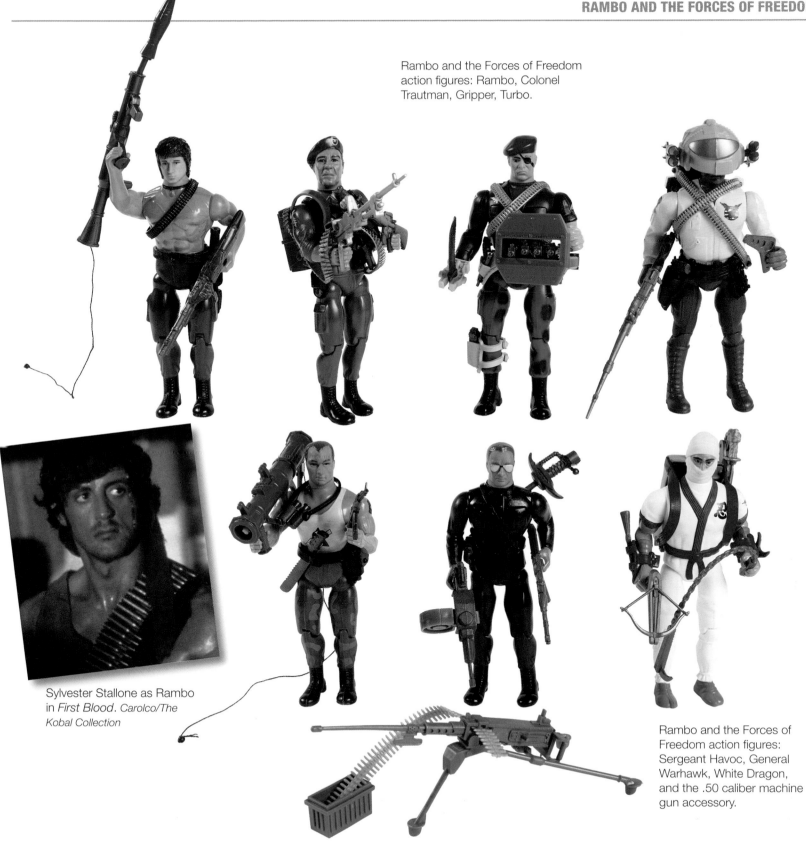

Rambo and the Forces of Freedom action figures: Rambo, Colonel Trautman, Gripper, Turbo.

Sylvester Stallone as Rambo in *First Blood*. *Carolco/The Kobal Collection*

Rambo and the Forces of Freedom action figures: Sergeant Havoc, General Warhawk, White Dragon, and the .50 caliber machine gun accessory.

Console Confidence Back

Nintendo Entertainment System ushers in new age of video gaming

NES accessories, from left: R.O.B. (Robotic Operating Buddy), and Advantage joystick.

After the "Great Video Game Crash" of 1983-84, it took a few years for consumer confidence to embrace console gaming once again. The one machine that ushered in a new age of video gaming was Nintendo Entertainment's premiere product of the 1980s: the aptly (and simply) titled Nintendo Entertainment System—the miraculous NES.

This third-generation console improved upon the designs of its predecessors, affording better protection for its cartridges while at the same time re-designing its entire system to allow for improved graphics and playability. Furthermore, allowing NES software to be licensed by third-party developers (a move traditionally frowned upon in the industry, much to Atari and Intellivision's vexation) such as Electronic Arts, Activision, and Ubisoft, Nintendo reaped the rewards of steady sales. Cartridges also introduced a wealth of new, marketable characters into the Nintendo universe including Donkey Kong and Donkey Kong Jr., Super Mario Bros., Zelda and Link, and the famous adventure hero, Megaman: these characters have endured for 30-plus years.

The NES system also included an electronic gun known as the "zapper," which allowed gamers to pretend to track and shoot ducks in the NES game *Duck Hunt* (initially bundled in a split-cartridge with the smash-hit Super Mario Bros.).

The NES was originally introduced with add-ons that were meant to restore consumer confidence in the industry after the crash of 1983-84, so although accoutrements such as R.O.B. (the NFS's Robotic Operating Buddy) were great fun as they allowed the NES to consistently garner new and interested gamers to their console, there was really no need; the quality of the system sold itself.

However, when the NES introduced products that complemented and improved upon the console's already near-flawless game play (in comparison to the Atari 2600 and Intellivision), the company hit a home run. The NES Advantage afforded those Generation Xers who grew up in arcades to play their NES games with the aid of an arcade-style controller: a huge joystick, opposed to the D ("directional" pad) on standard controllers, with oversized buttons and added options such as "turbo" and "slow motion" features.

The NES brought the video game console back onto children's Christmas wish lists, and Santa placed millions upon millions of units underneath Christmas trees for many years to come.

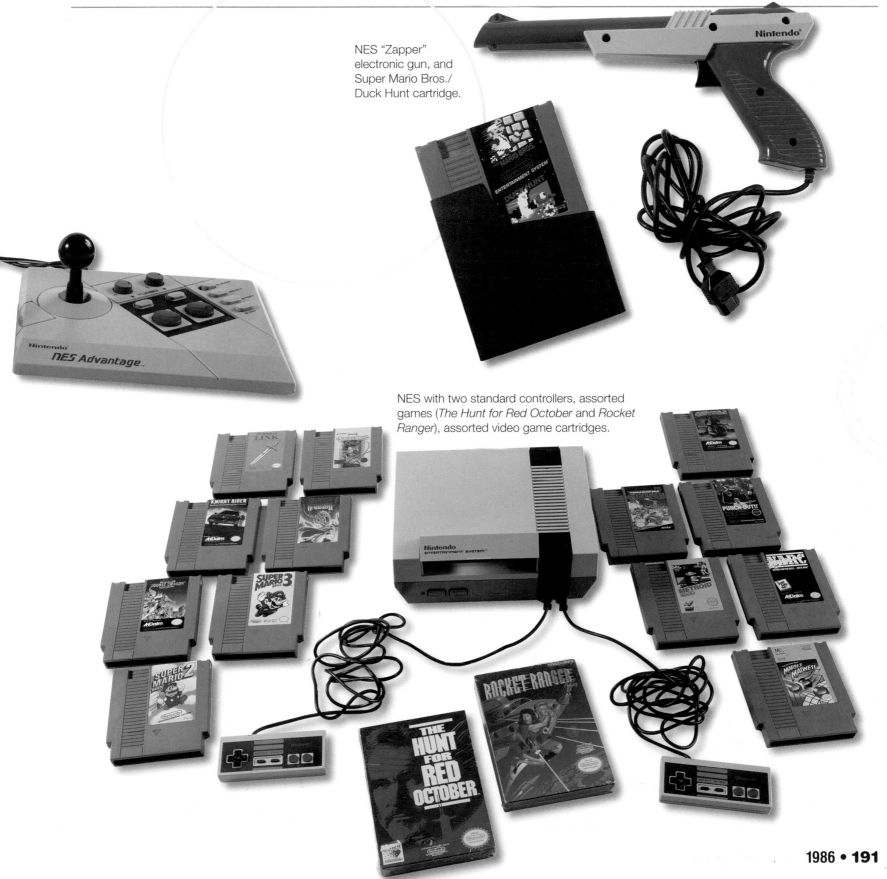

NES "Zapper" electronic gun, and Super Mario Bros./ Duck Hunt cartridge.

NES with two standard controllers, assorted games (*The Hunt for Red October* and *Rocket Ranger*), assorted video game cartridges.

'The Challenge Will Always Be There'

Sega Master System can't compete with Nintendo Entertainment System

Intended to be called the "Sega Base System" (sounds a bit mundane, doesn't it?), the Sega Master System was a third generation, 8-bit, cartridge-based console game that was released by Sega in 1986 to directly compete with the superior-selling Nintendo Entertainment System.

Bundled with two standard-sized controllers, a "Light Phaser," and the console itself (for a hefty $200), the game could not compete with the NES in terms of sales or popularity of titles. *The New York Times* reported on December 4, 1988 that Nintendo's end-of-the-year projections stated "…sales of $1.7 billion… increasing its market share to its present 83 percent." Sega simply couldn't compete.

Contributing to the Master System's decline was the fact that Nintendo would not allow its third-party game licensees to release titles that were smash-hits in the arcade to any competing systems, which frustrated Sega to no end. In light of the Master System's resounding defeat by the NES, Sega sold the rights to manufacturing their Master System to Tonka for a brief period of time; until the first year of the next decade. However, when Sega developed their Genesis console, their fortune reversed and the company asked Tonka to return the rights of the Master System to its originator.

Sega Master System with controller, Light Gun, and five games: *Ghostbusters*, *Spy vs. Spy*, *The Ninja*, *Reggie Jackson Baseball*, and *Monopoly*.

Part Human, Part Metal

Bionic Six created to battle evil forces

Bionic Six heroes Meg and Helen; villain Madame-O.

Produced by LJN toys in 1986, the Bionic Six line of action figures were toys licensed to support the animated program of the same name that borrowed conventions from many other cartoons of the 1980s.

The program and toy line met moderate success, yet LJN only produced a series of thirteen figures, which were, according to their package front, "fully poseable (with) durable die cast metal," one very rare headquarters/playset, and five hard-to-find vehicles.

The plot of the animated series was rendered as follows: a scientist, Professor Sharp, develops the technology to create humans with bionic parts. His first experimental human is Jack Bennett, and after a turn of events, Jack's family is damaged in an avalanche. Professor Sharp augments them all with bionic parts, and the "Bionic-Six" are created to battle hostile villains such as Dr. Scarab, Madame-O, and Glove.

'Evil That Lies Within'

Heroes defeat sinister Inhumanoids

The powerful Magnokor in his combined form.

One of the more singular action figure lines of the 1980s is Hasbro's excellently constructed Inhumanoids line, produced with the tag line, "The Evil That Lies Within."

Hasbro also developed a great back story to promote the toys, recounted in the 13-episode *Inhumanoids*, produced by Marvel and Sunbow Productions. A heroic group of government-funded geological scientists—the Earth Corps—encounters three subterranean monsters dubbed the Inhumanoids: Tendril, D'Compose, and leader Metlar, who wreak havoc on the surface of Earth. The Earth Corps scientists defeat the sinister Inhumanoids with the assistance of the kindly Mutores, another subterranean population of powerful beings including the twin being Magnokor, the Redwoods, and the Granites, led by Granok.

The four Earth Corps scientists were produced as "action ready" toys by Hasbro: they were molded inside their non-removable "exploration suits"; the only piece on each suit that is removable is the helmet. The Earth Corps scientists' brief biographies read as follows: Herc "Hooker" Armstrong is the leader of the Earth Corps who possesses an exosuit with a built-in grappling hook; Dr. Derek "Digger" Bright is the cool-headed, logical engineer of the Corps whose suit's main apparatus is a pair of grappling claws; Edward "Auger" Augutter, a former heavyweight boxer and current adventurer who is the more physical Earth Corps agent; and Johnathon "Liquidator" Slattery' s exploration suit shoots a jet of highly corrosive liquid, while his exoskeleton can withstand a heavy concussive force.

Each of Hasbro's four Earth Corps action figures possesses limited poseability (five points-of-articulation), an "Interchangeable Arm Implement" that can be used by any member of the Earth Corps team, and "Glow-in-the Light" helmets.

Assorted Inhumanoids action figures, action modes: Magnokor (dissembled), Earth Corps scientist Auger, and Granok.

Although essentially a tertiary toy line that lasted one short year, Hasbro's Inhumanoids action figures impressed many young collectors with their interesting aesthetics, fun action features, and sturdy designs that allowed kids to roughhouse with these toys to their hearts content. It also helped that—unintentionally—children may have learned a little bit about geology and Earth Science when playing with a group of four explorers dubbed "The Earth Corps."

Granok in rock mode.

Robots Morph into Colorful Rocks

Rock Lords have clever concept

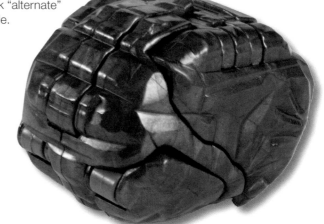

Rock Lords, Rockasaurs' Terra Rock "robot" mode.

Based on their appearance in the 1986 animated film *GoBots: Battle of the Rock Lords* (featuring the celebrity voices of Foster Brooks, Margot Kidder, Roddy McDowall, and Telly Savalas), Tonka's Rock Lords action figures captured the attention of children with a clever and unique concept: instead of creating robots that transform into vehicles (automobiles, ships, planes, etc.), why not have these detailed characters change into colorful rocks?

Derived from the molds of Japanese company Bandai's "Machine Robo" line of toys, the sales concept of the Rock Lords mimicked the successful pattern of the two most popular transforming robot franchises of the 1980s—Tonka's GoBots and Hasbro's Transformers. There were two warring factions of Rock Lords, the Good Rock Lords vs. the Bad Rock Lords, who were featured in three different series of toy releases. These are combined and delineated as follows, with a Rock Lord's actual "rock type" noted: Good Rock Lords—Boulder (Tungsten), Nuggit (gold), Granite (granite), Marbles (Cristobalite), Crackpot (azurite), Pulver Eyes (Dolomite); Bad Rock Lords: Magmar (Igneous), Tombstone (quartz), Sticks 'N Stones (anthracite and magnetite), Stoneheart (slate), Brimstone (brimstone), Slimestone (silver), and the insidious Sabrestone and Spearhead.

Beyond the first two series of "Good vs. Bad" GoBots Rock Lords action figures, Tonka also offered a set of furred companions to the line known as "Narlies." Along with these

Rock Lords, Rockasaurs' Terra Rock "alternate" mode.

Narlies (six "Evil" Narlies versus two "Good" characters), Tonka also produced a series of dinosaur companions to the Rock Lords—the Rockasaurs' Terra Rock ("Winged Flyer") and Spike Stone, with "horned nose and armored body."

Most importantly, and impressively, the crown jewels (if you'll pardon the pun) for the toy line were the Rock Lords' stunning Jewel Lords, although only three of these toys were released—Solitaire, Flamestone, and Sunstone. The toy line was rounded out with a few other sub-collections such as the Shock Rocks (Rock Roller, Rock Hook, and Stone Hook) whose action feature was to, well…roll on the ground.

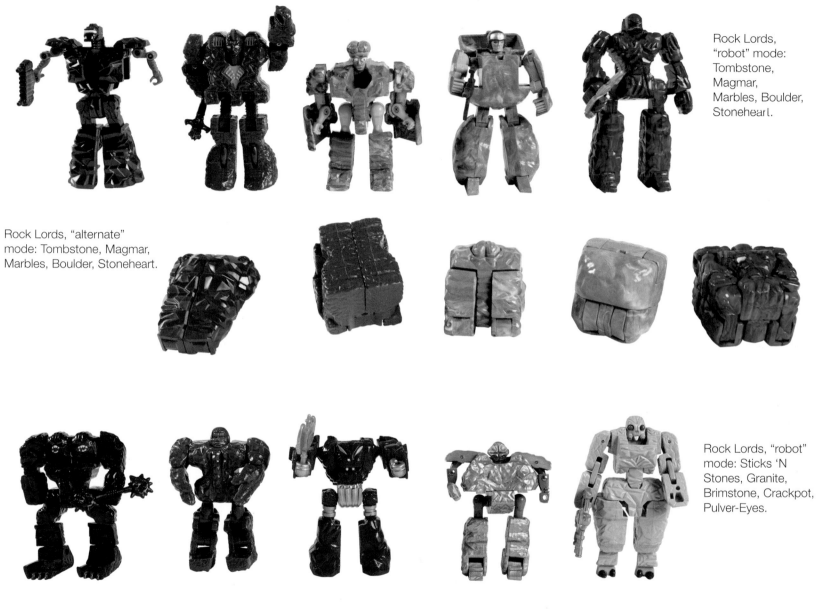

Rock Lords, "robot" mode: Tombstone, Magmar, Marbles, Boulder, Stoneheart.

Rock Lords, "alternate" mode: Tombstone, Magmar, Marbles, Boulder, Stoneheart.

Rock Lords, "robot" mode: Sticks 'N Stones, Granite, Brimstone, Crackpot, Pulver-Eyes.

Rock Lords, "alternate" mode: Sticks 'N Stones, Granite, Brimstone, Crackpot, Pulver-Eyes.

Barbie Gets Hip and Trendy

New dolls rock out

Barbie and the Rockers' punch-out posters.

Barbie and the Rockers Dana, Barbie, and Diva, complete with all accessories.

Although Barbie has functioned as Mattel's No. 1 selling product for many years, Hasbro's Jem and the Holograms line of figures (1985) gave the iconic fashion doll heavy competition. In response to the challenge Jem provided Barbie in terms of market share, Mattel leapt headfirst into mid-1980s American popular culture by launching a line of trendy, hip fashion dolls that reflected the sign of the times.

Dubbed "Barbie and the Rockers," Mattel offered fans of The Go-Go's and the Bangles an opportunity to own their very own female rock 'n' roll band whose motto was: "Dazzling Superstars Ready to Rock." With the support of a direct-to-video film created by D.I.C. entertainment, *Barbie and the Rockers: Out of This World* (1987), was a modest hit—yet the dolls sold spectacularly. With five dolls offered at retail, in two different series of releases, bandmates Dana, Dee Dee, Diva, and Derek, joined Barbie. With a good deal of well-crafted accessories and trendy "Barbie and the Rockers"-branded outfits and accoutrements such as concert T-shirts, cardboard gold record cutouts, concert tickets, iron-on patches, posters, and sheet music, Barbie collectors adored these stylish and chic fashion dolls.

Astronaut Barbie

Another stand out of Mattel's '80s Barbies capitalized on NASA's Space Shuttle program: the superbly detailed Astronaut Barbie, a toy whose tag line read: "We girls can do anything!" Inspired in part by the announcement that school teacher Christa McAuliffe would be involved in an upcoming space shuttle mission, this adventurous Barbie donned a hot pink space suit "with sparkly skirt and tights." Astronaut Barbie included the following items: a bubble space helmet, backpack with oxygen tanks, bodysuit, pants, mini skirt, tights, space boots (note the high heels!), purse, a computer, a flagpole and flag, jewelry, a hairbrush, and the following package punch-outs: two space maps and an "official" astronaut certificate.

Tragically, McAuliffe's space shuttle mission was a catastrophe. On January 28, 1986, the Space Shuttle Challenger broke apart less than two minutes after liftoff from Kennedy Space Center due to a faulty O-ring seal in the ship's solid rocket booster. Disintegrating over the Atlantic Ocean, all seven passengers of the Challenger were killed instantly. McAuliffe's profile as the first teacher in space attracted national media attention and because of this, many U.S. public schools were viewing the launch of the space shuttle live; according to a New York Times poll, 48 percent of nine to thirteen-year-old American school children watched the launch from their classrooms. The U.S. Space Shuttle program was grounded for nearly three years following this disaster.

Astronaut Barbie.

Barbie Travel Agency.

One of the added bonuses to Barbie collectibles in the '80s were the truly brilliant and timely toys offered by Mattel through Arco Ltd., a company responsible for many fine Barbie products that capitalized on modern culture through the years such as the Barbie and the Rockers Stage and Accessories (1986), and the Barbie Backyard playset (1986). Its finest piece: the Barbie Travel Agent playset. With an enormous full-color cardboard diorama backdrop and forty-two different accessories such as two large desks, a wall cabinet, a passport, six file folders, and dozens of perfectly rendered office accoutrements, no Barbie fan should be caught without this playset.

ENTERTAINMENT-O-RAMA:
1986 MOVIES, MUSIC, TELEVISION

In the science-fiction adventure *Aliens*, Ellen Ripley (Sigourney Weaver), the sole survivor from *Alien*, returns to battle more hostile monsters with the help of high-tech Colonial Marines. Weaver defined the action heroine in this edge-of-your-seat action movie. *20th Century Fox*

With its MTV-inspired visuals, rapid-fire action, and pop-music soundtrack, *Top Gun* took the top movie spot in '86 and propelled Tom Cruise to superstardom. In this high-flyin' flick, macho students of an elite US flying school for advanced fighter pilots compete to be the top of their class. *Paramount/The Kobal Collection/Stephen Vaughan*

Top Ten Films of 1986

1 *Top Gun* (Paramount)
2 *Crocodile Dundee* (Paramount)
3 *Platoon* (Orion)
4 *The Karate Kid Part II* (Columbia)
5 *Star Trek IV: The Voyage Home* (Paramount)
6 *Back to School* (Orion)
7 *Aliens* (Fox)
8 *The Golden Child* (Paramount)
9 *Ruthless People* (Buena Vista)
10 *Ferris Bueller's Day Off* (Paramount)

Best Picture: *Platoon* (Orion)

John Hughes' coming-of-age comedy, *Ferris Bueller's Day Off*, follows high school senior Ferris Bueller (Matthew Broderick), who decides to skip school and have some fun in the city of Chicago. Along for the ride are his girlfriend Sloane (Mia Sara) and his best friend Cameron (Alan Ruck). In between the fun, Ferris creatively finds ways to dodge his dean of students Edward Rooney (Jeffrey Jones), his resentful sister Jeanie (Jennifer Grey), and his parents. *Paramount/The Kobal Collection*

Top Ten Television Programs of 1986-87

1 *The Cosby Show* (NBC)
2 *Family Ties* (NBC)
3 *Cheers* (NBC)
4 *Murder, She Wrote* (CBS)
5 *The Golden Girls* (NBC)
6 *60 Minutes* (CBS)
7 *Night Court* (NBC)
8 *Growing Pains* (ABC)
9 *Moonlighting* (ABC)
10 *Who's the Boss?* (ABC)

After nearly being cancelled in its first season because of abysmal ratings, the sitcom *Cheers* rallied to become a ratings bonanza. The season 6 cast (1987-88) is pictured here. Back row, from left, are Rhea Pearlman, Woody Harrelson, Kelsey Grammer, and Debe Nouwirth; front row, from left: George Wendt, Kirstie Alley, Ted Danson and John Ratzenberger. *Paramount TV/The Kobal Collection.*

Singer Whitney Houston's career peaked in 1986, with two hit singles charting in the Billboard Top 20. Here she shows off her American Music Award. *AP Photo*

Top Ten Billboard Singles of 1980

1 "That's What Friends Are For," Dionne Warwick & Friends (*That's What Friends Are For*, 1986)
2 "Say You, Say Me," Lionel Richie (*Dancing on the Ceiling*, 1985)
3 "I Miss You," Klymaxx (*Meeting in the Ladies' Room*, 1985)
4 "On My Own," Patti Labelle & Michael McDonald (*Winner in You*, 1986)
5 "Broken Wings," Mr. Mister (*Welcome to the Real World*, 1986)
6 "How Will I Know," Whitney Houston (*Whitney Houston*, 1985)
7 "Party All the Time," Eddie Murphy (*How Could It Be*, 1985)
8 "Burning Heart," Survivor (*Rocky IV* soundtrack, 1985)
9 "Kyrie," Mr. Mister (*Welcome to the Real World*, 1985)
10 "Addicted To Love," Robert Palmer (*Riptide*, 1986)

1987

Matchbox's Pee-wee's Playhouse playset featuring Cowboy Curtis, the King of Cartoons, Reba the Mail Lady, Pee-wee Herman, Ricardo, Miss Yvonne, Magic Screen, Jambi, the Puppetland Band, and Pee-wee's scooter.

Pee-wee (Paul Ruebons) and Miss Yvonne (Lynn Marie Stewart) with some of the gang from *Pee-wee's Playhouse*, including Chairry, Pterri, Clockey, Randy, and Globey. *Pee Wee Pictures/Binder/RB Prods/The Kobal Collection*

Child-Like Character Becomes Pop-Culture Icon

The California Raisins' Sax Player has some mean licks.

PAUL REUBENS WAS THE RED-CHEEKED, audacious host of one of the hottest programs on television in 1987, *Pee-wee's Playhouse*. The show, no surprise, also spawned a toy line. Dinosaurs also made a comeback in toy form, while the trend of fusing man with bionic body parts continued with Silverhawks, and the supernatural melded with holograms in two different toy lines—Super Naturals and Visionaries, while some singing raisins controlled the airwaves.

On prime-time TV, few fans of NBC's ratings bonanza, *The Cosby Show*, would have pegged Denise Huxtable as its breakout star, yet Lisa Bonet made good for the network once again as she paired with Kadeem Hardison (playing the suave Dwayne Wayne) in the outstanding college sitcom, *A Different World*.

Robin Williams' transition from fast-talking Orkan in *Mork & Mindy* to fast-talking disc-jockey in *Good Morning, Vietnam* won him a Golden Globe for Best Actor. Cher abandoned her microphone to follow her heart (and Nicholas Cage) in *Moonstruck*, Sean Connery's Jimmy Malone was recognized by the Academy when the Scottish actor "bet" his $500,000 contract (and 10 percent of the film's gross) for the success of *The Untouchables*, while Richard Donner's *Lethal Weapon* helped skyrocket the career of the world's first "Sexiest Man Alive" (thanks to *People Magazine*): Mel Gibson. Relationships became somewhat complicated on the big screen: between Alex (Glenn Close) and Dan (Michael Douglas) in *Fatal Attraction*; Baby (Jennifer Grey) and Johnny (Patrick Swayze) in *Dirty Dancing*; and doubly so in the vampire comedy-horror movie *The Lost Boys*. And then there was *Planes, Trains & Automobiles*. Would any other director think to cast Steve Martin as a straight man? Rest in peace John Hughes.

Many iconic women come to mind when considering the music of 1987: Salt 'N Pepa's "Push It" still endures more than twenty years later, while Ann and Nancy Wilson as Heart sustained some Billboard heat. Grace Slick and Starship were on the rise, while Belinda Carlisle formed a solo career, breaking away from The Go-Go's. The red-headed, feather-haired Tiffany hypnotized young girls the world over with her cover of "I Think We're Alone Now." Yet it was Bon Jovi's *Slippery When Wet* and U2's *The Joshua Tree* that finally rewarded two drastically different yet remarkably hard-working bands. Billy Idol reaped his rewards with "Mony, Mony," while Ricky Rathman hosted the most iconic heavy metal music video request show of all time: *MTV's Headbanger's Ball,* which featured bands with good ol' "metal hair" such as Mötley Crüe, who climbed to international fame with their smash album, *Girls, Girls, Girls*.

It also appeared that political scandals were now common practice, as presidential candidate Gary Hart was caught in a relationship with Donna Rice; and Jim and Tammy Faye Baker's PTL Club scandal of lust and greed broke the papers.

Today's Secret Word is Comeback

Pee-wee's Playhouse resonates with kids *and* adults

Pee-wee Herman in action-figure form.

Paul Reubens developed his Pee-wee Herman character in order to survive as a stand-up comic in the late 1970s, yet he had no idea that his fictional personality would resound with so many children and adults throughout America. Attired in his trademarked gray glen plaid suit with high water slacks, a bow tie, powdered face with rosy red cheeks, and a closely-shorn haircut, Pee-wee Herman tested the mettle of American audiences via a stage show.

Hiring a number of comedians from his Groundlings days to round out the "nightclub" production, such as the brilliant Phil Hartman as Captain Carl and charming Lynne Marie Stewart as Miss Yvonne, Reuben's singular live stage performance, "The Pee-wee Herman Show," combined adult and children's humor and was an instant hit. Based on Reuben's newfound popularity, HBO approached him to tape a single performance of the stage show, and a one-hour special was created, again titled *The Pee-wee Herman Show* (1981). It appeared there was no stopping Reubens now: Pee-wee's brand of generation-defying comedy appealed to both viewers and critics alike and he exploded into American pop culture, and an eventual movie, *Pee-wee's Big Adventure*, became a cult smash and made him a star.

The success of this first feature film (sadly, 1988's *Big Top Pee-wee* grossed only half of *Adventure*'s revenue) caught the interest of network television, and in 1986, CBS proposed a Saturday morning program featuring Pee-wee. Reubens quickly assembled a cast of friends from his Groundlings days and recent nightclub show, and the incomparable *Pee-wee's Playhouse* was born. The revolutionary program ran from

Pee-wee's Playhouse ephemera: shopping bags, trading cards, tattoos, game, and stickers.

September 13 until November 19, 1990, with Reubens turning down a proposed sixth season due to fatigue and professional burnout; *Pee-wee's Playhouse* was not cancelled, as many would speculate, because of Reuben's unfortunate moral lapse and arrest on charges of indecent exposure in July of 1991.

Regardless, *Pee-wee's Playhouse* was appreciated by many different generations of fans: children loved Chairy, Corky, Jambi, the Puppet Land Band, and characters such as Cowboy Curtis (played by award-winning actor Laurence Fishburne), while their parents responded to Reuben's pop art sensibility, campiness, and unique musical score, provided by such composers as Danny Elfman, George Clinton, Dweezil Zappa, Todd Rundgren, and Mark Mothersbaugh of Devo. The program's aesthetics harkened to a better, vanished time, and regardless of age, you simply can't argue with a program that's won 22 Emmy Awards.

With a kooky opening theme song by Cyndi Lauper (credited anonymously as "Ellen Shaw"), *Pee-wee's Playhouse* was a Saturday morning sensation that became a staple for children of the 1980s; its mismatched combination of psychedelic and googie-style architecture and timeless sensibilities and message proved why the Matchbox toy company leapt at the chance to produce a series of action figures and collectibles under its Reubens' approved, "Official Pee-wee Brand."

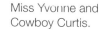
Miss Yvonne and Cowboy Curtis.

Pee-Wee Herman, King of Cartoons, Ricardo.

Constructed out of laminated chipboard, the playset provided kids with a wealth of action features that perfectly reflected what viewers witnessed on the program: Pee-wee's famous scooter with flag, a "Floory" character with pop-up floor, a "Clockey" with hands that turn, "Mr. Window" with a moving mouth, "Dancing Flowers" that move back-and-forth, a front door, an opening refrigerator with animated food stickers, a swinging open wall with flip-down chair, multiple action platforms, an island couch, television set, kitchen table, kitchen bench, and a vast amount of playable space.

The whole Playhouse playset folds back up for portability's sake, and allows you to carry the entire impressive line of 6-inch Pee-Wee action figures and Playhouse characters built to scale: Pee-wee himself, Cowboy Curtis, Miss Yvonne, the King of Cartoons, Reba the Mail Lady, Ricardo the soccer player, Jambi and the Puppetland Band, Randy and Globey, Pterri, Magic Screen, Conky, and Chairry. Although these action figures have limited poseability and accessories, their appeal continues to endure.

Heard it Through the Grapevine

The California Raisins become famous

The singing, dancing California Raisins, from left: Sax Player, Justin X. Grape, Ben Indasun, and Tiny Goodbite.

A group of singing, dancing, anthropomorphized raisins became a sensation after singing the 1968 Marvin Gaye song, "I Heard It Through the Grapevine," in a 1986 commercial for the California Raisin Advisory Board.

This was also the first time in history that a mere commercial spawned such a volume of merchandise, and in 1987, the California Raisins' popularity exploded after Hardee's created molded Raisins figurines to promote its cinnamon-raisin biscuits.

Combined with more TV ads, and even a music album, *The California Raisins Sing the Hit Songs*, the Raisins' images were everywhere, and a cultural phenomenon was born.

More TV ads, albums, and merchandise ranging from lunch boxes to clothing followed. They also eventually starred in an Emmy-nominated TV special, 1988's *Meet the Raisins*, and their own Saturday-morning cartoon on CBS, from 1989-90.

Not bad for little wrinkled pieces of fruit.

Cybernetic Do-Gooders

Silverhawks fight intergalactic bad guys

Silverhawks hero Moon Stryker with Tail-Spin,

Silverhawks villain Mumbo-Jumbo with Airshock.

With a 65-episode supporting animated series developed by Rankin/Bass, the producer of the famed *ThunderCats* cartoon (among others), *Silverhawks* was well-received, and Kenner produced a line of action figures to capitalize on this.

The narrative back story of the program took place in the fictional galaxy of Limbo, where the bionic police officer, Commander Stargazer, recruited a group of cybernetic heroes dubbed the "partly metal, partly real" Silverhawks—and led by Quicksilver—to fight an intergalactic mob of superhuman villains led by the evil Mon*Star." Each Silverhawk was once a human who was modified by Stargazer with bionic parts and an armored shell with mounted lasers; many of the members of the Silverhawks team also possess retractable masks and pop-up wings that allow them to fly.

Kenner produced two full series of Silverhawks figures, vehicles, and accessories between 1987 and 1988, featuring many of the major players from the animated canon. Each Silverhawks toy came complete with a power action feature and (usually) a "bird"-type accessory that assisted their respective action figure/character as a faithful companion. The first assortment of Silverhawks figures are Bluegrass with Sideman, Buzz-saw with Shredator, Copper Kid with Mayday, Flashback with Backlash, Hotwing with Gyro, Mo-Lec-U-Lar with Volt-ure, Mon*Star with Sky Shadow, Mumbo-Jumbo with Airshock, Quicksilver with Tally Hawk, Stargazer with Sly-Bird, Steelheart with Rayzor, and Steelwill with Stronghold. Series Two was subsequently comprised of Bluegrass with Ultrasonic Suit, Condor with Jet Stream, Hardware with Prowler, Moon Stryker with Tail-Spin, Steelwill with Ultrasonic Suit, Quicksilver with Ultrasonic Suit (a VERY rare toy), and Windhammer with Tuning Fork.

In addition to these action figures, six vehicles were made as well: the Silverhawks' enormous Maraj spacecraft; Mon*Star's Sky-Runner; Sky-Shadow, a larger out-of-scale version of Mon*Star's henchman/bird; Sprint Hawk, a one-man jet; Stronghold, another out-of-proportion companion figure (Steelwill's sidekick); and Quicksilver's popular and faithful Tally-hawk.

Silverhawks heroes: Copper Kidd with Mayday, Quicksilver with Tally Hawk, Steelwill with Stronghold, Steelwill with Rayzor, Bluegrass with Side Man.

Silverhawks action figures: Hotwing with Gyro, Condor with Jet Stream, Stargazer with Sly-Bird, Flashback with Backlash.

Silverhawks villains: Buzz-saw with Shredator, Mo-Lec-U-Lar with Volt-Ure, Windhammer with Tuning Fork, Mon*Star with Sky Shadow, Hardware with Prowler.

Prehistoric Power

Dino-Riders harness dinosaurs

Dino-Riders action figures: Deinonychus with Antor, and Quetzalcoatlus with Yungstar.

The back story of Tyco's Dino-Riders toy line, whose tag line read: "Harness the Power of Dinosaurs," pitted the noble Valorians (a play on the word "valor") against the sinister Rulons (i.e. "rulers"). The fourteen-episode animated program, airing as part of the Marvel Action Universe on USA, and its resultant toy line was concocted at the beginning of America's resurgent infatuation with dinosaurs.

In the 1980s, dinosaur-mania and the fascination with these "terrible lizards" held the attention of many American children, and Tyco capitalized on this by creating some of the best-sculpted and designed toys of the decade. So excellent were the designs of Dino-Riders, that Tyco was contacted by the Smithsonian Institution to create the National Museum of Natural History's "Dinosaur and Other Prehistoric Reptile Collection" of toys. Tyco went to great lengths to establish a dinosaur-themed toy line that smacked of authenticity, and this allowed the company to tap into the seemingly endless variety of pre-historic dinosaurs on which the company

based its designs: from Valorians' leader Questar's defense force of Diplodocus, Stegosaurus, and Woolly Mammoths, to the malicious Emperor Krulos' Rulon army of Triceratops, Ankylosaurus, and even the fierce Tyrannosaurus Rex, the premiere piece of the collection.

Yet Dino-Riders was not simply a line of 2-inch action figures that rode atop well-sculpted and accurately detailed 1/24th scale dinosaurs; each toy, even those offered at the smallest retail price point, included a complex and intricate array of futuristic accessories. Saddles, harnesses, bridles, laser cannons, and even a set of generic weapons for each figure packaged with their respective dinosaur.

Unfortunately, even though initial sales of the Dino-Riders were exceptional, the high production costs of such quality items (let's not forget the excellent packaging) was restrictive: the toys were simply too costly to produce while maintaining high quality standards.

Technologically Advanced Toys

Captain Power and the Soldiers of the Future

Captain Power and the Soldiers of the Future was a series of technologically advanced action figures, vehicles, and playsets released by Mattel Toys that afforded children the opportunity to "interact" with a live-action television program. More specifically, the toys themselves were constructed to react to sounds and images broadcast by Landmark Entertainment's *Captain Power and the Soldiers of the Future* syndicated television show, a program that, when revisited these many years later, possesses sophisticated story elements that suggests a narrative which was not entirely intended for children (e.g. romance, innuendo, profanity, and violent death).

However revolutionary this process was or how urbane the plot, written by such acclaimed writers as J. Michael Straczynski and Marv Wolfman, the lack of direction from a marketing standpoint became the property's undoing, and fans were left with a single season of twenty-two episodes; season two was scripted, but not produced.

Many pundits suggest that this oft-acclaimed television show and toy line floundered due to American parents viewing this program-to-toy interaction as far too violent, and it was the failure to retain a returning audience that marked Captain Power's doom. Yet, if I were to choose an '80s science-fiction program worth re-visiting, *Captain Power and the Soldiers of the Future* ranks near the top of the list. Although tracking down episodes is quite challenging, rewatching the adventures of Lt. Michael "Tank" Ellis, Major Matthew "Hawk" Masterson, Sgt. Robert "Scout" Baker, Lord Dread, Corporal Jennifer "Pilot" Chase, and Captain Jonathan Power himself, is worth the effort.

Captain Power and the Soldiers of the Future action figures: Corporal Pilot Chase and Captain Power.

Ghostly Warrior Holograms

Super Naturals has clever technology

Tonka's Super Naturals action figures: Lionheart and Eagle Eye.

What could be better than ghost warriors or holograms? A toy line that combines both!

The lone action figure line offered by Tonka in the 1980s was the Super Naturals: a series of "Ghost Warriors with double-channel holograms." Incorporating holography (holographic technology) into its design was clever on Tonka's part, as children truly responded to this advanced technology and found it fascinating. In place of a three-dimensional molded face and chest piece, each Super Naturals figure's mold was flattened, with a holographic sticker applied onto the plastic of the toy.

With a directive to "Release their hologram powers!"—where each character's hologram "transformed" from one image to the next (on both the figure and the figure's shield)—Super Naturals were only produced for one single series (1987), yet there was a good deal of product manufactured. The most popular Super Naturals toys were Tonka's six standard-sized action figures, each produced with one holographic shield accessory, a unique glow-in-the-dark weapon, and a mini-comic explaining the Super Naturals' back story: Eagle Eye—Heroic Warrior, whose hologram changes from Native American Chief to Soaring Eagle; Lionheart—Heroic Warrior, from King to Powerful Lion; Thunder Bolt—Heroic Warrior, from Viking to Lightning Warrior; Burnheart—Evil Warrior, from Evil Knight to Fiery Spirit; Snakebite—Evil Warrior, from Snake Charmer to Deadly Cobra; Skull—Evil Leader, from Pirate

to Skeleton with X-Ray Eye. It should be noted that each of these figures includes one more important accessory apart from their holographic shield, glow-in-the-dark weapon, and removable headgear; every large-scale Super Naturals figure possessed a removable piece of chest armor that functioned to hide a good deal of the toy's "hook"—its two-phase hologram sticker.

For consumers who wished to pick up a less expensive Super Naturals action figure at retail, Tonka created a series of smaller-scale toys. Packaged with removable cloaks, a single glow-in-the-dark sword, and a Super Naturals mini-comic, the Super Naturals' Ghostlings were sold at a slightly lower price point than the standard: Hooter—Heroic Ghostling, changes from Wizard to Wise Old Owl; Mr. Lucky—Heroic Ghostling, from Magician to Giant Rabbit; Rags—Evil Ghostling, from Egyptian to Ragged Mummy; Scary Cat—Evil Ghostling, from Wicked Witch to Hissing Cat; See-Thru—Heroic Ghostling, from Scientist to Invisible Man; Spooks—Heroic Ghostling, from Court Jester to Silly Spook; Vamp-Pa, from Vampire to Swooping Bat; and Weird Wolf—Evil Ghostling, from Weird Punk to Teenage Wolf. Tonka also released vehicles and playsets for its Super Naturals toy line: the Bat Bopper, Dark Dragon, Ghost Finder, Lion Wing, and the line's first playset—the Tomb of Doom, a fortress closely reminiscent of Mumm-Ra's Tomb Fortress from LJN's ThunderCats toy line.

Knights of the Magical Light

Whether hero or villain, Visionaries have three-dimensional excitement

Visionaries Spectral Knights: Arzon, Cryotek, Witterquick, Leoric, and Feryl.

"It is a time of when magic is more powerful then science, when evil Darkling Lords battle heroic Spectral Knights! For those who control the magic, control destiny! They are the Visionaries: Knights of the Magical Light!" echoes the toy packages and begins the opening credits of each episode of the short-lived *Visionaries* animated series.

Capitalizing on Colorforms' widely licensed and hugely popular Lazer Blazers holographic stickers, Visionaries combined the design of Hasbro's super-poseable G.I. Joe action figures with "new" holographic technology that was built into the characters' chest plates and accessory staffs. Each Visionaries' removable clip-in chest piece and staff had a holographic label applied to it that allowed the pieces to switch back-and-forth between two different three-dimensional images. These holograms were a huge selling point in the mid-'80s, so the Visionaries' packages touted the following proclamation: "Magic Holographic Powers! Single and dual holograms add magical 3-dimensional excitement!"

Each Visionaries figures stood 4-1/2 inches high (noticeably taller than standard 3-3/4" military and science-fiction action

figure fare of the 1980s), and in 1987, they captured kids' imaginations with their bright colors, excellent poseability (10 points of articulation), unique body sculpts (each figure had a totally original mold), and wonderful accessories.

Hasbro's Visionaries toy line was organized into two distinct groups: the "noble heroes"—known as the Spectral Knights—those brave and loyal characters that fight for liberty and justice on a world that (due to a cataclysmic event) has reverted back to medieval times. The second group is the villainous Darkling Lords: "evil villains" who have sworn fealty to their ruthless leader, Darkstorm, spreading mayhem and discord in their wake, taking advantage of the common folks inhabiting their magical land.

Regrettably, the Visionaries toy line was cancelled after one short year and a mere thirteen episodes of an excellent animated series. With only twelve action figures and four vehicles produced in total by Hasbro Inc., if you know a collector who is looking for an easy-to-obtain, highly playable vintage toy line to display proudly on your bookshelf, then these are the toys for you.

ENTERTAINMENT-O-RAMA: *1987* MOVIES, MUSIC, TELEVISION

Spending the summer in the Catskills with her family, Frances "Baby" Houseman (Jennifer Grey) falls in love with the camp's dancing teacher, Johnny Castle (Patrick Swayze). More women than just Baby were smitten not only with Johnny, but the movie itself, which became a cultural phenomenon. *Vestron/The Kobal Collection*

In *Lethal Weapon*, Mel Gibson is homicidal cop Martin Riggs, who, along with his partner, veteran cop Roger Murtaugh (Danny Glover), takes down a gang of drug smugglers. Along with *Die Hard*, *Lethal Weapon* is credited with setting new standards for urban action movies. *AP Photo*

Top Ten Films of 1987

1. *Three Men and a Baby* (Buena Vista)
2. *Fatal Attraction* (Paramount)
3. *Beverly Hills Cop II* (Paramount)
4. *Good Morning, Vietnam* (Buena Vista)
5. *Moonstruck* (MGM/Universal)
6. *The Untouchables* (Paramount)
7. *The Secret of My Success* (Universal)
8. *Stakeout* (Buena Vista)
9. *Lethal Weapon* (Warner Brothers)
10. *The Witches of Eastwick* (Warner Brothers)

Best Picture: *The Last Emperor* (Columbia)

Top Ten Television Programs of 1987-88

1 *The Cosby Show* (NBC)
2 *A Different World* (NBC)
3 *Cheers* (NBC)
4 *The Golden Girls* (NBC)
5 *Growing Pains* (ABC)
6 *Who's the Boss?* (ABC)
7 *Night Court* (NBC)
8 *60 Minutes* (CBS)
9 *Murder, She Wrote* (CBS)
10 *ALF* (NBC)

Debuting in 1983, *Who's the Boss?* was still going strong and would continue until 1992. The sitcom follows the lives of housekeeper Tony Micelli (Tony Danza), who works for career woman Angela Bauer (Judith Light), while their kids, Samantha (Alyssa Milano) and Jonathon (Danny Pintauro), and Angela's wacky mom Mona (Katherine Helmond) round out the cast. *ABC/Columbia Pictures/Embassy Pictures*

Groundbreaking Series

Max Headroom was one of the most groundbreaking and brilliant television programs ever created—a dystopic view of the future (do you recall Max Headroom featured on the "New Coke" advertisements?).

Performed by actor Matt Frewer in both commercials and on television, the short-lived but ground-breaking British-produced science fiction series was made for American TV and ran on ABC from 1987-88. It follows the exploits of an intrepid investigative TV reporter in the near future who does his job with the help of his colleagues and a computerized version of himself.

The series was based on the Channel 4 British TV pilot *Max Headroom: 20 Minutes into the Future*, and was the first cyberpunk series to run in the United States on one of the main broadcast networks in prime time. Like other science fiction, the series introduced the general public to new ideas in the form of cyberpunk themes and social issues.

Max Headroom. *Chrysalis/Lakeside/Lorimar Productions*

Top Ten Billboard Singles of 1987

1 "Walk Like an Egyptian," Bangles (*Different Light*, 1986)
2 "Alone," Heart (*Bad Animals*, 1987)
3 "Shake You Down," Gregory Abbott (*Shake You Down*, 1986)
4 "I Wanna Dance With Somebody (Who Loves Me)," Whitney Houston (*Whitney*, 1987)
5 "Nothing's Gonna Stop Us Now," Starship (*No Protection*, 1987)
6 "C'est La Vie," Robbie Nevil (*Robbie Nevil*, 1986)
7 "Here I Go Again," Whitesnake (*Whitesnake*, 1987)
8 "The Way It Is," Bruce Hornsby & the Range (*The Way It Is*, 1986)
9 "Shakedown," Bob Seger (*Beverly Hills Cop II* soundtrack, 1987)
10 "Livin' On A Prayer," Bon Jovi (*Slippery When Wet*, 1986)

Singer Jon Bon Jovi and his rock band, Bon Jovi, went from basic hair band to global superstars thanks to their album, *Slippery When Wet*, and singles including "You Give Love a Bad Name" and "Living on a Prayer." *AP Photo/Alan Greth*

Teenage Mutant Ninja Turtles: Raphael, Michaelangelo, Donatello, and Leonardo.

Turtle Power and the Future of Law Enforcement

C.O.P.S. Officer Bowzer.

THIS WAS THE YEAR KIDS COULD PRETEND they were mutant turtles battling petty criminals and villains; and also boldly set off on missions to go where no one has gone before. Other toy options included cyborg cops spawned from the 1987 movie *Robocop*, and a "bio-exorcist" named Beetlejuice.

On the small screen, Roseanne Barr brought her unique perspective of a contemporary lower-middle-class housewife to her self-titled *Roseanne*, essentially turning the modern sitcom—what was once considered a solely male province—on its head. Although in 1988, many programs would prefer to maintain the status quo rather than lose a loyal audience, *Roseanne* took a calculated risk, and broke away from the traditional patriarchal bonds established in situation comedy.

In the late 1980s, viewers would witness many different long-running programs forced to undergo re-inventions: when LJN's ThunderCats line began to fade, the *ThunderCats* cartoon was tweaked a bit to create *Silverhawks*, a cartoon that allowed similar revenue to fill the coffers of Rankin/Bass.

I suppose the same could be said for "Encounter at Farpoint," the premiere episode featuring Captain Jean-Luc Picard (Patrick Stewart) from *Star Trek: The Next Generation*. Although the Enterprise's mission is essentially the same, the cast of characters and their sensibilities are profoundly different.

In movies, 1988 featured New York cop John McClane (Bruce Willis) taking down terrorists in *Die Hard*, a toon-hating detective (Bob Hoskins) helping a cartoon rabbit to try and find out who's pinning a murder on him in *Who Framed Roger Rabbit*, incompetent Detective Frank Drebbin (Leslie Nielsen) foiling the assassination of Queen Elizabeth II in the zany *The Naked Gun: From the Files of Police Squad!*, and an obnoxious "bio-exorcist" named Beetlejuice (Michael Keaton) helping a newly deceased ghostly couple who try to get rid of the family that moves into their home in *Beetlejuice*. For those who liked a little drama with their comedy, there was the smash hit *Rain Man* that paired superstars Tom Cruise and Dustin Hoffman as brothers: one a selfish used car salesman and the other an autistic savant.

This was a complicated year for pop culture, as the street drug "crack" appeared in U.S. cities for the first time. George H.W. Bush was elected president, and although folks were wearing smiley buttons *enmasse*, N.W.A. released their seminal *Straight Outta Compton*, featuring Eazy-E, Ice Cube, Dr. Dre, MC Ren and DJ Yella. Gangsta rap was on the rise with Schooly D and Ice-T, as poor Mike Tyson's legacy fell apart, along with that of TV evangelist Jimmy Swaggart after an investigation revealed he solicited a prostitute for sex; he later admitted some of the allegations were true.

Teenage Mutant Ninja Turtles accessories: Retrocatapult, FlushoMatic, Double-Barreled Plunger Gun.

One word succinctly describes Playmates' expansive line of Teenage Mutant Ninja Turtles action figures, vehicles, and accessories: FUN. From the "high-tech toilet torture trap" known as the Flushomatic (with its toilet flushin' handle, and included can of Retromutagen ooze) to the "twin plungers of pounding force" dubbed the Double Barreled Plunger Gun (with its spring-loaded power and double barreled mutant plungers), TMNT fans reveled in these wonderful toys' imaginative designs.

Heroes in a Half Shell

Teenage Mutant Ninja Turtles have lasting legacy

The animated '80s cartoon Turtles top from left: Leonardo, Raphael, Michaelangelo, and Donatello. *Murakami Wolf Swenson/Fred Wolf Films/Mirage Studios/Surge Licensing*

"TMNT" is the more common appellation for the explosively popular quartet of anthropomorphic adolescent reptiles who follow the mysterious ways of ninjutsu: the Teenage Mutant Ninja Turtles. Although many aficionados of the Playmates toy line bought into the adventures of Donatello, Leonardo, Michelangelo, and Raphael via their Saturday morning animated adventures (from October 1, 1988 to September 23, 1989) as produced by Murakami-Wolf-Swenson and Shogakukan Studios, it wasn't until the show entered syndication that this risky venture by Playmates Toys in partnership with Mirage Studios caught heat.

Originally springing out of the brains of comic book artists and co-creators Kevin Eastman and Peter Laird in 1983, when the duo founded Mirage Studios, the two self-published *Teenage Mutant Ninja Turtles* as their flagship comic book. The comic parodied the clime of the grim and gritty comic book characters of the '80s: satirizing elements of Frank Miller's *Batman: The Dark Knight Returns*, *Batman: Year One*, *Daredevil*, and *Ronin*. The offbeat characters in *TMNT* reflected the new direction of comic book heroes present in that decade: from the re-invented Batman to the hyper-violent Punisher.

The original back story for *TMNT* has spawned a long-legged franchise of different media outlets for the *Turtles'* characters: three television series (two animated, one live-action), four films, a number of video games for different platforms, and a vast array of toys and collectibles.

The four core characters of the Teenage Mutant Ninja Turtles franchise are:

Leonardo, named after Leonardo DaVinci, Renaissance genius, is the blue-masked and blue-attired turtle who fights by wielding two katanas. Leonardo is depicted as the leader of the quartet, is the most disciplined in martial arts of the Turtles, is serious-minded, and of the four is closest to Splinter, their sensei.

Donatello, an allusion to early Renaissance Italian sculptor Donato di Niccolò di Betto Bardi, is the purple-masked turtle, who functions as the scientist/inventor of the team. Donatello wields a bo staff, which he uses to disarm adversaries, as he is often portrayed as the least aggressive of the four Turtles; he prefers to use intellect instead of brawn to solve problems.

Raphael, named after Italian high Renaissance architect and painter Raphael Sanzio da Urbino, is the red-masked turtle who functions as the team's resident rebel. Wielding two dangerous Okinawan sai (dagger-shaped, three-pronged truncheons), Raph's belligerent nature makes him difficult to control and quick to anger. However, his irrationality is often balanced by his role as the lighthearted jokester who often concocts witty remarks to cheer up his brethren.

Michelangelo, named for the Renaissance artist Michelangelo Buonarroti Simoni, is the fan-favorite orange-masked turtle who utilizes his infamous nunchaku to defeat enemy combatants (sometimes favoring a grappling hook, triple staff, tonfas, or even "thrown" pizzas). Michelangelo is known for his boundless

April O'Neil action figure.

energy and creativity, and for his reputation as the most laid-back and light-hearted member of the TMNT team. "Mikey" is often the source of not only comic relief, but for the popularization of many of the Turtles' catch phrases such as "Cowabunga, dudes!"

Other major characters in the canon are the Turtles' adoptive father, Splinter, who is skilled in martial arts, and represents the stereotypical sensei: wise, ethical, patient, spiritual, even-tempered, and soft-spoken; the willful red-headed television reporter April O'Neil, who was the first human to maintain continuous contact with the Turtles; and then there was the main antagonist of the cartoon, the sinister Shredder, portrayed as the standard evil-yet-incompetent Saturday-morning buffoon, as opposed to his more deadly and serious Mirage Studios' manifestation.

The Turtles also faced a bevy of wonderfully over-the-top villains who seemed to leap right from the pages of 1950s science-fiction fare including Krang, a super-intelligent disembodied brain sometimes housed in the torso of a giant exo-suit; and Bebop and Rocksteady, two curious bungling

Teenage Mutant Ninja Turtles Gags, Jokes, and Crazy Weapons No. 1-3.

evildoers. Bebop, named after a style of jazz, and Rocksteady, again a popular musical genre that originated in Jamaica; are Shredder's inept and incompetent henchmen. Bebop is a mutated warthog, while Rocksteady appears as a mutant rhinoceros.

There were many wonderful toys produced for the Teenage Mutant Ninja Turtles line by Playmates Toys. From Baxter Stockman to Storage Shell Don; from Mondo Gecko to Pizzaface, these action figures, vehicles, playsets, and accessories have stood the test of time.

In the spring of 1988, Eastman and Laird were approached by visionary licensing agent Mark Friedman, who advocated for their property by approaching Playmates Toys—a company interested in producing action figures for the first time. Playmates agreed to produce action figures of the Turtles if a television program would support the toy line. Although a

calculated risk, a concerted effort was made by Eastman and Laird, Friedman, Playmates' toy designers, Murakami-Wolf-Swenson's animators, and other agents and invested parties helped to guarantee the Turtles' success in both animated and action figure form. The results were Playmates Toys' excellent and inspired interpretations of Teenage Mutant Ninja Turtles characters from their plucky animated form into three-dimensional plastic toys.

Although rendered considerably more cartoonish than their dark roots (since the animated series was family oriented), Playmates' Teenage Mutant Ninja Turtles action figures were like nothing else offered on the action figure market at the time—from the colorful figures themselves to their odd yet appropriate accessories to the brilliant toy packages which touted memorable catch-phrases such as "Heroes in a Half Shell" and "Turtle Power!"

Usagi Yojimbo, Casey Jones, Metalhead, General Traag, Leatherhead, and the Rat King.

The Turtles' sensei, Splinter, in action-figure form.

Going Boldly

Star Trek: The Next Generation

Villains Selay, Antican, Q, and Ferengi.

As always, with a successful science-fiction franchise comes an action figure line. This year it was in honor of *Star Trek: The Next Generation*.

Premiering in 1987 to 27 million people, when the opening credits were spoken by new Enterprise Captain Jean-Luc Picard, I knew this "sci-fi/action-adventure" program would be something different than the standard science-fiction dreck.

Our story begins with Captain Picard (Patrick Stewart), who possessed an illustrious career as an accomplished diplomat and tactician, and had just taken over command of the new Enterprise-D. Well-spoken and admired by every member of his crew, Picard is a true Renaissance Man. Commander William Thomas "Will" Riker (Jonathan Frakes) is the smarmy yet charming second-in-command. Known for his unorthodox solutions to problems, Riker frequently exhibits a lighter touch when commanding the Enterprise. The third most visible member of the crew is not human at all, "he" is a Soong-type android—a sentient artificial life-form created to resemble a human. Lieutenant Commander Data (Brent Spiner) is roughly equivalent to Spock on the original *Star Trek* show, yet Data overtly desires to be human, and this, combined with his innocence and honesty, appealed to many fans. Lieutenant Geordi La Forge (LeVar Burton) is sight-impaired and wears a visor over his eyes which allows him to "see" into the electromagnetic spectrum.

One of the more shocking changes on the Bridge is the addition of security officer, Lieutenant Worf (Michael Dorn). Worf is the first Klingon crew member added to a Federation Starship, since the United Federation of Planets is now at peace with the Klingons in the 24th Century. Perhaps the most progressive aspect of the new members of the *Star Trek* canon was the addition of a much larger female cast: with Marina Sirtis as Lieutenant Commander Deanna Troi, ship's counselor, Gates McFadden as Commander Dr. Beverly Crusher, chief medical officer, and Denise Crosby as the efficient, tough and secretive Lieutenant Natasha "Tasha" Yar, chief of security. These strong, capable, and uncompromising female characters attracted numerous women to the long-lived franchise.

The license for creating toys in these characters' likenesses was briefly given to Galoob, which produced two different series of ten action figures and two small spacecrafts. Series One consisted of Captain Jean-Luc Picard, Commander William Riker, Lieutenant Commander Data, Lieutenant Tasha Yar, Lieutenant Worf, and Lieutenant Geordi La Forge. In Series Two, only villains were included in the assortment, with an Antican, Selay, Ferengi, and the diabolical "Q" rounding out the set. The two vehicles offered by Galoob were small in stature, but would accommodate any of the 3-3/4-inch figures from the two series: the Shuttlecraft Galileo fit all six Federation crew members, while the Ferengi Fighter accommodated two Ferengi pilots.

Plastic Athletes

Starting Lineup lets children collect sports superstars

Starting Lineup Baseball figures: Vince Coleman, Gary Carter, Ozzie Smith, Tim Raines.

One of the final revolutionary toy lines introduced exclusively by Kenner was its ingenious Starting Lineup action figures, featuring an ambitious roster of 132 different baseball players. Starting Lineup was the brainchild of former professional football player Pat McInally, and Kenner delivered the following inspired idea: 1) each Starting Lineup toy was officially licensed by Major League Baseball and included official MLB brands and logos, 2) every toy package included a unique collector's card similar to a standard-sized baseball card (with "Sports Super Star Collectible" player statistics on the back of each card), and 3) the company did its best to represent the 132 MLB player names they acquired as accurately as possible. Although this stable of players shared similar molds (figures were constructed by swapping and re-casing parts in different colors with different uniform logos), Kenner provided a few little touches that "personalized" every figure; for instance, if a player possessed a moustache, Kenner painted one on the action figure; if an athlete was speedy when running the bases, the company chose to portray the player's toy as he was sliding into second base.

In 1988, Kenner's Starting Lineup toy line provided fans with action figures for all 26 current Major League Baseball teams: twelve from the National League: St. Louis Cardinals (6), Chicago Cubs (7), New York Mets (7), Philadelphia Phillies (6), Pittsburgh Pirates (6), Houston Astros (6), Atlanta Braves (5), Los Angeles Dodgers (6), San Francisco Giants (4), San Diego Padres (5), Cincinnati Reds (6), and the lowly Montreal Expos (1); and fourteen from the American League: Milwaukee Brewers (5), Cleveland Indians (5), Baltimore Orioles (6), Boston Red Sox (5), Detroit Tigers (6), Minnesota Twins (6), California Angels (5), Oakland A's (4), Seattle Mariners (5), Texas Rangers (5), Kansas City Royals (5), Chicago White Sox (5), Toronto Blue Jays (1), and the New York Yankees (5).

The line met with such success that Kenner eventually incorporated as many different sports as possible into its Starting Lineup franchise, acquiring the licenses for NFL Football (1988-2000), NHL Hockey (1993-2000), NBA Basketball (1988-1995), and legends from various other sports institutions such as WBC & WBA boxing and PGA golf. Unfortunately, due to the fact that Kenner's Starting Lineup toys were released in 1988, we never had a chance to witness the most famous American sports team of the decade, the 1980 U.S. Olympic Hockey Team, translated into action figure form after the amateur players' triumphed over a heavily favored professional Russian powerhouse on February 22, 1980's "Miracle on Ice."

Starting Lineup figures provided children with the opportunity to own a plastic representation of their favorite superstar athlete—the first time this feat was ever accomplished by a toy company.

'Ghost with the Most'

Beetlejuice a big success

Lydia and Beetlejuice from the animated cartoon.
Geffen Film Company/Nelvana/Tim Burton Incorporated/
Warner Bros. Television

Adam Maitland and
"Spinhead" Beetlejuice.

Most Tim Burton fans fondly remember 1988's *Beetlejuice* as the first offering by the acclaimed director to truly "smack" of his darkly unfettered style, other than the revered short, *Frankenweenie* (1984), that would later inform his terrifically popular hits such as *Batman* (1989), *Edward Scissorhands* (1990), *The Nightmare Before Christmas* (1993), *Charlie and the Chocolate Factory* (2005), and most recently, *Alice in Wonderland* (2010).

In the film, a young married couple—Adam Maitland (Alec Baldwin) and his wife, Barbara (Geena Davis)—get in a car accident and veer off a bridge, falling into the icy water of the river below. Upon returning to their home, the hearth fire is already lit, yet they have no memory of how they stoked the fire or returned to the house after the car crash. Furthermore, after stepping off their front porch, it appears they have access to

another dimension. After a series of odd events, the two realized that they perished and are, in fact, now ghosts. As ghosts, they mean to deter anyone interested in buying their home and begin haunting the house's new inhabitants, the ostentatious Deetze family: the high-strung Charles (Jeffrey Jones of *Ferris Bueller's Day Off* fame), the stuffy Delia (Catherine O'Hara), and the out-of-the-ordinary Lydia Deetz (memorably portrayed by Winona Ryder).

The titular role of Beetlejuice—a perverse, cunning trickster with a heart of coal—is played by Michael Keaton, who makes the most of the character, and skyrocketed to superstardom with his display of dazzling physical comedy. Burton's direction and expert production quality combined with Keaton's performance made Beetlejuice a critical and commercial success. And a success on the big screen led to the creation of an animated series in 1989.

The *Beetlejuice* animated program was initially a breakout hit for ABC—and then for FOX's weekday afternoon schedule—lasting a full four seasons through 1991. As a bi-modal cartoon similar to CBS's Burton-inspired live-action *Pee-wee's Playhouse* (1986-90), *Beetlejuice*'s humor could be discerned on two levels: on the surface, the program could be understood and digested by children who could easily follow the eccentric plots, yet if watched by adults, there were certain jokes and allusions weaved into the narrative that only "grown-ups" could understand.

Kenner, hoping to capitalize off of the success of the film, created two full series of figures, opting to translate characters from the movie rather than the animated series. This line of toys is quite underappreciated, as the accurate sculpting (for the 1980s), amazing colors, inspired design, and unusual accessories are all first-rate. Many fans of Kenner's Real Ghostbusters line took notice that these two licenses easily merged together, allowing Peter, Ray, Egon, and Winston to hunt the most famous ghost of the 1980s: Beetlejuice. Series

Beetlejuice Vanishing Vault playset with "disappearing" Micro-Beetlejuice ("Showtime" Beetlejuice sold separately).

One of Kenner's Beetlejuice line featured Adam Maitland (the Headless Ghost with Beakface Mask and Creepy Crawler), Harry the Haunted Hunter (with Terrible Tarantula), Otho the Obnoxious (with Loathsome Lizard), Shish Kebab Beetlejuice (with Scary Skewers), Showtime Beetlejuice (with Rotten Rattler), Spinhead Beetlejuice (with Creepy Cockroach), and of course…the Beetlejuice Vanishing Vault playset, with Disappearing "Micro" Beetlejuice.

"Shishkebab" Beetlejuice, Harry the Haunter Hunter, and Otho the Obnoxious & Loathsome Lizard.

Live Action and Animation

Who Framed Roger Rabbit revolutionary movie-making

Who Framed Roger Rabbit LJN "Flexies" assortment: Judge Doom, Baby Herman, Eddie Valiant, Roger Rabbit, Jessica, and Smartguy (Boss Weasel).

Taking place in 1947—a time when the Golden Age of animation peaked with such talented designers as Fritz Freleng, Tex Avery, and Bob Clampett at the helm—the plot of 1988's *Who Framed Roger Rabbit* centers around the murder of popular animated film star, Roger Rabbit (who bears a passing similarity to Bugs Bunny), and the resulting conspiracy and cover-up. Starring the always-brilliant Bob Hoskins as detective/gumshoe Eddie Valiant, Kathleen Turner, who voices the seductress-turned-widow Mrs. Jessica Rabbit, and Christopher Lloyd as Judge Doom (fresh off his role as absentminded professor, Dr. Emmett Brown in Zemeckis' *Back to the Future*), the all-star cast assured a successful production. Although many films since this venture have combined live actors with CGI characters, most viewers will attest to the fact that none of these characters have been rendered more effectively than those in the revolutionary *Who Framed Roger Rabbit*.

Producing such an intricate and ambitious film was risky; it would be the most expensive animated movie ever produced at that time, with production costs soaring to more than $70 million. Thankfully, it grossed more than four times that amount; a whopping $330 million. In order to capitalize upon the phenomenal film, LJN toys bought the license to concoct two different series of action figure-related products: Who Framed Roger Rabbit "Flexies," and "Animates." Even though the Animates line was most similar to the standard action figure offerings littering toy store shelves in the late 1980s, it was LJN's Flexies line that sold quite well. With a small assortment of characters—Roger Rabbit himself, Smartguy (Boss Weasel), Baby Herman, Judge Doom, Eddie Valiant, and of course, the voluptuous Jessica Rabbit—kids could re-enact all the action or create their own adventures.

Rumors abound that there will be a sequel to *Who Framed Roger Rabbit* produced in the near future, as a script is "in development," but only time will tell.

Cyborg Law Enforcer

RoboCop and Ultra Police

Many science-fiction films of the 1980s did not fare well critically. *RoboCop*, however, was well-received by reviewers and viewers alike, grossing $54 million on a budget of a mere $13 million—a lucrative success for a film with such dark sensibilities.

With a pessimistic vision of the future of "New Detroit"—a nihilistic, decadent den of iniquity—and a desperate desire for the police force to take their city back from the powerful street gangs, a police officer injured in the line of duty is transformed into a cybernetic super-sheriff: RoboCop.

Released in three different series, each member of Kenner's RoboCop and the Ultra Police toy line features a minimum of five points of articulation, a roll-cap firing system built into the figure itself (or into a weapon or accessory), two rolls of standard blue roll caps, and a unique weapon (rifle, pistol, etc.). The following six characters were released in Series One of Robocop and the Ultra-Police: Robocop, part man, part robot, the unstoppable leader of the Ultra Police; remove his helmet to reveal his true identity; "Wheels" Wilson, having no fear of speed, is the Ultra Police high speed pursuit officer and defends himself with a Blast-Zooka and captures criminals with his Ultra-Cuffs; Birdman Barnes, whose knack for heights allows him to control Ultra Police air operations, and for his own high elevation work he always carries an Ultra-Grappling gun and hook; and Ace Jackson, the tough Ultra Police weapons expert, armed with shoulder cannon and Ultra Stick.

There were also two villain figures released in Series One, members of the world's worst criminals: Headhunter, the "King of Crime" and leader of the Vandals, who doesn't think anybody can stop him with his Magnum Rifle and Electro-Crowbar; and Nitro, Headhunter's henchman, always trying to outdo his boss'

RoboCop and the Ultra Police action figures: "Torpedo" Thomspon, RoboCop Nightfighter, "Birdman" Barnes.

criminal deeds using his Nitro-Pincher and Dyno-Bomb.

Series One possesses a few select vehicles and accessories, such as: Robo-1, the futuristic police car specially designed for the Ultra Police with special weaponry including a swiveling, rear-mounted, missile launcher and a Robo-Armor shield; and the Robo-Cycle, a sleek turbo-charged bike used for chasing down the Vandals, which nothing can stop with its front-mounted pulse cannon and Robo-Armo shield. The final vehicle was the Skull Hog, Headhunter's favorite street machine because of its surprise spring-loaded cruise missile.

The line continued for another year and encompassed two full series of products: Series Two added four more figures, and one more vehicles to the line: Anne Lewis, Sergeant Reed, Chainsaw, Dr, McNamara, and the Robo-Copter. Series Three saw six new figures: "Torpedo" Thompson, RoboCop Nightfighter, "Claw" Callahan, Gatlin' Blaster Robocop, Scorcher, and Toxic Waster; and the addition of a few vehicles—the Robo-Tank, Robo-Jailer, Vandal 1, ED-209, Robo-Hawk, Robo-Glove (role play), Robo-Command, and the Robo-Helmet and Blaster (role play).

'Fighting Crime in a Future Time!'

C.O.P.S. 'N Crooks capitalizes on fascination with law and order

C.O.P.S. Bullet-Proof.

C.O.P.S. Blitz, Officer Bowser's faithful dog.

C.O.P.S. 'N Crooks' Big Boss.

Hasbro's C.O.P.S. 'n Crooks action figures sold well initially, possessing as they did excellent articulation and first-rate accessories, and the toy line endured for two full series with the support of both a comic book and animated series.

A *C.O.P.S.* comic series tie-in was handled by DC Comics, who put together an excellent book in large part due to a crackerjack creative team of Doug Moench, creator of *Moon Knight*, and penciling responsibilities handled at various times by Pat Broderick, Bart Sears, and the versatile Alan Kupperberg.

Both the comic book and the animated series followed the same basic back story: in the year 2020, Empire City is facing a criminal uprising. The criminal association responsible for the disturbance: the "Crooks," led by Brandon "Big Boss" Babel, channeling Edward G. Robinson from *Little Caesar* (1930). Big Boss is a nefarious gangster who dresses in a white suit jacket with blue slacks, carries a cane that has been modified to function as a machine gun, and is rarely without his evil pet weasel, Scratch. Big Boss' Crooks (Buttons McBoomBoom, Rock Crusher, Berserko, Dr. Badvibes, and others) are deterred from committing their crimes because Empire City is under protection by the C.O.P.S. organization: the Central Organization of Police Specialists.

C.O.P.S. is led by honorable federal agent Baldwin P. Vess, code-named "Bullet-Proof," a nickname given to him because of a hidden metal-plated cybernetic suit of armor.

Bullet-Proof dresses in a tan trench-coat, canary-yellow shirt and black tie, and trademark dark sunglasses. His troopers are among the elite police officers of Empire City: Highway, Sundown, Barricade, Longarm, Sgt. Mace, and Officer Bowser and his dog, Blitz. With these colorful characters, Hasbro's C.O.P.S.-against-Crooks back story played out similarly to the Autobots versus the Decepticons or G.I. Joe against Cobra narratives. To that end, Hasbro hired Larry Hama, author of the G.I. Joe line's file card biographies, to construct the action figures "C.O.P.S. I.D. Cards" and Crooks' "Wanted: Criminal Data Files." Commenting upon this process, veteran comic writer/artist Hama said, "Constructing the dossiers was a lot more tongue-in-cheek than writing G.I. Joe bios. Sort of like the attitude of the Warren Beatty Dick Tracy movie. I named a character Tommy Tu-Tone (after the power pop-rock bad of the early '80s)."

A unique feature of Hasbro's 6-inch scale C.O.P.S. 'n Crooks action figures, with the tag-line, "Fighting Crime in a Future Time!", was their cap-firing action: each figure possessed a weapon or attachment on the figure itself that allowed the toy to activate an included roll of standard paper caps which produced a loud noise and smoke when triggered by a striking mechanism. This use of standard rolls of caps allowed children to purchase extra boxes of caps at a toy store when the caps included with the toy were completely fired.

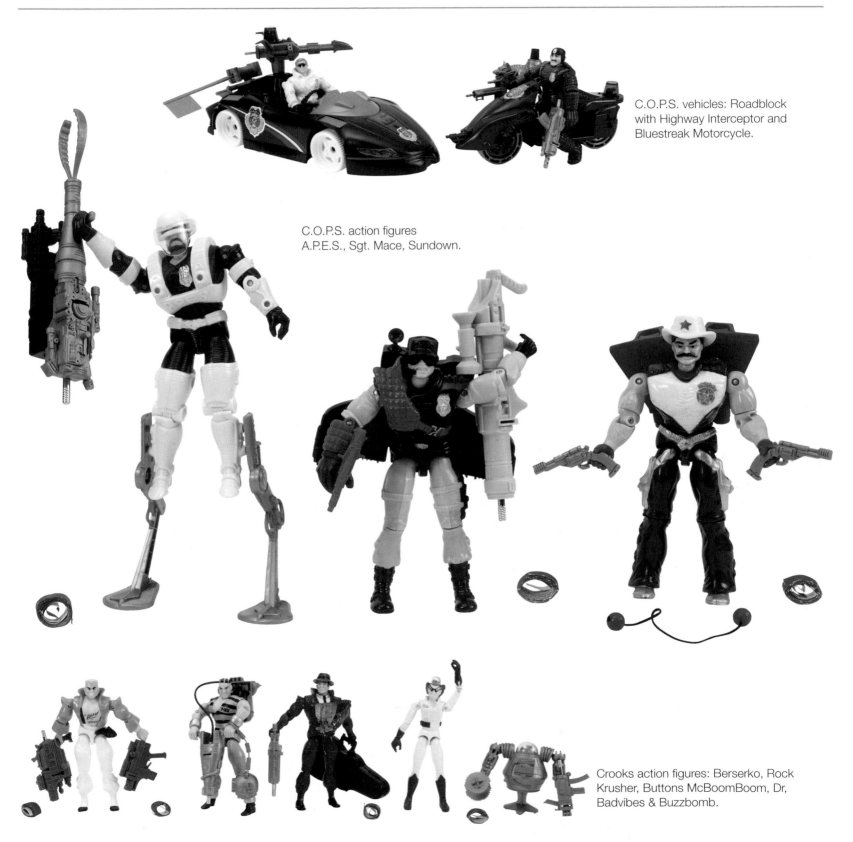

C.O.P.S. vehicles: Roadblock with Highway Interceptor and Bluestreak Motorcycle.

C.O.P.S. action figures A.P.E.S., Sgt. Mace, Sundown.

Crooks action figures: Berserko, Rock Krusher, Buttons McBoomBoom, Dr, Badvibes & Buzzbomb.

ENTERTAINMENT-O-RAMA: 1988 MOVIES, MUSIC, TELEVISION

Top Ten Films of 1988

1. *Rain Man* (MGM/Universal)
2. *Who Framed Roger Rabbit* (Buena Vista)
3. *Coming to America* (Paramount)
4. *Big* (Fox)
5. *Twins* (Universal)
6. *Crocodile Dundee II* (Paramount)
7. *Die Hard* (Fox)
8. *The Naked Gun: From the Files of Police Squad!* (Paramount)
9. *Cocktail* (Buena Vista)
10. *Beetlejuice* (Warner Brothers)

Best Picture: *Rain Man* (MGM/Universal)

The zany and eye-popping *Who Framed Roger Rabbit* is a landmark film, combining animation with live action. A toon-hating detective (Bob Hoskins) is a cartoon rabbit's only hope to prove his innocence when he is accused of murder. *Touchstone/Amblin/The Kobal Collection*

In Tim Burton's twisted and clever black comedy *Beetlejuice*, Michael Keaton plays the "ghost with the most," the mischievous and maniacal Beetlejuice. A newly deceased couple (Geena Davis and Alec Baldwin) now ghosts themselves, hire him to get rid of the yuppie family who moves into their house. They eventually end up trying to get rid of Beetlejuice himself after he unleashes an evil scheme involving the yuppies' morose daughter (Winona Ryder). *Geffen/Warner Bros/The Kobal Collection*

Top Ten Television Programs of 1988-89

1 *The Cosby Show* (NBC)
2 *Roseanne* (ABC)
3 *A Different World* (NBC)
4 *Cheers* (NBC)
5 *60 Minutes* (CBS)
6 *The Golden Girls* (NBC)
7 *Who's the Boss?* (ABC)
8 *Murder, She Wrote* (CBS)
9 *Empty Nest* (NBC)
10 *Anything But Love* (ABC)

While most TV shows retained their status quo, Roseanne Barr brought her special brand of comedy to TV in *Roseanne*. The series centered on a working-class family, the Connors, struggling with problems common to all families: marriage, money, children, work, and in-laws. *Carsey-Werner/Wind Dancer Productions*

Guns N' Roses' major label debut album, *Appetite for Destruction*, has sold in excess of 28 million copies worldwide and reached No. 1 on the United States Billboard 200, thanks to such hits as "Welcome to the Jungle" and "Sweet Child of Mine." The band's debut was no fluke, as their third album, *Use Your Illusion*, led to the Michael Jackson Video Vanguard Award for "November Rain," at the 1992 MTV Video Music Awards. From left are Michael "Duff" McKagan, Dizzy Reed, Axl Rose, Slash, and Matt Sorum. *AP Photo/Kevork Djansezian*

Top Ten Billboard Singles of 1988

1 "Faith," George Michael (*Faith*, 1987)
2 "Need You Tonight," INXS (*Kick*, 1987)
3 "Got My Mind Set On You," George Harrison (*Cloud Nine*, 1988)
4 "Never Gonna Give You Up," Rick Astley (*Whenever You Need Somebody*, 1987)
5 "Sweet Child O' Mine," Guns N' Roses (*Appetite for Destruction*, 1987)
6 "So Emotional," Whitney Houston (*Whitney*, 1987)
7 "Heaven Is a Place on Earth," Belinda Carlisle (*Heaven on Earth*, 1987)
8 "Could've Been," Tiffany (*Tiffany*, 1987)
9 "Hands to Heaven," Breathe (*All that Jazz*, 1988)
10 "Roll With It," Steve Winwood (*Roll with It*, 1988)

1989

The *Batman* Batcave playset was a standout in the movie's toy line. It possesses the following eleven unique features: a falling boulder, multiple removable bridges, a climb up platform, button activated jail cell, secret hideaway, carry handle (to transport the playset from place-to-place), a lever-activated collapsing bridge (which leads to a "bottomless pit"), a sliding elevator, a hinged door, and a rotating computer with five action-packed movie scenes.

The Dark Knight Rises Again, Marvel Universe Begins Anew

Batman: The Killing Joke. © 1988 DC Comics, Inc.

THE DARK KNIGHT OF GOTHAM CITY continued his war on criminals, both in Tim Burton's *Batman*, which brought back the super-hero genre in a big way, and children's imaginations when the toy tie-ins soon followed.

Kids could also create their own "excellent" adventures with the help of two head bangin' slackers and a new line of Marvel super-heroes was created, while with Nintendo's new hand-held device, you could play video games almost anywhere.

In 1989, the rise of voyeuristic television continued with the program *America's Funniest Home Videos*, which also heralded the premature death of scripted television. Yet, did the dumbing down of American television begin in the late 1980s with the multitude of ingenious FOX reality programming? Was FOX the sole culprit, as we are led to believe? Of course this is untrue. Apart from FOX's rise to prominence, Fred Savage (as Kevin Arnold) and Danica McKellar (as Winnie Cooper) in *The Wonder Years* (1988-1993) shot us back into the age of innocence—the late 1960s—while David Hasselhoff returned to television in the dramatic adventures of *Baywatch* with Pamela (Lee) Anderson and Erika Eleniak. As critically panned as *Baywatch* was in the U.S.—the show was cancelled after only the 1989 season—other investors saw its potential in syndication and revived the program, where, according to the *Guinness Book of World's Records*, *Baywatch* is the most watched TV show in the world

of all time, with over 1.1 billion viewers turning in per week.

Regarding the movie industry in 1989, we witnessed Sean Connery portraying Dr. Henry Jones, Indiana's father in Harrison Ford's *Indiana Jones and The Last Crusade*. Like *The Last Crusade*, there were quite a few eminently re-watchable and touching films produced in '89: both Ron Howard's *Parenthood* and Peter Weir's *Dead Poets Society* tugged at my heartstrings, while *Bill & Ted's Excellent Adventure* is amazingly relevant to this very day.

It appears in 1989 that the rise of boy bands and female "mall" singers were taking a pop-starved America by storm. Between Bobby Brown, Tiffany, Debbie Gibson, New Kids on the Block, former-Laker Girl Paula Abdul, and Milli Vanilli (who would have their Grammy Award rescinded), we should all thank our lucky stars that performers with true talent would rescue music from languishing in the depths of mediocrity: the songs of Janet Jackson, Bette Midler, and Madonna continue to endure.

With the fall of the Berlin Wall in the autumn of '89, there was a sense of hope and prevailing optimism that was reflected in our day-glow pastel-colored clothing, and in our voyeuristic reality TV moguls such as Phil Donahue and Sally Jesse Raphael, whose "tabloid talk shows" took the place of hard news.

Caped Crusaders Overhauled

Batman and the DC Comics Super-Heroes

Batman: The Dark Knight.
© 1986 DC Comics, Inc.

Batman's star was rising with comics collectors and the mainstream media in the 1980s, and with acclaim being heaped upon Frank Miller's *The Dark Knight Returns* (1986) and Alan Moore's *Batman: The Killing Joke* (1988), the super-hero was championed by aficionados. Therefore, it was a risky move for a major studio to take a character from a comic book, as popular as Batman currently was with his devoted fans, and translate him onto the silver screen in '89.

Although Warner Brothers had decided that Tim Burton was the proper director for *Batman*, based on his successful and plucky *Pee-wee's Big Adventure* (1985), the studio still wished to wait until Michael Keaton and Burton's *Beetlejuice* performed well at theaters in 1988 before principal shooting for the new Batman film began. Beyond financial concerns, many speculators were worried about Burton's casting of the film's major roles. Since it would take some big-name actors with cache to heighten public interest in the movie, the director cast a strong yet controversial ensemble: Keaton, an actor known for his comedic choices and fresh off of his role as a mental patient with delusions of grandeur in the endearing but unconventional film *The Dream Team* (1989) was cast as Bruce Wayne/Batman; sex-symbol Kim Basinger, who had recently finished two comedies—*Nadine* (1987) and as the lead in the quirky comedy science-fiction flick, *My Stepmother is an Alien* (1988)—was cast as the protagonist's love interest, Vicki Vale;

and the Emmy- and Oscar-winning actor Jack Palance arrived to the film immediately after his role as Lawrence G. Murphy in *Young Guns* (1988), playing the intimidating crime boss of Gotham City, Carl Grissom.

Yet the "big get" for *Batman* was Jack Nicholson. Following one of the most productive periods in his career that garnered him a slew of award-winning roles—in *Terms of Endearment* (1983), *Prizzi's Honor* (1986), *The Witches of Eastwick, Broadcast News*, and *Ironweed* (all 1987)—Nicholson was one of the most requested, acclaimed, and bankable stars in all of Hollywood. Cast as Batman's arch-nemesis, the Joker, audiences were treated to the '80s lunatic interpretation of the character as the Joker appeared in Miller's *The Dark Knight Returns* and Moore's chilling *The Killing Joke*. Nicholson would not play the role as Caesar Romero did in the 1960s; this was not your father's goofy, harmless Batman villain: Nicholson's Joker was a psychopathic killer—a sociopath without scruples.

Released on June 23, *Batman* set a precedent for successive films in the super-hero genre; it defied expectations and was an international smash-hit, translating well to a non-comic book reading audience. The movie reaped a hefty reward at the box office and became the top-grossing film of 1989, earning $411 million in box office receipts to date, with an extra $150 million profit in VHS and DVD sales. In a mere 2 hours and 6 minutes, this first installment triggered what would become the epic *Batman* franchise, which also includes *Batman Returns* (1992), *Batman Forever* (1995), *Batman & Robin* (1997), and the more recent *Batman Begins* (2005) and *The Dark Knight* (2008).

For the first time in many years—since Kenner's Star Wars heyday of the early '80s—a toy company had a major motion picture to latch onto in order to promote its product. Unfortunately, the company producing the action figures for the *Batman* film had little experience in that arena. The few figures and vehicles (and lone playset) capitalizing on the movie were some of Toy Biz's first retail offerings, and as such, they had low quality sculpts, poor poseability, and limited amounts of poorly constructed accessories. However, eventually Toy Biz would grow to dominate the action figure aisles of retail stores from 2002-present with its much-lauded Marvel Legends and other Marvel Comics super-hero toys. Regardless, the first series of Toy Biz's DC offerings were based on characters taken directly from the *Batman* film and the packaging for these toys reflects this choice.

The first selection in Toy Biz's *Batman* line, Batman himself, possessed two different face sculpts—one that was fairly generic, while the other emulated the likeness of Keaton. Veteran character actor Tracey Walter, the Joker's lead henchman "Bob the Goon," was the second figure; and the final offering was, of course, the Joker. This toy came replete with removable hat, cane, and a bellows and hose with which to work his "squirting flower" action feature.

Batman (the movie) action figures Bob the Goon and the Joker.

Upon reviewing the first two waves of Toy Biz's Batman and DC Super-Heroes action figures, it will become apparent to action figure fans that many of the figures' designs are simple re-casts of Kenner's Super Powers action figures from 1984-86: the Joker's body, Mr. Freeze, Penguin, Robin, Superman, Wonder Woman, and the Riddler (a poor re-sculpt of Super Powers Flash).

Beyond the re-sculpting, the two waves of figures that Toy Biz produced following the initial Batman movie line were created with DC Comics' more iconic comic book characters in mind, and these toys' packages were labeled "DC Comics Super Heroes" instead of "Batman."

DC Comics Super-Heroes:
Wonder Woman, Superman, Robin.

DC Comics Super-Heroes: Flash, Green Lantern, Aquaman.

DC Comics Super-Heroes villains: Lex Luthor, Riddler, Mr. Freeze, Penguin.

DC Comics Super-Heroes: Hawkman, Two-Face (villain).

Bricks and Pocket Monsters

Nintendo Game Boy proves its endurance

Nintendo Game Boy with the following cartridges: *F1 Race*, *Mega Man II*, *Tetris*, *Kirby's Dream Land*, *Final Fantasy Legend*, and *Super Mario Land*.

A fourth-generation video game, the Nintendo Game Boy, nicknamed "The Brick" or "Brick Boy" because of its durability and similarity to a small gray brick, was the brain-child of Gunpei Yokoi and Nintendo's Research & Development 1 staff. The original Game Boy combined the features of the best-selling Nintendo Entertainment System (1986) and the Game & Watch, a combination of video game, LCD screen, clock and alarm (i.e., the "game" and "watch").

One of the first handheld games to utilize different cartridges that were inserted into the machine to access different games, the Game Boy has proven its endurance by outselling and outlasting its (sometimes superior) competitors during its lengthy run at retail, and now exists in specialty stores that deal in "vintage" video games.

When released domestically on July 31, 1989, bundled together with the famous game, the "killer app" *Tetris*, the Nintendo Game Boy's only competitor was the Atari Lynx, yet there was little competition. The Lynx cost nearly $100 more than the Game Boy (Lynx retailed for $185.99; the Game Boy $89.99), and required 6 AA batteries, which provided a mere five hours of game play—a substantial extraneous purchase for such limited play time when using a hand-held video game. Nintendo sold an external rechargeable battery pack/AC adapter for $29.99 which, unless you played your Game Boy 24-7, allowed near-unlimited power for your Game Boy system.

Therefore, when compared to the monochromatic Game Boy, the full-color Atari Lynx was still relegated to a second-rate ranking. Heck, the monochromatic element of the Game Boy actually extended the battery life of the machine: the device boasted anywhere from 12 to 25 hours of battery life on only 4 AA batteries by using a non-backlit monochrome screen and a low-power 8-bit processor.

Before ceasing production of the most popular hand-held video game of all time, Nintendo's Game Boy and Game Boy Color had sold 118 million units worldwide combined; this ridiculous sales number does not include revenues from the popular Game Boy Advance, which would add another 82 million units to the total. Nintendo provided world-class software for the Game Boy console for more than a decade, thanks to popular and enduring franchises such as *Metroid*, *Zelda*, *Super Mario Bros.*, and, especially, *Pokémon*—those little "pocket monsters" that may have rescued the Game Boy console, and the Nintendo Corporation itself, from irrelevancy more than once.

R.A.M.S. vs P.O.R.K.S.

Barnyard animals become action commandos

The Barnyard Commandos action figure line was produced by toy-maker Playmates and supported by a four-episode animated series.

Crafted by the same company that gave us the *Teenage Mutant Ninja Turtles* cartoon (Murakami-Wolf-Swenson), the voice talent on the animated program was first-rate, yet these farm animals did not catch on with children like TMNT.

The Barnyard Commandos, mutant anthropomorphized sheep and pigs, were the result of remnants of a secret military experiment buried for many years.

After eating Farmer Bob's latest crop of grain, the animals started acting kind of funny. Some started driving the tractors around like tanks, others started digging trenches. Soon after, an all out war erupted between the Barnyard Commandos.

The two warring factions of Commandos were the R.A.M.S (Rebel Army of Military Sheep) and the P.O.R.K.S (Platoon of Rebel Killer Swine), enemies who fought against one another in military fashion, as reflected in their appellations: Sergeant Woolly Pullover, Commodore Fleece Cardigan, Major Legger Mutton, and Pilot Fluff Pendleton versus General Hamfat Lardo,

Barnyard Commandos Commodore Fleece Cardigan and General Hamfat Lardo.

Private Side O'Bacon, Sergeant Shoat N. Sweet, and Captain Tusker Chitlins.

Although the premise for the line was interesting, the action figures themselves possessed little poseability, which may have caused retail sales to suffer when children were confronted with a myriad of more popular (and poseable) choices at their local toy store. Despite poor sales, the Barnyard Commando toy line continues to tickle the funny bone of many a toy collector.

Perhaps the most interesting toy released by Hasbro for its Official New Kids on the Block line was the stage playset, allowing fans of the band to recreate their own pretend concerts. Rarely do fashion doll playsets compare with action figure playsets in terms of detail or design, yet Hasbro's playset is stunning in its detail with the following action features and accoutrements: a moving platform that allowed kids to move figures across the stage, photos of NKOTB that could be displayed as a backdrop for the stage, stage steps, keyboard with stand, a small snare drum, a large snare drum, a bass drum, cymbal, two drumsticks, drum stand base, two drum stands, a cymbal stand, bass guitar with strap, rhythm guitar with strap, lead guitar with strap, microphone stand, five microphones, bass amplifier, two small amplifiers, three spotlights, three instrument cords, six cardboard panels, a label sheet, and a chipboard NKOTB logo.

They Got It (The Right Stuff)

New Kids on the Block

Hasbro New Kids on the Block 12-inch fashion dolls: Donnie Wahlberg, Danny Wood, and Jordan Knight

Although many pundits would recommend categorizing New Kids on the Block as a phenomenon of the 1990s, since they garnered two American Music Award wins in 1990 for Favorite Pop/Rock Band, Duo or Group and Favorite Pop/Rock Album, this boy-band is indeed a product of the decade of excess. However, success was not initially so easy for the group. Their 1986 self-titled debut album—chock full of bubblegum-pop laden tunes—flopped, even in the "Kids" native city of Boston, MA.

Released by Hasbro for the 1989 Christmas season, the five New Kids on the Block were translated into "official" plastic, fashion doll form featuring the band members in a variety of different outfits. Jordan and Jonathan Knight, Joey McIntyre, Donnie Wahlberg, and Danny Wood were each released in two different sets of outfits: as "Hangin' Loose" action figures, where they're dressed in the "street look that's so awesome," and a set of "In Concert" fashion figures, wearing concert clothing, replete with cassettes of exclusive interviews.

Selling over two million units in just a few months of solicitation, Hasbro's New Kids on the Block fashion dolls were a rousing success for the company.

Marvel Universe Begins Anew

Super-heroes stars of line

These days, it may be quite difficult to walk into any department store and NOT find Marvel Comics' super-hero action figures hanging on retail pegs. They're simply everywhere, thanks in large part to the success of Marvel's super-hero films.

But apart from Mego's iconic Official World's Greatest Super-Heroes line that was "officially" discontinued in 1982 and Mattel's fantastic yet short-lived Marvel Super-Heroes Secret Wars toy line (1984-85), there was little Marvel toy product to speak of in the '80s. Marvel's television and movie production studio of the 1980s, Marvel Productions Limited, truly concocted some enduring and bona-fide programming hits during this decade such as *G.I. Joe: A Real American Hero*, *Transformers*, *Spider-Man and His Amazing Friends*, *Jim Hensons' Muppet Babies*, and *The Incredible Hulk*, yet the company reaped the benefits of licensed action figures from only a few of these productions.

In retrospect, one failed component of Marvel Productions in the 1980s was its toy division, as headed by Toy Biz, and due to the company's lack of experience in the action figure world when initially receiving both the Marvel and DC Comics licenses. When Toy Biz first produced toys based on Marvel's action figures, the results were poorly received due to their sub-par sculpting, lack of realism, and poor poseability.

Toy Biz's Marvel Super Heroes line (1990-1994) was in the planning stages in early 1989, yet did not infiltrate retail stores until early 1990. Regardless, I have included these toys in this book because they are some of the few Marvel Comics action

Marvel Super-Heroes action figure Iron Man.

figures to enter the market during a lengthy ten-year time period. Furthermore, they were released hot on the heels of Toy Biz's DC Comics action figure offerings, which, although similar in design to the Marvel toys, were a bit more successful. I gladly bought these figures at retail because this was the first time that the Punisher, the Silver Surfer, and Venom were created in action figure form.

Although the sculpts of these figures were considered sub-par by today's standards (and by the super-high standards created by Toy Biz/Marvel Toys with the production of Marvel Legends action figures in the 00s), some of the action features incorporated into the Marvel Super-Heroes figures were truly amazing: the Green Goblin actually came with his goblin glider, Iron Man's arm, leg, and chest pieces were removable, and the slime that was included with the first edition of Venom was tinted black to match his alien symbiote's costume color.

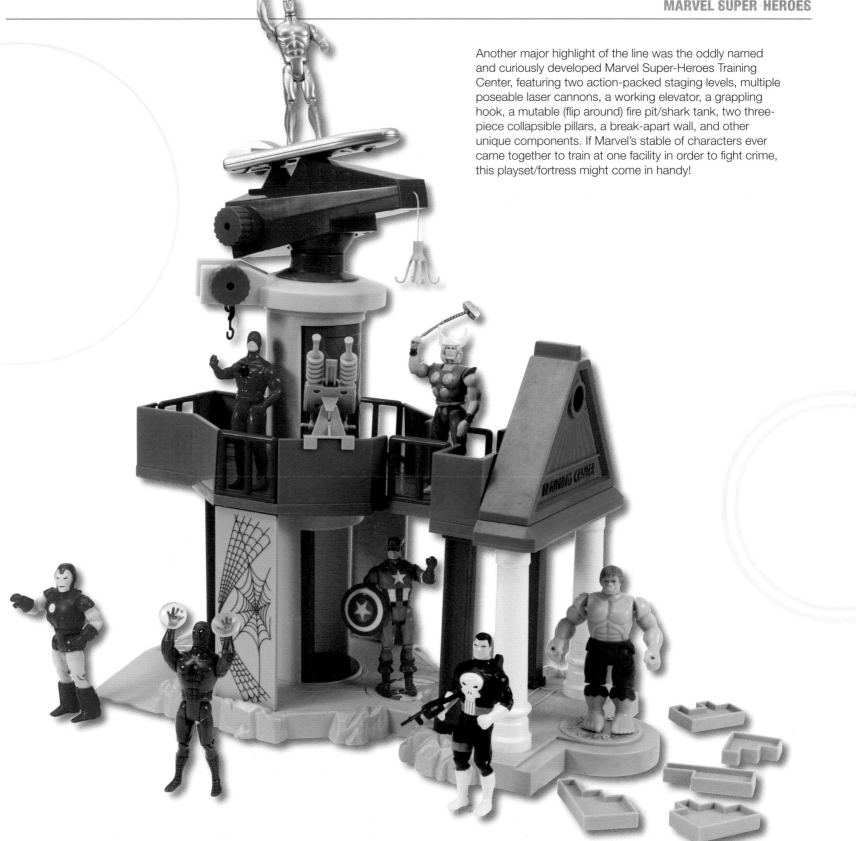

Another major highlight of the line was the oddly named and curiously developed Marvel Super-Heroes Training Center, featuring two action-packed staging levels, multiple poseable laser cannons, a working elevator, a grappling hook, a mutable (flip around) fire pit/shark tank, two three-piece collapsible pillars, a break-apart wall, and other unique components. If Marvel's stable of characters ever came together to train at one facility in order to fight crime, this playset/fortress might come in handy!

Marvel Super-Heroes action figures, Series Three:
Green Goblin, Venom, Thor, Iron Man.

Marvel Super-Heroes action figures:
Venom, Green Goblin, Thor.

Marvel Super-Heroes action figures, Series One:
Captain America, Spider-Man, Dr. Doom, Dr. Octopus.

Marvel Super-Heroes action
figures, Series Two: Silver Surfer,
Hulk, Daredevil, Punisher.

Nothing Bogus Here

Bill & Ted's Excellent Adventure(s)

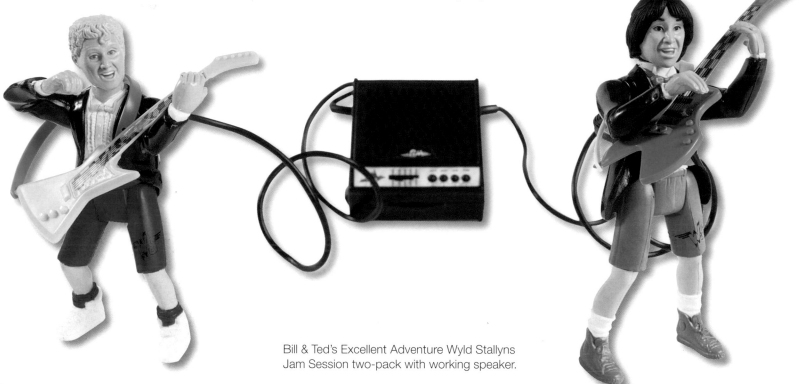

Bill & Ted's Excellent Adventure Wyld Stallyns
Jam Session two-pack with working speaker.

Although the action figures for Bill & Ted's Excellent Adventures (note the "s") were produced by Kenner in late 1990/early 1991 for the CBS (and later FOX) animated series, the toys were—in essence—an extension of the characters concocted for the break-out cult films *Bill & Ted's Excellent Adventure* (1989) and *Bill & Ted's Bogus Journey* (1991). Any child growing up in the late 1980s couldn't avoid the impact and cultural influence that the characters of Bill and Ted provided, and the plot of the first film is indelibly etched onto our consciousness.

Many comedies of the 1980s often fall apart when being viewed decades later, but the lighthearted plot, decent production quality, and quirky nature of the film *Bill & Ted's Excellent Adventure* still retains its magic. The plot: two head-

banging slackers living in San Dimas, California—William S. Preston Esquire ("Bill," played by Keanu Reeves) and Theodore Logan ("Ted," Alex Winters)—are ordered by a fascinating being from the future (deftly portrayed by George Carlin) to use a technologically advanced phone booth to travel back in time in order to make sure that the two underachievers' metal band— Wyld Stallyns—does not break up. The Utopian society of the future depends upon the band's continuance and endurance, as their entire philosophy of non-violence ("Be excellent to each other") is an extension of the ideas permeating the Wyld Stallyns' lyrics and music. Therefore, Bill and Ted's friendship must never be ruined, yet there is a threat: if Ted fails his upcoming history test, his father will ship him off to military school, breaking up the band.

WYLD STALLYNS JAM SESSION TWO-PACK

AGES 4 AND UP
NO. 54210

CAUTION:
NOT RECOMMENDED FOR
CHILDREN WHO STILL PUT
OBJECTS IN THEIR MOUTHS.
CONTAINS SMALL PARTS.

INCLUDES
BILL & TED FIGURES
WITH
SPEAKER AND CASSETTE TAPE!
6 NEW WYLD STALLYNS TUNES!

BILL & TED PLAY MUSIC!
with your portable
tape player
(sold separately)

NOTE: PARENTS SHOULD REMOVE AND DISCARD
PLASTIC SHIPPING PIECE PRIOR TO PLAYING CASSETTE.

Kenner.

SAFETY TESTED — meets or
exceeds ASTM F963-86

Bill & Ted's Excellent
Adventure Wyld
Stallyns Jam Session
two-pack.

Utilizing the time-traveling phone booth, Bill and Ted journey into the past to learn about history for their exam, and encounter many famous historical figures in humorous situations including Napoleon, Billy the Kid, Socrates, Princesses Joanna and Elizabeth, Sigmund Freud, Beethoven, Genghis Khan, Joan of Arc, and Abraham Lincoln. As we all know, the pair of lovable metal-heads pass their history test with the assistance of the aforementioned historical figures, and save the future.

Season one of the animated series (1990) was a logical extension from the plot of the first film, and was a rare and phenomenal achievement in casting for a cartoon: producers Hanna-Barbera brought in "big guns" to provide character voices: Reeves, Winter, Carlin, and Bernie Casey all returned to voice their proper characters. Although an ambitious project, the program was not a ratings success, and Hanna-Barbera handed the reins of the show to D.I.C. Entertainment, which produced only an eight episode second season.

Bill (Alex Winter) and Ted (Keanu Reeves) are a couple of head-bangin' Valley boys who spend so much time forming their band, Wyld Stallyns, that they find themselves flunking history. Enter a guardian angel from the future (George Carlin), who devises a time-traveling phone booth they use to go back in time and learn about history firsthand from the people who made it. Whoa! *Orion/The Kobal Collection*

ENTERTAINMENT-O-RAMA:
1989 MOVIES, MUSIC, TELEVISION

Top Ten Films of 1989

1 *Batman* (Warner Brothers)
2 *Indiana Jones and the Last Crusade* (Paramount)
3 *Lethal Weapon 2* (Warner Brothers)
4 *Look Who's Talking* (Columbia/TriStar)
5 *Honey, I Shrunk the Kids* (Buena Vista)
6 *Back to the Future Part II* (Universal)
7 *Ghostbusters II* (Columbia)
8 *Driving Miss Daisy* (Warner Brothers)
9 *Parenthood* (Universal)
10 *Dead Poets Society* (Buena Vista)

Best Picture: *Driving Miss Daisy* (Warner Brothers)

The blockbuster hit of 1989, Tim Burton's *Batman*, gave the famed caped crusader an overhaul in keeping with the super-hero's evolution in DC Comics. Michael Keaton is the brooding Dark Knight, and Jack Nicholson is the wildly crazy and maniacal Joker. The movie helped establish the modern-day super-hero genre. *Warner Bros/DC Comics/The Kobal Collection*

You couldn't turn on a radio in '89 and not hear songs by Janet Jackson and Paula Abdul. Where Abdul's debut album, *Forever Your Girl*, was full of pure pop song, including chart-toppers "Straight Up" and "Cold Hearted," Jackson's fourth studio album, *Rhythm Nation 1814*, explored racism, poverty, substance abuse, and other social issues. *AP Photo/Harrison Funk*

Top Ten Billboard Singles of 1989

1 "Look Away," Chicago (*Chicago 19*, 1988)
2 "My Prerogative," Bobby Brown (*Don't Be Cruel*, 1988)
3 "Every Rose Has Its Thorn," Poison (*Open Up and Say... Ahh!*, 1988)
4 "Straight Up," Paula Abdul (*Forever Your Girl*, 1988)
5 "Miss You Much," Janet Jackson (*Janet Jackson's Rhythm Nation 1814*, 1989)
6 "Cold Hearted," Paula Abdul (*Forever Your Girl*, 1988)
7 "Wind Beneath My Wings," Bette Midler (*Beaches* soundtrack, 1988)
8 "(Girl) You Know It's True," Milli Vanilli (*All or Nothing*, 1988)
9 "Baby, I Love Your Way/Freebird Medley (Free Baby)," Will To Power (*Will to Power*, 1988)
10 "Giving You the Best That I Got," Anita Baker (*Giving You the Best That I Got*, 1988)

Top Ten Television Programs of 1989-90

1 *The Cosby Show* (NBC)
2 *Roseanne* (ABC)
3 *Cheers* (NBC)
4 *A Different World* (NBC)
5 *America's Funniest Home Videos* (ABC)
6 *The Golden Girls* (NBC)
7 *60 Minutes* (CBS)
8 *The Wonder Years* (ABC)
9 *Empty Nest* (NBC)
10 *Monday Night Football* (ABC)

The new, charming series, *The Wonder Years*, which deftly mixed comedy with pathos, harkened back to an innocent time of first crushes and kisses. Taking place in the late 1960s/early '70s, the show centers around Kevin (Fred Savage), his best friend Paul (Josh Saviano), and his childhood friend and budding girlfriend, Winnie (Danica McKellar). *New World/Black-Marlens/The Kobal Collection*

Although NBC's *Baywatch* was cancelled after one season due to low ratings, the series about attractive lifeguards who patrol a crowded recreational beach and are led by David Hasselhoff, was resuscitated in syndication and has gone on to become the most watched television show in world history. From left are Traci Bingham, Donna D'Errico, Yasmine Bleeth, Gena Lee Nolin, and Nancy Valen. *Baywatch Co/Tower 12 Productions/The Kobal Collection*

Bibliography

Chapter Introductions, In-Text Allusions, and Chapter Conclusions

In this book, all references regarding the chart position of American music; e.g., chapter introductions, in-text allusions, and chapter finales ("Top Ten Billboard Singles of…") were acquired from Billboard.com's "View Chart Archives" search function, since the Billboard Hot 100 (which tracks best-selling singles) and Billboard 200 (which ranks best-selling albums) are the official trade archives for the music industry.

The meticulously maintained database available at Box Office Mojo (www.boxofficemojo.com) was utilized to document and determine each film's box office gross in Totally Tubular's chapter introductions, chapter finales ("Top Ten Films of…"), and throughout all textual references.

Finally, Nielsen TV Research audience measurement systems (en-us.nielsen.com), used in conjunction with the American History and World History Web site at www.historycentral.com, were employed throughout this book's chapter introductions, conclusions, et al. to chart the popularity of American television broadcasts in the 1980s.

Books

Barton, Matt, and Bill Loquidice. *Vintage Games: An Insider Look at the History of Grand Theft Auto, Super Mario, and the Most Influential Games of All Time.* Boston: Focal Press/Elsevier, 2009.

Guinness World Records. *Guinness World Records 2010: The Book of the Decade.* New York: Guinness World Records Press Ltd., 2009.

Gygax, Gary. *Advanced Dungeons and Dragons Player's Handbook.* Lake Geneva, Wisconsin: TSR, Inc. 1978.

Hayes, Summer. *The My Little Pony G1 Collector's Inventory: an unofficial full-color illustrated collector's price guide to the first generation of MLP including all U.S. ponies, playsets and accessories released before 1997.* New Jersey: Priced Nostalgia Press, 2008.

Kalter, Suzy. *The Complete Book of M*A*S*H.* New York: Harry N. Abrams, Inc., 1988.

Kent, Stephen L. *The Ultimate History of Video Games: From Pong to Pokemon—The Story Behind the Craze That Touched Our Lives and Changed the World.* New York: Three Rivers Press, 2001.

Mantlo, Bill and Mark Texeira. *Sectaurs: Warriors of Symbion.* Issues 1-8. New York: Marvel Comics, June 1985-September 1986.

Miller, Frank, Klaus Janson, and Lynn Varley. *Batman: The Dark Knight Returns.* Issues 1-4. New York: DC Comics, February-June, 1986.

Moench, Douglas, et al. *C.O.P.S.* Issues 1-15. New York: DC Comics, August 1988-August 1989.

Moore, Alan and Brian Bolland. *Batman: The Killing Joke.* New York: DC Comics, 1988.

Rettenmund, Michael. *Totally Awesome 80s: A Lexicon of the Music, Videos, Movies, TV Shows, Stars, and Trends of that Decadent Decade.* New York: St. Martin's Griffin, 1996.

Shooter, Jim, et. al. *Marvel Super Heroes Secret Wars.* Issues 1-12. New York: Marvel Comics, May 1984-April 1985.

Smith, Carl. *The Shady Dragon Inn*. Lake Geneva, Wisconsin: TSR. Inc., 1983.

Kellner, Douglas. *Television and the Crisis of Democracy*. Boulder, Colorado: Westview Press, 1990.

Films

Batman. Dir. Tim Burton. Perf. Michael Keaton, Jack Nicholson. Warner Bros., 1989. DVD.

Bill & Ted's Excellent Adventure. Dir. Herek, Stephen. Perf. Keanu Reeves. Alex Winter. DEG Ent., 1989. DVD.

Ghostbusters. Dir. Ivan Reitman. Perf. Bill Murray, Dan Aykroyd, Harold Ramis, Ernie Hudson. Columbia Pictures, 1984. DVD.

Gremlins. Dir. Joe Dante. Warner Bros., 1984. DVD.

Karate Kid. Dir. John G. Alvidson. Perf. Ralph Macchio, Pat Morita. Columbia Pictures, 1984. DVD.

Mazes & Monsters. Dir. Steven Hilliard Stern. Perf. Tom Hanks. CBS Television, 1982. DVD.

The Best of She-Ra Princess of Power (includes the Feature Film *The Secret of the Sword*). Dir. Ed Friedman et al. Filmation Associates, 1985. DVD.

Star Wars Episode IV: A New Hope. Dir. George Lucas. Twentieth Century Fox, 1977. VHS.

Star Wars Episode V: The Empire Strikes Back. Dir. George Lucas. Twentieth Century Fox, 1980. VHS.

Star Wars Episode VI: Return of the Jedi. Dir. George Lucas. Twentieth Century Fox, 1983. VHS.

Tron. Dir. Steven Lisberger. Perf. Jeff Bridges, Bruce Boxleitner. Buena Vista, 1982. DVD.

Who Framed Roger Rabbit. Dir. Robert Zemeckis. Perf. Bob Hoskins, Christopher Lloyd, Kathleen Turner. Amblin Entertainment, 1988.

Interviews

Albano, (Captain) Louis. "Wrestling Superstars and the History of the WWF." Personal Interview. Dec. 2, 2006.

Bozigian, H. Kirk. "G.I. Joe: A Real American Hero." E-mail Interview. July 27, 2005.

Budiansky, Bob. "Transformers and Marvel Comics." E-mail Interview. January 30, 2010.

Budiansky, Bob. "Transformers: Tech Specs." E-mail Interview. February 4, 2010.

Glut, Donald F. "He-Man and the Masters of the Universe." E-mail Interview. January 30, 2010.

Hama, Lawrence. "C.O.P.S.' I.D. Cards and Crooks' Wanted Files." Telephone Interview. July 31, 2009.

Hama, Lawrence. "G.I. Joe: A Real American Hero." Telephone Interview. May 24, 2005.

Rudat, Ronald. "G.I. Joe Lead Designer from 1981-1987." E-mail Interview. May 20, 2005.

Shooter, Jim. "*Marvel Super-Heroes Secret Wars*." Personal Interview conducted by Tim Hartnett. *Silver Bullet Comics* (www.silverbulletcomicbooks.com).

Newspaper and Magazine Articles

Anonymous. "Rubikmania." *Time Magazine*, December 7, 1981: 35.

Broad, William J. "The Shuttle Explodes: 6 in Crew and High School Teacher are Killed 74 Seconds after Liftoff." *New York Times, Special to the New York Times*. January 29, 1986: A1.

Cocks, Jay. "Why He's a Thriller." *Time Magazine,* March 19, 1984: 54.

Parelese, Jon. "Michael Jackson at 25: A Musical Phenomenon." *New York Times*, January 14, 1984, late edition: A11.

Kieszkowski, Elizabeth. "Those ThunderCats Just Keep On Coming Back." *Honolulu Advertiser.* July 4, 2000: E14.

Television Programs

ALF: Season One. NBC. Sept. 1986-May 1987. Lions Gate, August 2004. DVD.

The A-Team: Season One. NBC. Jan. 1983-May 1983. Universal Studios, June 2004. DVD.

Beetlejuice: [The Animated Series] Volume 1. Writ. Tim Burton. ABC. Sept. 1989-Sept. 1989. Warner Home Video, Dec 1993. DVD.

Centurions. April 1986. Ruby-Spears Productions, 1994. VHS.

Fraggle Rock: Complete Series Collection. Dir. Jim Henson, et. al. HBO. Jan. 1983-March 1987. Jim Henson Company, Nov. 2009. DVD.

Inhumanoids: The Evil That Lies Within (Episodes 1 thru 5). Sunbow Productions. Sept. 1986-Oct. 1986. Rhino/Wea, April 2001. DVD.

Inspector Gadget: Go-Go Gadget Collection. DIC Entertainment, 1983, assorted release dates. 20th Century Fox, Sept. 2009. DVD.

*M*A*S*H: Season 9 Collector's Edition.* CBS. Nov. 1980-May 1981. 20th Century Fox, Dec 2005. DVD.

*M*A*S*H: Season 10 Collector's Edition.* Oct. 1981-April 1982. 20th Century Fox, May 2006. DVD.

*M*A*S*H: Season 11 Collector's Edition.* CBS. Oct. 1982-Feb 1983. 20th Century Fox, Nov 2006. DVD.

M.A.S.K.: Illusion is the Ultimate Weapon, Collection One. DIC Entertainment. Sept. 1985-Nov. 1985. Madman Entertainment. Nov. 2006. DVD.

Pee-Wee's Playhouse #1 (Season One and Two). Sept. 1986-1987. Image Entertainment. November 2004. DVD.

The Real Ghostbusters: Complete Collection. DIC Enterprises. Sept. 1986-Oct. 1989. Time Life Entertainment. Sept. 2009. DVD.

Robotech: Protoculture Collection. Harmony Gold & Tatsunoko. March 1985-July 1985. Section 23 Studios, Nov. 2005. DVD.

The Best of She-Ra, Princess of Power [Includes the Feature Film *The Secret of the Sword*]. Filmation. 1985. BCI/Eclipse, July 2006. DVD.

Silverhawks: Volume One. Rankin/Bass. Sept. 1986-Oct. 1986. Warner Home Video, Oct. 2008. DVD.

Star Trek: The Next Generation: Complete Series. Paramount Television. Sept. 1987 (Stardate: 41153.7)-May 1994 (47988.1). Paramount, Oct. 2007. DVD.

ThunderCats, Volume One. Rankin/Bass. Jan. 1985-Nov. 1985. Warner Home Video, August 2005. DVD.

Visionaries, "Feryl Steps Out." Sunbow Productions. Oct. 1987. Anchor Bay, May 1989. VHS.

Voltron: Defender of the Universe, Collection One [Blue Lion]. World Events Productions/Toei Animation. Sept. 1984-Oct. 1984. Anime Works, Sept. 2006.

Web sites

Action Figure Archive—A vintage 70s & 80s action figure collectors guide, online store & forums. 2003. Web. Visionaries, Jan. 2010. Rambo & the Forces of Freedom, Dec. 2009. Super Naturals, Jan. 2010 (www.action-figures.ca).

All Chuck Norris Facts & Jokes / Chuck Norris Facts. Spreadshirt.com. Web. Dec. 2009 (www.chucknorrisfacts.com).

Bickmore, Alex. Alex Bickmore's Super Toy Archive. Alex Bickmore, Mac Bickmore, et al., 1997. Web. Battle Beasts, Jan. 2010, GoBots and Rock Lords, Jan. 2010.

Cabbage Patch Kids. Original Appalachian Artwork, Inc., 1983-2010. Web. Dec. 2009. (www.cabbagepatchkids.com).

Davis, Jim. Garfield and Friends—The Official Site featuring Today's Comic, Games, News, Videos and more. Paws, Inc. Web. Feb 2010 (www.garfield.com).

Dino-Riders.com—The Dino Riders Authority! Dino-Riders. com, 2004. Web. Nov. 2009 (www.dinoriders.com).

Famous Artists of Italy: Italian Renaissance Artists. Oracle Thinkquest Education Foundation. Web. Dec. 2009 (library. thinkquest.org).

Gifford, James. Max Headroom Chronicles. Version 0.69. 2005. Web. Nov. 2009 (www.maxheadroom.com).

Harris, David Daniel. The California Raisins. DIzzo Designs. Web. Jan. 2010 (www.thecaliforniaraisins.com).

Like Totally 80s—1980s Culture, Music, Movies, and Fashion. Like Totally 80s, Inc.. Web. Jan. 2010 (www.liketotally80s.com).

Madeline. Care Bears Forever…keep the spirit alive forever! Care Bears Forever, 2007. Web. Jan 2010 (www.wishbear.net).

Newwell, Nathan. Nathan's M.U.S.C.L.E. Blog. Blogger.com, April 1998. Web. Jan. 2010 (nathansmuscleblog.blogspot.com). The Official TMNT Web Site! Mirage Studios, 2008. Web. Dec. 2009 (www.ninjaturtles.com).

Penello, Albert. Welcome to the Kenner M.A.S.K. Page [at] Albert Penello.com. Albert Penello, Jan. 1999. Web. Nov. 2009 (www.albertpenello.com).

ROBOTECH.COM—The Official Robotech Site! "Robotech Infopedia." Harmony Gold USA, 1985-2007. Web. Jan. 2010.

Thompson, Janice. Captain Power and the Soldiers of the Future. [Affiliated with] Landmark Entertainment, April 1999. Web. Dec. 2009 (www.captainpower.com).

Voltron: The Official Website of the Voltron Universe. Version Two. Koplar Communication/World Events Productions, Ltd., 2003. Web. Jan 2010.

Wales, Jimmy and Angela Beesley. Muppet Wiki: Fraggle Rock. Wikia Entertainment. Jan. 2010. Web. Jan. 2010 (muppet.wikia. com/wiki/Fraggle_Rock).

Wikipedia

"A-Team." Wikipedia: The Free Encyclopedia. Wikimedia Foundation, Inc. Nov 22, 2009. Web. Nov. 22, 2009.

"ALF (TV Series)." Wikipedia: The Free Encyclopedia. Wikimedia Foundation, Inc. Dec. 4, 2009. Web. Dec. 5, 2009.

"Alvin and the Chipmunks." Wikipedia: The Free Encyclopedia. Wikimedia Foundation, Inc. Jan. 3, 2010. Web. Jan. 3, 2010.

"Batman (1989 film)." Wikipedia: The Free Encyclopedia. Wikimedia Foundation, Inc. Feb. 21, 2010. Web. Feb. 22, 2010.

"Beetlejuice (TV Series)." Wikipedia: The Free Encyclopedia. Wikimedia Foundation, Inc. Feb. 13, 2010. Web. Feb. 14, 2010.

"Bill & Ted's Excellent Adventure." Wikipedia: The Free Encyclopedia. Wikimedia Foundation, Inc. Jan. 1, 2010. Web. Jan. 1, 2010.

"Buck Rogers." Wikipedia: The Free Encyclopedia. Wikimedia Foundation, Inc. Nov. 5, 2009. Web. Nov. 5, 2009.

"Buck Rogers in the 25th Century (TV Series)." Wikipedia: The Free Encyclopedia. Wikimedia Foundation, Inc. Jan. 30, 2010. Web. Feb. 1, 2010.

"The California Raisins." Wikipedia: The Free Encyclopedia. Wikimedia Foundation, Inc. Dec. 29, 2009. Web. Jan. 2, 2010.

"Care Bears." Wikipedia: The Free Encyclopedia. Wikimedia Foundation, Inc. Nov. 22, 2009. Web. Nov. 22, 2009.

"Challenge of the Gobots." Wikipedia: The Free Encyclopedia. Wikimedia Foundation, Inc. Feb. 2, 2010. Web. Feb. 2, 2010.

"Chuck Norris." Wikipedia: The Free Encyclopedia. Wikimedia Foundation, Inc. Oct. 9, 2009. Web. Oct. 10, 2009.

"Clash of the Titans (1981 film)." Wikipedia: The Free Encyclopedia. Wikimedia Foundation, Inc. Nov. 2, 2009. Web. Nov. 2, 2009.

"Disney's Adventures of the Gummi Bears." Wikipedia: The Free Encyclopedia. Wikimedia Foundation, Inc. July 22, 2004. Web. May 3, 2010.

"Dukes of Hazzard." Wikipedia: The Free Encyclopedia. Wikimedia Foundation, Inc. Dec. 19, 2009. Web. Dec. 19, 2009.

"Garbage Pail Kids." Wikipedia: The Free Encyclopedia. Wikimedia Foundation, Inc. Feb. 11, 2010. Web. Feb. 12, 2010.

"Knight Rider (1982 TV Series)." Wikipedia: The Free Encyclopedia. Wikimedia Foundation, Inc. Feb. 5, 2010. Web. Feb. 6, 2010.

"Lazer Tag." Wikipedia: The Free Encyclopedia. Wikimedia Foundation, Inc. Jan. 22, 2010. Web. Jan. 29, 2010.

"Mr. T." Wikipedia: The Free Encyclopedia. Wikimedia Foundation, Inc. Jan. 1, 2010. Web. Jan. 1, 2010.

"MTV Video Music Awards ["Moonman"]." Wikipedia: The Free Encyclopedia. Wikimedia Foundation, Inc. Jan. 16, 2010. Web. Jan. 16, 2010.

"Jim Henson's Muppet Babies." Wikipedia: The Free Encyclopedia. Wikimedia Foundation, Inc. Dec. 5, 2009. Web. Dec. 6, 2009.

"MacGyver." Wikipedia: The Free Encyclopedia. Wikimedia Foundation, Inc. Dec. 2, 2009. Web. Dec. 6, 2009.

"My Little Pony." Wikipedia: The Free Encyclopedia. Wikimedia Foundation, Inc. Dec. 26, 2009. Web. Dec. 26, 2009.

"New Kids on the Block." Wikipedia: The Free Encyclopedia. Wikimedia Foundation, Inc. Nov. 11, 2009. Web. Nov. 13, 2009.

"North American Video Game Crash of 1983." Wikipedia: The Free Encyclopedia. Wikimedia Foundation, Inc. Nov. 4, 2009. Web. Nov. 8, 2009.

"Pee-wee Herman." Wikipedia: The Free Encyclopedia. Wikimedia Foundation, Inc. Dec. 23, 2009. Web. Dec. 23, 2009.

"Rainbow Brite." Wikipedia: The Free Encyclopedia. Wikimedia Foundation, Inc. Jan. 23, 2010. Web. Jan. 25, 2010.

"Rambo and the Forces of Freedom." Wikipedia: The Free Encyclopedia. Wikimedia Foundation, Inc. Dec. 2, 2009. Web. Dec. 6, 2009.

"The Smurfs." Wikipedia: The Free Encyclopedia. Wikimedia Foundation, Inc. Jan. 2, 2010. Web. Jan. 2, 2010.

"Starting Lineup (Toy Line)." Wikipedia: The Free Encyclopedia. Wikimedia Foundation, Inc. Nov. 27, 2009. Web. Nov. 30, 2009.

"Star Wars: Droids." Wikipedia: The Free Encyclopedia. Wikimedia Foundation, Inc. Jan. 12, 2010. Web. Jan. 12, 2010.

"Star Wars: Ewoks." Wikipedia: The Free Encyclopedia. Wikimedia Foundation, Inc. Jan. 12, 2010. Web. Jan. 12, 2010.

"Superfriends." Wikipedia: The Free Encyclopedia. Wikimedia Foundation, Inc. Feb. 21, 2010. Web. Feb. 21, 2010.

"Teddy Ruxpin." Wikipedia: The Free Encyclopedia. Wikimedia Foundation, Inc. Jan. 9, 2010. Web. Jan. 13, 2010.

"Tim Burton." Wikipedia: The Free Encyclopedia. Wikimedia Foundation, Inc. Feb. 21, 2010. Web. Feb. 21, 2010.

"Trivial Pursuit." Wikipedia: The Free Encyclopedia. Wikimedia Foundation, Inc. Feb. 5, 2010. Web. Feb. 8, 2010.

"Tron (franchise)." Wikipedia: The Free Encyclopedia. Wikimedia Foundation, Inc. Jan. 20, 2010. Web. Jan. 23, 2010.

"V." Wikipedia: The Free Encyclopedia. Wikimedia Foundation, Inc. Dec. 4, 2009. Web. Dec. 6, 2009.

"Who Framed Roger Rabbit." Wikipedia: The Free Encyclopedia. Wikimedia Foundation, Inc. Dec. 17, 2009. Web. Dec. 20, 2009.

FIND TREASURES AMONG TOYS

Barbie A Rare Beauty

This hardcover book, with its 350+ stunning photographs and authoritative details from renowned Barbie doll expert Sandi Holder, is truly a visual feast and a collector's delight. It features some of the finest Barbie dolls ever created in the more than 50 year history of this American icon. You'll enjoy a rich and interesting overview of Barbie doll history, an in-depth review of the rare Ponytail Barbie No. 1, and a decade-by-decade exploration of all things Barbie, including rare dolls, prototypes, licensed items, trend-setting fashions, and notable series of Barbie dolls. 224p.

Item# Z7611 • $30.00

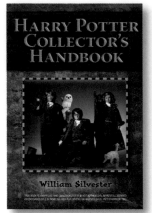

Harry Potter Collector's Handbook

This one-of-a-kind handbook to all things Harry Potter will bewitch you with fantastic color photographs and current values of the multitude of licensed products from the franchise of the famous boy wizard, his charming chums and nefarious foes. Inside this spellbinding book you'll find 1,000+ listings for everything from action figures, books and costumes to lunch boxes, toys and ornaments with size, identifying features and manufacturer information. This glorious guide takes you into the enchanting world of "Pottermania" unlike any other guide can. 272 p.

Item# Z6611• $17.99

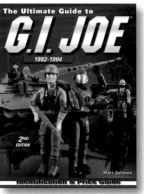

The Ultimate Guide to G.I. Joe, 2nd Ed.

Your G.I. Joe collection isn't complete without this premiere guide. In this book you'll find unmatched details and photographs for every domestically-made 3-3/4" G.I. Joe toy produced between 1982 and 1994. Every accessory, action figure, playset, and vehicle is listed in this guide and represented within the 1,300+ color photographs featured. Plus, you'll also find current pricing, in up to four condition grades, for each item. Written by the ultimate authority on G.I. Joe, nothing compares to this book. 304 p.

Item#Z3600 • $26.99

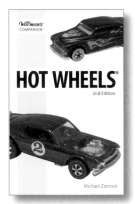

Hot Wheels Warman's Companion

This affordable and portable book is the perfect companion when you're shopping or searching for Hot Wheels. Fits easily and comfortably in a bag, jacket pocket, and even some back pockets, this guide contains identifying data, collector value and photographs of some of the most popular Hot Wheels Redline, Blackwall and Number Pack cars ever made. Plus, you'll find an inspiring and informative interview with legendary Hot Wheels designer Larry Wood. 288 p.

Item#Z3047 • $18.99